WHEN WE DEAD AWAKEN

AND

THREE OTHER PLAYS

THE PLAYS OF HENRIK IBSEN
(1828–1906)

WITH THEIR DATES OF COMPOSITION

Cataline (1849)

The Warrior's Barrow
    (1849–50)

Norma (1851)

St. John's Eve (1852)

Lady Inger of Oestraat (1854)

The Feast at Solhaug (1855)

Olaf Liljekrans (1856)

The Vikings at Helgeland
    (1857)

Love's Comedy (1862)

The Pretenders (1863)

Brand (1865)

Peer Gynt (1867)

The League of Youth (1868–69)

Emperor and Galilean (1864–73)

The Pillars of Society (1875–77)

A Doll's House (1879)

Ghosts (1881)

An Enemy of the People (1882)

The Wild Duck (1884)

Rosmersholm (1886)

The Lady from the Sea (1888)

Hedda Gabler (1890)

The Master Builder (1892)

Little Eyolf (1894)

John Gabriel Borkman (1896)

When We Dead Awaken (1899)

HENRIK IBSEN, the most influential dramatist since Shakespeare, was born at Skien, Norway, in 1828. After years of failure and poverty, he emigrated at the age of thirty-six to Italy, and there wrote *Brand,* which brought him immediate fame. He remained in self-imposed exile for twenty-seven years, living in Rome, Dresden, and Munich. In 1891 he returned to Norway, and spent the last fifteen years of his life in Christiania (now Oslo). He died there in 1906 at the age of seventy-eight. Ibsen wrote twenty-six plays, sixteen of which are still performed in England and America.

MICHAEL MEYER, the translator, was born in London in 1921. After studying at Oxford he was for three years lecturer in English Literature at Upsala University in Sweden and now lives partly in Stockholm and partly in London. Author of one novel, two plays, and one television play, he is best known as a translator from the Scandinavian languages and has established a unique reputation for himself in this field in England.

The Lady from the Sea
The Master Builder
John Gabriel Borkman
When We Dead Awaken

BY

HENRIK IBSEN

NEWLY TRANSLATED FROM
THE NORWEGIAN BY
MICHAEL MEYER

Anchor Books
Doubleday & Company, Inc.
Garden City, New York

COVER DRAWING BY ROBERT VICKREY
COVER DESIGN BY SYDNEY BUTCHKES
TYPOGRAPHY BY SUSAN SIEN

ACKNOWLEDGMENTS

Permission to quote from Ibsen's letters and from the letters written by Magdalene Thoresen has been kindly granted by Gyldendal Norsk Forlag of Oslo, Norway.

Mrs. Reginald Orcutt has given her permission for the use of the quotations from Basil King's articles concerning Ibsen and Emilie Bardach in the introduction to THE MASTER BUILDER.

Permission to use the material from the George Bernard Shaw review of the first performance of JOHN GABRIEL BORKMAN in England has been granted by the Public Trustees, London, England, and The Society of Authors, London, England.

CONTENTS

FOREWORD

Henrik Ibsen wrote twenty-six plays, covering a span of half a century. Of these, sixteen, at least, are still theatrically valid: all those from *The Pretenders* onwards, with the single exception, in my opinion, of *The League of Youth*. The remaining ten, though they offer a fascinating insight into the mind of a great dramatist striving to rid himself of the theatrical conventions of nineteenth-century romanticism, are chiefly of literary and documentary interest, and I hardly think any of them could hold the stage today.

In Ibsen's early plays, up to and including *Love's Comedy*, erotic themes occupy a central place. He wove fantasies about a central male character whom attractive women were drawn to and competed for. But after his marriage in 1858, at the age of thirty, he turned away from erotic themes and concentrated on social problems and struggles of the will. Then, as he approached sixty and began to achieve international recognition, young women entered his private life; and his last plays, like his first, are dramas of passion.

The four plays contained in this volume belong to Ibsen's final period; he wrote them between the ages of sixty and seventy-one. *The Lady from the Sea* is about a woman obsessed by a man she knows to be evil. *The Master Builder*, *John Gabriel Borkman* and *When We Dead Awaken* are studies of arrogant men of genius who destroy the happiness of those closest to them. In these plays, Ibsen created some of his most memorable portraits of women: Ellida, drawn to her demon lover as though by a tide drawing her out to sea; Hilde Wangel, first seen in *The Lady from the Sea* as a child starved of affection, then as the predatory young woman who drives the Master Builder to his death; Ella and Gunhild, the twin sisters whom John Gabriel Borkman destroys; and Irene in *When We Dead Awaken,* the deranged relic of a former beauty. Around these central characters, some of the most powerful ever created by any dramatist, move sharply observed minor characters, some comic, some tragic. *The Lady from the Sea, The Master Builder* and *John Gabriel Borkman* show Ibsen at the height of his powers and in complete command of the technique to the perfecting of which he had devoted fifty years; while in *When We Dead Awaken* we see him, at the age of seventy-one, moving into a new and experimental field into which, a dozen years later, James Joyce, who had been much excited by the play as a young man, was to follow him.

London, 1959

MICHAEL MEYER

The Lady from the Sea

INTRODUCTION

THE LADY FROM THE SEA represents an important turning-point in Ibsen's work. He wrote it in 1888, at the age of sixty; chronologically, it was the twenty-first of his twenty-six completed plays.

Twenty years before, having explored the possibilities of poetic drama in *Brand* (1865) and *Peer Gynt* (1867), and of historical drama in a string of early plays culminating in *Emperor and Galilean* (begun in 1864 and finished in 1873), he had turned to the business of exposing the vanities and weaknesses of contemporary society. *The League of Youth* (1869) attacked the hollowness of radical politicians; *The Pillars of Society* (1877) attacked with equal vehemence the hollowness of conservatism. Then, turning his attention from the hypocrisy of politicians to the hypocrisy of social conventions, he wrote *A Doll's House* (1879), *Ghosts* (1881), and *An Enemy of the People* (1882). The three plays that followed, *The Wild Duck* (1884), *Rosmersholm* (1886), and THE LADY FROM THE SEA (1888) were less studies of social problems than of the sickness of the individual; and this is also true of the five mighty dramas of his old age, *Hedda Gabler* (1890), *The Master Builder* (1892), *Little Eyolf* (1894), *John Gabriel Borkman* (1896), and *When We Dead Awaken* (1899).

THE LADY FROM THE SEA, more than any other of his plays, impressed Ibsen's contemporaries as signifying a change of heart. Within a few days of its publication Ibsen's earliest pioneer in England, Edmund Gosse, wrote: "There is thrown over the whole play a glamour of romance, of mystery, of landscape beauty, which has not appeared in Ibsen's work to anything like the same extent since *Peer Gynt*. And moreover, after so many tragedies, this is a comedy . . . THE LADY FROM THE SEA is connected with the previous plays by its emphatic defence of individuality and its statement of the imperative necessity of developing it; but the tone is quite unusually sunny, and without a tinge of pessimism. It is in some respects the reverse of *Rosmersholm;* the bitterness of restrained and baulked individuality, which ends in death, being contrasted with the sweetness of emancipated and gratified individuality, which leads to health and peace."

Later, in a speech delivered in Norway in 1906, the year of Ibsen's death, the Danish critic, Georg Brandes, recalled a conversation he had had with Ibsen shortly before the latter began to write THE LADY FROM THE SEA. "I remember that, after Ibsen had written *Rosmersholm*, he said to me one day: 'Now I shan't write any more polemical plays.' Good God, I thought, what will become of the man? But, as we know, he kept his word. His last plays are not polemical, but are plays about families and the individual. The difference between these two groups of [prose] plays is shown by the fact that of the first six (*The Pillars of Society, A Doll's House, Ghosts, An Enemy of the People, The Wild Duck,* and *Rosmersholm*), only one, *An Enemy of the People,* is named after its chief character, while all the plays in the group beginning with THE LADY FROM THE SEA, except the last [*When We Dead Awaken*], have as their title the name or nickname of a person."

To understand the reasons for this change of heart, we must go back three years from the time Ibsen wrote THE LADY FROM THE SEA, to 1885.

In the summer of that year, he had returned to Norway from his self-imposed exile in Italy and Germany for only the second time in twenty-one years. His previous visit (to Christiania, in 1874) had not been altogether happy; but on this occasion, he proceeded beyond the capital to the little seaside town of Molde, high up on the northwest coast. Although he had been born by the sea, in the village of Skien, and had spent all his youth and early manhood within sight of it, he had since 1864 been living in Rome, Dresden, and Munich and—apart from that one brief visit to Christiania— had not seen the sea; for he did not count the quiet waters of the Mediterranean. Molde brought back to him memories of Grimstad and Bergen, and it is related that he stood for hour after hour gazing down into the fjord, or out at the rough waters of the Atlantic.

People in Molde told him strange stories about the sea, and the power it had over those who lived near it. Two stories in particular remained in his mind. One, told him by a lady, was of a Finn who, by means of the troll-power in his eyes, had induced a clergyman's wife to leave husband, children, and home, and go away with him. The other was of a seaman who left home and stayed away for many years, so that his family believed him dead; suddenly he returned, and found his wife married to another man.

The former story must have reminded Ibsen of his own mother-in-law, Magdalene Thoresen, who had fled from her native Denmark to escape from a love affair with an Icelandic poet, and had married a widowed clergyman seventeen years her senior. In one of her letters, she has left a vivid account of what happened. "While I was studying in Copenhagen, I met a young man, a wild, strange, elemental creature. We studied together, and I had to yield before his monstrous and demonic will. With him, I could have found passion and fulfilment; I still believe that . . . Now I have never regretted that he let me go, for as a result I met a better person, and have lived a better life. But I have always been conscious that he could have nurtured into flower that love of which my spirit was capable. So I have lived my life oppressed by a feeling of want and longing. . . ." Of her husband she said: "Thoresen was my friend, my father and my brother, and I was his friend, his child. . . . He was a man to whom I could openly and unhesitatingly say anything and be understood." She had already told him of "a tragic incident in my restless life. But I begged him to regard the past, those years when I had been ignorant, helpless and unprotected, years which I found it impossible to explain either to myself or to anyone else, as a closed book. I begged him to accept me as I was as the result of that struggle and, if he thought me worthy of it, to let the rest be blotted out. He accepted me."

Magdalene Thoresen was powerfully affected by the sea, and could hardly live away from it. Even in old age, she had to go down every day to bathe in the surf. "People in Norway," Ibsen said to a German friend while he was writing THE LADY FROM THE SEA, "are spiritually under the domination of the sea. I do not believe other people can fully understand it."

During the winter of 1885, after his return from Molde, Ibsen was occupied with planning *Rosmersholm*. As usual, he did not actually put pen to paper until the summer, and completed it in September 1886. Certain traits in the character of Rebecca West in *Rosmersholm* are plainly influenced by Ibsen's stay in Molde. She is obsessed by the sea, Ulric Brendel calls her "a mermaid," and she compares herself to the sea-trolls which, according to legend, clung to ships and hindered their sailing.

Ibsen had determined to revisit the northern sea again the following summer, but in the meantime a chain of events occurred which, though unconnected with the sea, were also to leave their mark on his next play.

In December 1886, shortly after he had completed *Rosmersholm*, Ibsen was invited by Duke George II of Saxe-Meiningen to visit Liebenstein for a theatrical festival, in the course of which, among other plays, *Ghosts* was to be performed. Duke George was the patron and inspirer of the famous Meiningen troupe which, under its producer, Kronek, so influenced theatrical managers all over Europe during the eighteen-eighties (including Antoine, Otto Brahm, Stanislavsky and Henry Irving, who was much impressed by their lighting and grouping when he saw them in London in 1881). It was not the first time Ibsen had been a guest of the Duke, for as long ago as 1876 he had visited him to see a performance of *The Pretenders*—a performance which may very possibly have influenced his subsequent writing. This time, however, the Duke showed Ibsen signs of especial favour which evidently left a deep impression on him. In his letter of thanks, Ibsen speaks of "a long and deeply cherished dream" having been fulfilled, and says that the memories of his stay at Liebenstein will remain with him to enrich his remaining days. During the next few months, his plays were performed with success in town after town throughout Germany; he was repeatedly feted, three books were published about him, and eminent German authors praised him and wrote poems in his honour. In France, too, and even England, people were beginning to take serious notice of him at last. He had of course attracted attention in these countries through *A Doll's House* and *Ghosts*, but hitherto his reputation outside Scandinavia had still been largely that of a revolutionary. Now he was beginning to be looked upon as an altogether larger and more permanent figure; and Ibsen, like most revolutionary writers, was much gratified at being at last accepted by what is nowadays known as "the Establishment."

Next summer (1887), Ibsen returned again to the north; but this time he chose, not Norway, but Denmark. At first he went to Frederikshavn, but "I was frightened away from that town, which has become a colony for artistic coteries," and he moved after ten days to the little town of Saeby, on the east coast of north Jutland. He found this much more to his liking and, as at Molde two years before, spent hours each day gazing out to sea. A nineteen-year-old Danish girl named Engelke Wulff, who was also staying at Saeby, noted on the beach "a little, broad-shouldered man, with grey sidewhiskers and eyebrows. He stood staring out across the water, with his hand shading his eyes. He had a stick with him with which he supported himself while he took a book out and wrote something in it. From where I sat and watched him, I supposed him to be drawing the sea." Ibsen saw her, too, as she sat doing her handiwork, and after a time got into conversation with her. She told him of her longing to see the world, and of her love of the theatre, and he promised that he would put her into his next play. One thinks immediately of Bolette; but in fact, when they met by chance in a street in Christiania some years later, he called her "my Hilde," and one must assume that some of Hilde's lines in THE LADY FROM THE SEA, if not her character, stemmed from his conversations with Engelke Wulff on the beach at Saeby.

Another young lady from Saeby imprinted herself in Ibsen's memory, though he never met her, for the good reason that since 1883 she had been lying in Saeby churchyard. Her name was Adda Ravnkilde; she was a talented young writer who had killed herself at the age of twenty-one, leaving behind her several stories and a novel, which was later published with a foreword by Georg Brandes. One theme recurs throughout her writings; the unsuccessful efforts of a young girl to free herself of her obsession for a man who she knows is not worthy of her. Ibsen read her writings, and visited her home and her grave. Her story, like the one he had heard in Molde, must have made him think of Magdalene Thoresen; she had succeeded in escaping from her obsession, but if she had not she might have suffered the same fate as this young girl.

On September 12, 1887, Ibsen made a speech at Gothenburg in the course of which he said that his polemical interests were waning and, with them, his eagerness for battle. Twelve days later, in a speech in Stockholm, he startled his audience by describing himself as an "optimist," declaring that he believed the world was entering a new epoch in which old differences would be reconciled and humanity would find happiness. On October 5, he attended a dinner in the Copenhagen home of his publisher, Hegel. In his address of thanks, Ibsen said that this summer, in Denmark, he had "discovered the sea; that the smooth and pleasant Danish sea, which one could come close to without feeling that mountains cut off the approach, had given his soul rest and peace, and that he was carrying away memories of the sea which would hold significance for his life and his writing."

In addition to his rediscovery of the sea, and the international recognition that was now being accorded him, a third mollifying influence should be mentioned. During the eighteen months that elapsed between the completion of *Rosmersholm* and the beginning of work on THE LADY FROM THE SEA, Ibsen held a number of conversations with Henrik Jaeger, who was preparing the first authorised biography for publication in 1888, in honour of Ibsen's sixtieth birthday. In the course of these conversations, Ibsen recalled many old memories, to help Jaeger with the early chapters. These memories included some which Ibsen had tried to forget; but now, when he dragged them out into the daylight, he found that they no longer had the power to frighten him. Consequently, as Professor Francis Bull has remarked, Ibsen must have felt impelled to ask himself whether it did not lie within a man's power to drive away "ghosts" and "white horses," of whatever kind, provided he had the courage to look his past in the face and make his choice between the past and the present, a choice taken "in freedom and full responsibility." In *Rosmersholm*, a potentially happy relationship between two people is destroyed by the power of the past; in THE LADY FROM THE SEA, Wangel and Ellida overcome that power, and it may be that Ibsen's conversations with Jaeger gave him a new confidence, if only a temporary one, in man's ability to escape from the terror of his own history.

A fourth influence, though scarcely a mollifying one, was the increasing interest of scientists during the eighteen-eighties in the phenomena of hypnosis and suggestion. Throughout Europe during this decade, writers were being infected with this interest; Ibsen's preliminary jottings for *The Wild Duck* in 1884 contain references to "the sixth sense" and "magnetic influence," and Strindberg's *Creditors*, written in the same year as THE LADY FROM THE SEA, is closely concerned with "magnetism" and hypnosis.

It was Ibsen's practice to allow eighteen months to elapse after the completion of a play before beginning to write another; he would meditate long on a theme before putting pen to paper. Consequently, it was not until June 5, 1888, that he made the first rough notes for *Rosmersholm's* successor, which he provisionally entitled *The Mermaid*. Five days later, he began the actual writing. It took him nine weeks to complete his first draft, and since in his manuscript he dated each act we can tell exactly how long the various stages of the play took him. Act I is dated June 10–16; Act II, June 21–28; Act III, July 2–7; Act IV, July 12–22; and Act V, July 24–31. Early in August, he began to revise the play, and by August 18 he had corrected the first two acts to his satisfaction. Two days later, he began to revise the third act, and on August 31 he started on the fourth. We do not know when he finished his revision, but on September 25 he posted his final

manuscript to Hegel, and on November 28, 1888, the play
was published by Gyldendal in Copenhagen under the new
title of THE LADY FROM THE SEA, in a first printing of 10,000
copies. It was first performed on February 12, 1889, simultaneously at the Christiania Theatre, Christiania, and at the
Hoftheater, Weimar.

When THE LADY FROM THE SEA first appeared, most of the
critics were puzzled, especially in Norway, and apart from a
production at the Schauspielhaus in Berlin in 1889 the play
seems never really to have succeeded in Ibsen's lifetime. Its
psychology struck his contemporaries as fanciful and uncon-
vincing, although Kierkegaard had long ago asserted, as
Freud was shortly to assert, the importance of allowing someone who is psychologically sick to be faced with some kind
of choice and to make his own decision. When, however, THE
LADY FROM THE SEA was revived in Oslo in 1928, on the occasion of the centenary of Ibsen's birth, Halvdan Koht wrote:
"It was a surprise to find how fresh the play seemed. . . . No
one could but be struck by how closely the whole conception of the play was related to the very latest scientific psychology, both that which Pierre Janet had originated in the
nineties, and the 'psycho-analysis' which Sigmund Freud had
founded at the same time, and which became universally
known shortly after the beginning of the twentieth century.
THE LADY FROM THE SEA instantly acquired a new meaning
and new life. Science had in the meantime seized on all mor-
bid activities of the soul, had penetrated into all its border
lands, and had tried to follow all the suppressed impulses in
their subconscious effect, the strife between original, suppressed will or desire, and acquired, thought-directed will.
With poetic insight, Ibsen had seemed to foresee all this.
He envisaged a woman who felt hampered and bound in her
marriage because she had married, not for love, but for material support, and in whom there consequently arose a series
of distorted imaginings which gripped her mind like witch-
craft. She needed a doctor, so Ibsen made her husband one
—he had at first intended to make him a lawyer. Moreover,
Ibsen discovered the remedy for Ellida; he gave her back
her full sense of freedom. . . . As early as *Love's Comedy*

(1862), he had declared war on all marriage which was not built upon full freedom, and now he wished to picture a marriage which, from being a business arrangement, became a free and generous exchange. Ellida was to experience what Nora (in A Doll's House) missed—'the miracle'."

Ibsen's rough notes and draft of THE LADY FROM THE SEA provide some interesting revelations of the dramatist's mind at work. At first, as already explained, he intended to make Wangel a lawyer "refined, well-born, bitter. His past stained by a rash affair. In consequence, his future career is blocked." But he abandoned this conception, and Wangel became instead a kindly and understanding doctor. His wife first appears as Thora (perhaps after Magdalene Thoresen), but Ibsen changed this to Ellida. In The Saga of Frithiof the Bold, there is a ship named Ellide, "which," Halvdan Koht points out in his biography of Ibsen, "there means something like 'the storm-goer.' Such a name gave a stronger suggestion of storm and mysterious troll-powers; the ship Ellidi in the saga was almost like a living person fighting its way against evil spirits that tried to drag it down." Ibsen originally intended that Ellida should have broken her engagement with the seaman because of social and moral prejudices derived from his upbringing; but, significantly, he discarded this motive, and the conflict between Wangel and the Stranger became instead a struggle to gain control over the subconscious powers of her soul. Ibsen also planned at first to have an extra group of characters who would represent the outside world and be contrasted with the inhabitants of the little town, but he scrapped this idea, presumably to achieve stronger dramatic concentration.

Lyngstrand, the consumptive sculptor, had made a phantom appearance four years earlier in Ibsen's first notes for The Wild Duck. Bolette and Hilde seem to have been present in Ibsen's mind while he was planning Rosmersholm, for his early notes for that play contain mention of Rosmer's two daughters by his dead wife, the elder of whom "is in danger of succumbing to inactivity and loneliness. She has rich talents, which are lying unused," while the younger daughter is "sharply observant; passions beginning to dawn."

Among the characters Ibsen considered putting into THE
LADY FROM THE SEA, but subsequently discarded, was "an
old married clerk. In his youth wrote a play, which was performed once. Is continually touching it up, and lives in the
illusion of getting it published and becoming famous." This
character, who appears to have been based on a friend of
Ibsen's youth named Vilhelm Foss, turned up four plays later
as Vilhelm Foldal in *John Gabriel Borkman*. Hilde Wangel
was to reappear formidably in *The Master Builder*.

The early notes for THE LADY FROM THE SEA also contain
mention of a "strange passenger," visiting with the steamer,
who "once felt a deep attachment to her [Ellida] when she
was engaged to the young sailor." This character was clari-
fied into Hesler, a civil servant; then Ibsen altered his name
to Arenholdt, Askeholm, and finally, Arnholm, and turned
him from a civil servant into a schoolmaster.

The "young sailor" does not figure in Ibsen's first cast-list,
and Ibsen seems to have intended that he should not appear;
then he hit on the notion of making him, and not Arnholm,
"the strange passenger," or, as he finally called him, "the
Stranger." The Stranger is (unless one reckons Ulric Brendel
in *Rosmersholm* as such) the predecessor of those Intruders
from the Outside World who enter so importantly into Ibsen's
later plays: Hilde in *The Master Builder*, The Rat Wife in
Little Eyolf, Mrs. Wilton in *John Gabriel Borkman*, the Nun
in *When We Dead Awaken*. After several productions had
failed to portray the Stranger satisfactorily, Ibsen issued a
directive that this character "shall always stand in the background, half concealed by the bushes; only the upper half of
his body visible, against the moonlight." In a letter to Julius
Hoffory, he stressed that the Stranger "has come as a passenger on a tourist steamer. He does not belong to the crew. He
wears tourist dress, not travelling clothes. No-one knows what
he is, or who he is, or what his real name is." At Weimar,
where he thought the production "quite admirable," though
Wangel and Lyngstrand were disappointing, he allowed himself an unusual luxury in way of praise. "I cannot wish for,
and can hardly imagine, a better representation of the Stranger than the one I saw here. A long, lean figure, with a hawk
face, black, piercing eyes, and a splendid deep, quiet voice."

The incident of the rings which Ellida and the Stranger throw into the sea as a token of betrothal was borrowed from Ibsen's own experience. Thirty-five years before, in his early days as an apprentice at the theatre in Bergen, he had fallen in love with a fifteen-year-old girl named Rikke Holst, and they had betrothed themselves to each other in just this way. Rikke's father had broken off the match and, three years before he wrote THE LADY FROM THE SEA, Ibsen had re-encountered his former fiancée, now married to a rich businessman and surrounded by numerous children. That meeting, too, left its mark on the play.

The objection most commonly raised against THE LADY FROM THE SEA is the difficulty of making the climactical moment of Ellida's choice seem convincing. In this connection, Dr. Gunnar Ollén has written: "No-one who saw the production in Vienna in the spring of 1950, with Attila Hörbiger as Wangel and Paula Wessely as Ellida, will share the opinion that Ellida's choice is implausible. The way Hörbiger played the scene in which he gives Ellida her freedom, her choice seemed utterly natural. He became red in the face, and had difficulty in enunciating his words, standing absolutely motionless and upright, with tears streaming down his cheeks. Quite simply, a stronger emotional power emanated from her husband than from the sailor. She . . . stared at Wangel as though seeing him for the first time, and then walked slowly across to him as though magnetically drawn. It was as if two hypnotists were fighting to gain control of a medium."

Pirandello particularly admired THE LADY FROM THE SEA, and Ellida was Eleonora Duse's favourite role among the many of Ibsen's in which she excelled. She chose it both for her "farewell performance" in 1909, and for her comeback twelve years later. In 1923, she played it in London, at the New Oxford Theatre, and James Agate has left a memorable description of her performance:

"This play is a godsend to a great artist whose forte is not so much doing, as suffering that which Fate has done to her. With Duse, speech is silver, and silence golden. . . . The long second act was a symphony for the voice, but to me the scene of greatest marvel was the third act. In this, Duse scaled incredible heights. There was one moment when, drawn by every fibre of her being to the unknown irresistible of the Stranger and the sea, she blotted herself behind her husband and took comfort and courage from his hand. Here terror and ecstasy sweep over her face with that curious effect which this actress alone knows—as though this were not present stress, but havoc remembered of past time. Her features have the placidity of long grief; so many storms have broken over them that nothing can disturb again this sea of calm distress. If there be in acting such a thing as pure passion divorced from the body yet expressed in terms of the body, it is here. Now and again in this strange play, Duse will seem to pass beyond our ken, and where she has been there is only a fragrance and a sound in our ears like water flowing under the stars."

M.M.

CHARACTERS

DR. WANGEL, a country doctor
ELLIDA, his second wife
BOLETTE ⎫
HILDE ⎭ his daughters by a previous marriage
ARNHOLM, a schoolmaster
LYNGSTRAND
BALLESTED
A STRANGER
YOUNG PEOPLE FROM THE TOWN
TOURISTS AND VISITORS

The action takes place during the summer in a small town by a fjord in northern Norway.

This translation of THE LADY FROM THE SEA *was first performed on August 24, 1958, on BBC Television, with the following cast:—*

DR. WANGEL	Claes Gill
ELLIDA	Rosalie Crutchley
BOLETTE	Avril Elgar
HILDE	Jill Dixon
ARNHOLM	Robert Harris
LYNGSTRAND	Donald Bradley
BALLESTED	George Howe
A STRANGER	Harold Lang

Produced by Casper Wrede and Michael Elliott
Settings by Norman James

ACT ONE

DR. WANGEL's *house. On the left, a large verandah, roofed. In the foreground, and surrounding the house, is a garden. Below the verandah, a flagstaff. On the right, in the garden, an arbour, with a table and chairs. In the background is a hedge, containing a small gate. Behind the hedge, a path along the shore, shaded by trees. Through the trees we can see the fjord, with high mountain ranges rising to peaks in the distance. It is a hot and brilliantly clear summer morning.*

BALLESTED, *middle-aged, dressed in an old velvet jacket and a broad-brimmed artist's hat, is standing beneath the flagstaff busying himself with the line. The flag itself is lying on the ground. A short distance away stands an easel with a canvas on it. Beside it is a folding chair, on which lie brushes, a palette, and a paintbox.*

BOLETTE WANGEL *comes out through the open doors leading on to the verandah. She is carrying a big vase of flowers, which she puts on the table.*

BOLETTE. Hullo, Ballested. Can you manage all right with that?

BALLESTED. Oh yes, Miss Bolette. It's quite a simple matter really. If I may be so bold as to ask—are you expecting visitors today?

BOLETTE. Yes, we're expecting Dr. Arnholm this morning. You know, the schoolmaster.

BALLESTED. Arnholm? Wait a moment! Wasn't there a gentleman called Arnholm who used to be—ah—tutor here a few years ago?

BOLETTE. That's right, my old tutor. He arrived in town last night.

BALLESTED. So he's in these parts again?

BOLETTE. Yes, that's why we want the flag up.

BALLESTED. Very proper.

BOLETTE goes back into the garden room. A few moments later LYNGSTRAND comes up the path from the right, and stops, interested, on catching sight of the easel and painting materials. He is a thin young man, shabbily but decently dressed and of delicate appearance.

LYNGSTRAND, *from the other side of the hedge.* Good morning.

BALLESTED, *turning.* Oh! Good morning.

Hoists the flag.

There now! Up she goes!

Makes the line fast and gets busy at the easel.

Good morning, sir. I don't think I've had the pleasure——

LYNGSTRAND. You're a painter, are you?

BALLESTED. Er—conceivably. Why not a painter, *inter alia?*

LYNGSTRAND. Why not indeed? Can I come inside for a moment?

BALLESTED. You wish to look at my work?

LYNGSTRAND. Yes, I'd like to very much.

BALLESTED. There's nothing much to see yet. Still, if you'd really like to. Pray step in.

LYNGSTRAND. Thank you.

He comes in through the gate.

BALLESTED, *painting.* Just now I'm working on that stretch of the fjord—there, you see, between the islands.

LYNGSTRAND. Yes, I know.

BALLESTED. I haven't begun on the figure yet, though. It's impossible to secure a model in this town.

LYNGSTRAND. Are you going to have a figure as well?

BALLESTED. Yes. On this rock—here in the foreground. I'm going to have a mermaid. Half dead.

LYNGSTRAND. Why half dead?

BALLESTED. She's wandered in from the sea, and can't find her way back. So here she lies, dying in the brackish waters of the fjord. You follow me?

LYNGSTRAND. Yes, I see.

BALLESTED. It was the lady of the house here who put the idea into my head.

LYNGSTRAND. What are you going to call this picture when you've finished it?

BALLESTED. I'm thinking of calling it "The Death of the Mermaid."

LYNGSTRAND. Very appropriate. You should be able to make something really good out of this.

BALLESTED, *looking at him.* A—ah—fellow-forager, perhaps?

LYNGSTRAND. Er—painter, you mean?

BALLESTED. Yes.

LYNGSTRAND. No, I'm not a painter. I'm going to be a sculptor, actually. My name is Lyngstrand—Hans Lyngstrand.

BALLESTED. So you're going to be a sculptor? Yes, yes—sculpture's a fine art too—very fine. I think I've seen you in the town once or twice. Have you been around here long?

LYNGSTRAND. No, only a fortnight. But I'm going to stay the whole summer, if I can manage to.

BALLESTED. And enjoy the bathing amenities, no doubt.

LYNGSTRAND. Yes, that's why I came. To regain my strength.

BALLESTED. Oh? You don't look—ah—infirm.

LYNGSTRAND. I am a little—infirm, as you say. Nothing dangerous. My chest, you know. Just a shortness of breath now and then.

BALLESTED. That's nothing. Er—perhaps you should consult a doctor all the same—a good doctor.

LYNGSTRAND. I thought—Dr. Wangel—if I get an opportunity.

BALLESTED. Yes, I should.

Glances left.

There's another steamer coming in. Bursting with passengers. It's quite phenomenal how the tourist traffic has increased here these last few years.

LYNGSTRAND. Yes, I've noticed you get a lot of trippers.

BALLESTED. Ah, and a lot of people come for the whole summer too. I often fear our little town may lose its character with all these strangers coming here.

LYNGSTRAND. Were you born here?

BALLESTED. No, but I've accli—acclimatised myself. I've been here so long and got so much into the ways of the place that I feel like one of the natives.

LYNGSTRAND. Then you've been here a long time?

BALLESTED. Seventeen years. No—eighteen! I came with a theatrical company. But we got into financial difficulties, so the company broke up. Scattered to the four winds.

LYNGSTRAND. But you stayed.

BALLESTED. Yes, I stayed. And did quite nicely, really. My forte in those days used to be decoration and design.

BOLETTE *comes out with a rocking chair, which she sets down on the verandah.*

BOLETTE, *talking to someone in the garden room.* Hilde, see if you can find that embroidered footstool for Father, will you?

LYNGSTRAND *goes to the verandah and greets her.* Good morning, Miss Wangel.

BOLETTE, *leaning over the rail.* Why, hullo, Mr. Lyngstrand, is it you? Good morning. Forgive me a moment, I must just—

Goes back into the house.

BALLESTED. You know the family, then?

LYNGSTRAND. Not really. I've just met the young ladies once or twice here and there. And exchanged a few words with Mrs. Wangel the last time they had a concert up on the hill. She suggested I should come and call on them some time.

BALLESTED. You must cultivate their acquaintance.

LYNGSTRAND. I thought I'd pay them a call. A visit, as they say in England. I've been trying to think up some excuse.

BALLESTED. Excuse! Bah!

Glances away left.

Oh, confound it! The steamer's almost alongside now. I must get along to the hotel. The new arrivals may need my services. I run a little line as haircutter and *friseur*, I must tell you.

LYNGSTRAND. You're very versatile.

BALLESTED. Well, one's got to ac—climatise oneself. One's got to learn to do a bit of everything in a little place like this. If you should ever need anything in that line—pomade, or suchlike—just ask for Monsieur Ballested, the dancing master.

LYNGSTRAND. Dancing master?

BALLESTED. Chairman of the Horn Society, if you like. We're giving a concert up on the Prospect this evening. Goodbye, goodbye!

He goes out through the garden gate with his painting materials and disappears, left. HILDE *comes out of the house with the footstool,* BOLETTE *follows her with more flowers.*

LYNGSTRAND, *down in the garden, raises his hat.*

HILDE, *coming to the verandah railing. She does not acknowledge his greeting.* Bolette tells me you've actually ventured into the garden today.

LYNGSTRAND. Yes, I have taken that liberty.

HILDE. Been walking all morning?

LYNGSTRAND. No, actually, I've just——

HILDE. You've been swimming, then, I suppose?

LYNGSTRAND. Yes, I had a little dip. I saw your mother down there. She was just going into her bathing-hut.

HILDE. Who, do you say?

LYNGSTRAND. Your mother.

HILDE. Oh, I see what you mean.

She puts the footstool down in front of the rocking chair.

BOLETTE, *quickly.* Did you see anything of Father's boat out on the fjord?

LYNGSTRAND. Yes, I thought I saw a boat sailing this way.

BOLETTE. That would be Father. He's been visiting some patients on the islands.

She busies herself at the table.

LYNGSTRAND, *climbing on to the first step of the stairs to the verandah.* How splendid you're making it look with all these flowers.

BOLETTE. Yes, it looks rather nice, don't you think?

LYNGSTRAND. Wonderful. As though you were celebrating some sort of red letter day.

HILDE. We are.

LYNGSTRAND. I guessed as much. Your father's birthday, I presume?

BOLETTE, *warningly to* HILDE. Ssh!

HILDE, *ignoring her.* No, Mother's.

LYNGSTRAND. Really? Your mother's?

BOLETTE, *softly, but angrily.* Hilde——

HILDE. Leave me alone.

To LYNGSTRAND.

Well, I suppose you'll be going back to your hotel for lunch now?

LYNGSTRAND *steps down.* Yes, I ought to be getting a bite of something.

HILDE. I suppose the food up there seems wonderful to you.

LYNGSTRAND. I don't live at the hotel any longer. I found it too expensive.

HILDE. Where do you live now, then?

LYNGSTRAND. Up at Mrs. Jensen's.

HILDE. Which Mrs. Jensen?

LYNGSTRAND. The midwife.

HILDE. Really, Mr. Lyngstrand, I have better things to do——

LYNGSTRAND. Ah, of course. I ought not to have said that.

HILDE. Said what?

LYNGSTRAND. What I said just now.

HILDE. I haven't the faintest idea what you're talking about.

LYNGSTRAND. No, no. Well I'd better say *au revoir* to you and Miss Bolette.

BOLETTE, *coming down the steps.* Goodbye, Mr. Lyngstrand, goodbye! Do please excuse us today. Some other time— when you have nothing to do—you must come and look round the house and see Father and—the rest of us.

LYNGSTRAND. Yes, thank you very much. I should love to.

He raises his hat and goes out through the garden gate. As he goes down the path to the left, he raises his hat again up towards the verandah.

HILDE, *half aloud. Au revoir*, monsieur! Give my love to Mother Jensen.

BOLETTE, *quietly, shaking her by the arm.* Hilde, you little beast! Are you mad? He could easily have heard you.

HILDE. Do you think I care if he did?

BOLETTE, *glancing right.* Here's Father.

DR. WANGEL, *in travelling clothes, with a small bag in his hand, comes up the path from the right.*

WANGEL. Well, young ladies, here I am again.

Enters through garden gate.

BOLETTE, *going down into the garden to meet him.* Oh, Father! It's good to have you back!

HILDE, *also running down to him.* Are you free for the day now, Father?

WANGEL. Oh no, I shall have to go down to the surgery for an hour or two. Tell me, has Arnholm arrived yet?

BOLETTE. Yes, he got into town last night. We heard from the hotel.

WANGEL. You haven't seen him, then?

BOLETTE. No. But I expect he'll come here this morning.

WANGEL. Yes, I'm sure he will.

HILDE, *pulling his arm.* Father! Look!

WANGEL, *looking up at the verandah.* Why yes, child. I see. How very gay.

BOLETTE. Don't you think we've made it look pretty?

WANGEL. I should say you have. Is your—are there just the three of us at home now?

HILDE. Yes, she's gone down to——

BOLETTE, *quickly.* Mother's gone down to bathe.

WANGEL *gives* BOLETTE *an affectionate glance, and pats her head. Then he says awkwardly.* But tell me, young ladies, are you going to have the house looking like this for the rest of the day? With the flag flying and everything?

HILDE. Father! Of course!

WANGEL. I see. But——

BOLETTE, *with a wink.* Of course, you know we've really done all this for Dr. Arnholm. When such an old friend comes to pay his first——

HILDE, *shaking his arm playfully.* He used to be Bolette's tutor, Father!

WANGEL, *with a half smile.* What a couple of rogues you are! Well, well! I suppose it's inevitable that we should spare a thought now and then for her who is no longer with us. All the same—— Here, Hilde!
Gives her the bag.
Run down with that to the surgery, there's a good girl. No, children, I don't like this—the way you—every year—— Ah, well. I suppose it must be so.

HILDE, *about to go through the garden with* WANGEL's *bag, stops, turns, and points.* Isn't that Dr. Arnholm?

BOLETTE, *looking in the same direction.* That?
Laughs.
Silly! He's much too old for Arnholm.

WANGEL. Upon my soul, I think it is he! Yes, it is, yes!

BOLETTE *stares, amazed.* Good heavens, I think you're right.

DR. ARNHOLM, *the schoolmaster, elegantly dressed in morning clothes, with gold spectacles and a slender cane, comes up the path, from the left. He looks overworked. He glances*

*into the garden, gives a friendly wave and comes in through
the gate.*

WANGEL, *going to greet him.* Welcome, my dear fellow!

Warmly.

Welcome home!

ARNHOLM. Thank you, Dr. Wangel, thank you. You are too
kind.

*They shake hands warmly and go together across the
garden.*

And here are the children!

Holds out his hands and looks at them.

I should hardly have recognised them.

WANGEL. No—I don't suppose you would.

ARNHOLM. Except—Bolette perhaps. Yes, I think I should have
known Bolette.

WANGEL. Really? It must be eight or nine years since you
last saw her. Ah, yes. A great deal has changed here in
that time.

ARNHOLM, *looking round.* I was just thinking the opposite. Except that the trees are a little taller—and that arbour——

WANGEL. Ah, yes, externally——

ARNHOLM, *smiling.* And now you have two eligible grown-up
daughters.

WANGEL. Well—one.

HILDE. Oh, Father!

WANGEL. Shall we go and sit on the verandah? It's cooler
there.

Indicates to ARNHOLM *to precede him up the steps.*

ARNHOLM. Thank you, my dear doctor, thank you.

They go up. WANGEL *waves* ARNHOLM *into the rocking
chair.*

WANGEL. There, now. Just sit back and take things easy. You
look quite exhausted after your long journey.

ARNHOLM. Oh, that's nothing. The air here is so——

BOLETTE, *to* WANGEL. Shall we bring some seltzer and some

lemonade into the garden room? It'll soon be too hot to sit out here.

WANGEL. Yes, do that, will you, children? Bring us some seltzer and some lemonade. And some brandy, too, perhaps.

BOLETTE. You want some brandy, too?

WANGEL. Just a drop. In case anyone should feel like it.

BOLETTE. Yes, of course. Hilde, take Father's bag to the surgery, will you?

BOLETTE *goes into the garden room and closes the door behind her.* HILDE *takes the bag and walks through the garden and out behind the house, to the left.*

ARNHOLM, *who has watched* BOLETTE *go out.* What a lovely girl—er—your daughters have grown into.

WANGEL, *sitting.* Yes, they have, haven't they?

ARNHOLM. Yes. I'm amazed at Bolette—and Hilde too. But now, tell me about yourself, my dear doctor. Have you decided to settle here for good?

WANGEL. Oh yes, I think so. I was born and bred here, as they say. And here I spent those unbelievably happy years with her—the few years we were allowed. You met her when you were here before, Arnholm.

ARNHOLM. Yes. Yes.

WANGEL. And now I have found a new happiness here with— my new wife. Yes, all in all I must confess that Fate has been kind to me.

ARNHOLM. You have had no children by your second marriage?

WANGEL. We had a little boy two—no, two and a half years ago. But we didn't keep him long. He died when he was four or five months old.

ARNHOLM. Is your wife not at home today?

WANGEL. Yes, she'll be here soon. She's down at the fjord bathing. She goes every day now. Whatever the weather.

ARNHOLM. You speak as if there were—something the matter with her.

WANGEL. There's nothing exactly the matter with her. She's been very nervous these past few years. Off and on, you know. I can't make up my mind what's behind it. Bathing in the sea has become a—a kind of passion with her.

ARNHOLM. Yes. I remember she used to be like that.

WANGEL, *with an almost imperceptible smile.* Of course, you knew Ellida when you taught out at Skjoldviken.

ARNHOLM. Yes. She used to come to the vicarage. And I met her quite often when I went out to the lighthouse to see her father.

WANGEL. The life out there has never loosed its hold on her. The people here can't fathom her. They call her: "The Lady from the Sea."

ARNHOLM. Do they really?

WANGEL. Yes. That's why—— Talk to her about the old days, Arnholm. It will do her so much good.

ARNHOLM, *glancing uncertainly at him.* You have some special reason for thinking that?

WANGEL. Yes.

ELLIDA'S *voice, from the garden, offstage right.* Is that you, Wangel?

WANGEL, *getting up.* Yes, my dear.

ELLIDA WANGEL *comes through the trees by the arbour, wearing a large, lightweight bathing wrap, her hair wet and spread over her shoulders.* DR. ARNHOLM *gets to his feet.*

WANGEL, *smiling and stretching out his hands to her.* Well, here she is, our lady from the sea.

ELLIDA *goes quickly up to the verandah and clasps his hands.* Thank heaven you're back! When did you arrive?

WANGEL. Just now—a few minutes ago.

Indicates ARNHOLM.

Well, aren't you going to greet an old friend?

ELLIDA, *holding out her hand to* ARNHOLM. You've come, then? Welcome! Forgive me for not being here when you——

ARNHOLM. Please. You mustn't put yourself to any trouble——

WANGEL. How was the water today? Fresh and clean?

ELLIDA. Fresh? Dear God, the water here is never fresh. Ugh! The water is sick here in the fjord.

ARNHOLM. Sick?

ELLIDA. Yes—sick. And poisonous, I sometimes think.

WANGEL *smiles.* Well, you're certainly doing your best to recommend the amenities of the place.

ARNHOLM. No, I rather think that Mrs. Wangel has a special affinity to the sea and everything connected with it.

ELLIDA. But have you noticed how beautifully the girls have arranged everything in your honour?

WANGEL, *embarrassed.* Hm.

Looks at his watch.

Well, I must be getting off.

ARNHOLM. Is all this really in my honour?

ELLIDA. Certainly. You don't think we do this sort of thing every day? Ugh—how stiflingly hot it is under this roof.

Goes down into the garden.

Come down here. There's at least some air down here.

Sits in the arbour.

ARNHOLM, *going to her.* I think the air's quite fresh up here.

ELLIDA. Oh, you're used to that dreadful city air. It's quite suffocating in summer, I'm told.

WANGEL, *who has also come down into the garden.* Well, Ellida, my dear, now you must entertain our good friend by yourself for a while.

ELLIDA. Have you work to do?

WANGEL. Yes, I must go to the surgery—and change my clothes, too. I shan't be long, though.

ARNHOLM, *seating himself in the arbour.* Please don't hurry yourself, my dear doctor. Your wife and I will manage to pass the time.

WANGEL *nods.* Yes, I'm sure you will. Well—see you later.

Goes out left, through the garden.

ELLIDA, *after a brief silence.* It's pleasant sitting here, don't you think?

ARNHOLM. Very pleasant, I think—now.

ELLIDA. We call this my arbour. Because I made it. Or rather, Wangel made it for me.

ARNHOLM. And this is where you like to sit?

ELLIDA. Yes, I sit here most of the day.

ARNHOLM. With the girls, I suppose?

ELLIDA. No, the girls stay on the verandah.

ARNHOLM. And Wangel himself?

ELLIDA. Oh, Wangel comes and goes. Half an hour with me, half an hour with the children.

ARNHOLM. Did you make that arrangement?

ELLIDA. I think it suits us all best. We can call across—when we have anything to say to each other.

ARNHOLM, *after a moment's thought.* When I last saw you— out at Skjoldviken, I mean—— Hm. That's a long time now.

ELLIDA. At least ten years.

ARNHOLM. Yes. But when I remember you as you used to be out there in that lighthouse—the old priest used to call you "The Heathen" because your father had given you the name of a ship instead of an honest Christian name, he used to say——

ELLIDA. Yes—well?

ARNHOLM. The last thing on earth I could have imagined would have been that I should ever see you here as Mrs. Wangel.

ELLIDA. Yes, then Wangel was still—the girls' mother was alive. Their real mother, I mean.

ARNHOLM. Yes, of course. But even if he hadn't been—even if he'd been a bachelor—I could never have guessed that this would happen.

ELLIDA. Nor could I. Not for a moment. Then.

ARNHOLM. Wangel is such a good man. So honourable—so good and kind to everyone.

ELLIDA, *warmly and affectionately.* Yes!

ARNHOLM. But he must be so very different from you, I should have thought.

ELLIDA. He is.

ARNHOLM. How did it happen then? How did it happen?

ELLIDA. Oh, my dear Arnholm, you mustn't ask me that. I

couldn't begin to explain to you. And even if I could, you could never begin to understand.

ARNHOLM. Hm.

More subdued.

Have you ever told your husband anything about me? I mean, of course, regarding that foolish proposal I once made to you?

ELLIDA. No! Of course not. I've never breathed a word to him about that.

ARNHOLM. I'm glad. I was a little worried at the thought that you might have——

ELLIDA. Well, you needn't be. I have merely told him the truth, which is that I was very fond of you, and that you were the best and truest friend I had out there. Have you ever thought of marrying anyone else?

ARNHOLM. Never. I have remained faithful to my memories.

ELLIDA, *half jestingly.* Oh, Arnholm! Let those sad old memories rest! You ought to look round for a wife who could make you happy.

ARNHOLM. I shall have to begin soon, then, Mrs. Wangel. I'm already thirty-seven, you know.

ELLIDA. All the more reason to lose no time then.

She is silent for a moment, then continues earnestly and in a subdued voice.

Arnholm, my dear, listen. I want to tell you something I could never have told you—at the time—not if my life had been at stake.

ARNHOLM. What?

ELLIDA. When you made that—when you asked—what you spoke of just now—— I couldn't have replied in any other way than I did.

ARNHOLM. I know. You had nothing to offer me except friendship. I know that.

ELLIDA. But you don't know that all my thoughts and feelings were already directed elsewhere.

ARNHOLM. Already?

ELLIDA. Yes.

ARNHOLM. But that's impossible! Why, you didn't even know Wangel then.

ELLIDA. I'm not speaking of Wangel.

ARNHOLM. Not Wangel? But at that time—when you were out at Skjoldviken—I can't think of anyone else you could possibly have become attached to.

ELLIDA. No, I suppose not. The whole thing was so insane.

ARNHOLM. Tell me more.

ELLIDA. All that matters is that I was already in love with someone else. Well, now you know.

ARNHOLM. But if you hadn't been in love with someone else?

ELLIDA. Yes?

ARNHOLM. Would you have replied differently to my letter?

ELLIDA. How can I tell? When Wangel came I replied differently to him.

ARNHOLM. Then why do you bother to tell me this?

ELLIDA *rises to her feet, as though in pain.* Because I've got to have someone to confide in. No, don't get up.

ARNHOLM. Then your husband knows nothing about this?

ELLIDA. I told him from the first that I had once been in love with someone else. He has never demanded to know any more. And we've never discussed the matter. In any case the whole thing was insane. And it soon passed over—in a way——

ARNHOLM, *rising to his feet.* In a way! Not completely?

ELLIDA. Yes, yes, completely! Oh, Arnholm, it's not as you think. It's all quite inexplicable. I don't know how I could begin to tell you. You would only think I was ill or mad.

ARNHOLM. My dear Mrs. Wangel, you must and shall tell me the whole truth.

ELLIDA. Very well. I'll try. Tell me; how, as a sensible man, can you explain this?

Glances away and breaks off.

I'll tell you later. Someone is coming.

LYNGSTRAND *comes down the path from the left, and enters the garden. He is wearing a flower in his buttonhole and is carrying a large and splendid bouquet, wrapped in paper and tied with ribbon. He halts and hesitates uncertainly beneath the verandah.* ELLIDA, *coming to the edge of the arbour.*

Are you looking for the girls, Mr. Lyngstrand?

LYNGSTRAND, *turning.* Ah, is that you, Mrs. Wangel?

Raises his hat, and comes towards her.

No, I wasn't looking for the girls, Mrs. Wangel—it was you I wanted to see. You were so kind as to suggest that I might pay a visit some time——

ELLIDA. Why, yes, so I did. You are always welcome here.

LYNGSTRAND. Thank you so much. Well, seeing that it happened to be rather a special occasion here today——

ELLIDA. Oh, you know about that?

LYNGSTRAND. Yes. So I thought I'd be so bold as to ask you to accept this.

He bows and offers her the bouquet.

ELLIDA, *with a smile.* But, my dear Mr. Lyngstrand, don't you think you ought to give your beautiful flowers to Dr. Arnholm yourself? It's he who——

LYNGSTRAND, *glancing uncertainly from one to the other.* Forgive me, but I don't know this gentleman. I only came because of the—the birthday.

ELLIDA. Birthday? You have made some mistake, Mr. Lyngstrand. It's nobody's birthday here today.

LYNGSTRAND *beams happily.* Oh, I know all about it. I didn't realise it was meant to be a secret, though.

ELLIDA. What do you know all about?

LYNGSTRAND. That it's your birthday, Mrs. Wangel.

ELLIDA. Mine?

ARNHOLM. Today? Surely not?

ELLIDA, *to* LYNGSTRAND. What makes you think it is?

LYNGSTRAND. Miss Hilde let it out. I was here for a few moments earlier today. I asked the young ladies why they'd got everything to look so smart with flowers and flags——

ELLIDA. I see.

LYNGSTRAND. And Miss Hilde said: "It's because today is Mother's birthday."

ARNHOLM. Ah!

He and ELLIDA *exchange a glance of understanding.*

Well, since this young gentleman knows, Mrs. Wangel——

ELLIDA, *to* LYNGSTRAND. Yes, since you know——

LYNGSTRAND, *offering her the bouquet again.* May I then have the honour to offer my congratulations?

ELLIDA, *taking the flowers.* It's very kind of you. Won't you come in and sit down for a minute, Mr. Lyngstrand?

ELLIDA, ARNHOLM, *and* LYNGSTRAND *sit down in the arbour.*

This business—about my birthday—was meant to be a secret, Dr. Arnholm.

ARNHOLM. I know. It wasn't meant to be revealed to us outsiders.

ELLIDA, *putting the bouquet down on the table.* No, that's right. Not to outsiders.

LYNGSTRAND. I promise I shan't breathe a word about it to a living soul.

ELLIDA. It's really of no importance. But tell me, how are you? You're looking better than when I last saw you.

LYNGSTRAND. Yes, I think I'm making good progress. And next year, when I get down to the south—the Mediterranean, that is—if I manage to——

ELLIDA. That's arranged, the girls tell me.

LYNGSTRAND. Yes, I hope so. I've got a benefactor in Bergen who's very good to me. He's promised he'll help me next year.

ELLIDA. How did you come to meet him?

LYNGSTRAND. A most extraordinary piece of luck. I happened to go to sea once in one of his ships.

ELLIDA. Really? So you loved the sea?

LYNGSTRAND. No, not in the least. But when my mother died, my father didn't want to have me hanging round the house any longer, so he made me go to sea. Well, on the way home our ship was wrecked in the English Channel. Luckily for me.

ELLIDA. Why do you say luckily?

LYNGSTRAND. Well, it was as a result of the shipwreck that I got this chest trouble. I was such a long time in the water before they picked me up. And it was terribly cold—cold as ice. So then I had to leave the sea. Yes, it was a great stroke of luck for me.

ARNHOLM. Oh, do you really think so?

LYNGSTRAND. Why, yes. This chest of mine isn't at all dangerous. And now I can become a sculptor, which is what I really want. Clay's so beautiful—the way it takes shape beneath your fingers.

ELLIDA. What are you going to do? Mermaids? Or Vikings?

LYNGSTRAND. No, nothing like that. As soon as I can, I want to try my hand at something really big. A group. A composition.

ELLIDA. Really? What is this composition to represent?

LYNGSTRAND. Well, it's got to be something I've experienced myself.

ARNHOLM. Quite right! Always stick to your own experiences.

ELLIDA. Tell us about it.

LYNGSTRAND. Well, what I have in mind is a young girl, a sailor's wife, lying asleep—but restlessly, strangely restlessly. She's dreaming. I think I'll be able to manage it so that you can see she's dreaming.

ARNHOLM. But you said a composition.

LYGNSTRAND. Yes, I'm going to have another figure. Symbolic, don't you know? Her husband, whom she's been unfaithful to while he's been away. He's been drowned—drowned in the sea.

ELLIDA. Drowned?

LYGNSTRAND. Yes. Drowned on a sea-voyage. But he came home to her all the same. One night. And there he stands by her bed, staring at her. Wet and sodden as—as only a drowned man can be.

ELLIDA, *leaning back in her chair.* That's strange. Wonderfully strange. Yes. I can see it so vividly.

ARNHOLM. But for heaven's sake, Mr.—Mr.—— I thought you said this composition was to represent something that had once happened to you.

LYNGSTRAND. Yes. It did happen to me. In a manner of speaking.

ELLIDA. What exactly happened, Mr. Lyngstrand?

LYNGSTRAND. We were just about to sail for home from a town called Halifax when the boatswain fell ill, and we had to leave him behind in hospital. So we signed on another fellow instead, an American. Well, this new boatswain——

ELLIDA. The American?

LYNGSTRAND. Yes. One day he borrowed a bundle of old newspapers from the captain, and spent every minute he could reading them. He said he wanted to learn Norwegian.

ELLIDA. Yes! And then?

LYNGSTRAND. Well, one evening a terrible storm blew up. All the men were on deck except the boatswain and me. He'd sprained a foot, so that he couldn't walk. I wasn't feeling well either, and was lying in my bunk. Well, there he was sitting in the cabin, re-reading one of these old newspapers——

ELLIDA. Yes, yes?

LYNGSTRAND. Well, as he's sitting there, I hear him give a kind of howl. And when I look at him, I see his face has gone as white as chalk. Then he crumples the paper together and pulls it into a thousand pieces. But he did it all so quietly. So quietly.

ELLIDA. Didn't he say anything? Not a word?

LYNGSTRAND. Not at first. But after a bit he said to himself: "Married. To another man. While I was away."

ELLIDA *closes her eyes and says half audibly.* He said that?

LYNGSTRAND. Yes. And, would you believe it, he said it in really good Norwegian. He must have had a wonderful ear for languages, that man.

ELLIDA. What then? What else happened?

LYNGSTRAND. Well, then this extraordinary thing happened which I shall never forget. He said, still in the same calm voice: "But mine she is, and mine she shall always be. And she will come to join me, even though I go as a drowned man to claim her."

ELLIDA *pours herself a glass of water. Her hand trembles.* Ugh! How close it is!

LYNGSTRAND. And the way he said it made me think he would do it too.

ELLIDA. Do you know what—what has become of this man?

LYNGSTRAND. Ah, Mrs. Wangel, he's dead, I'm sure.

ELLIDA, *passionately.* Why do you think that?

LYNGSTRAND. Well, it was just after that that we got wrecked in the Channel. I managed to get into the big lifeboat with the captain and five others. The mate got into the dinghy. And the American and one other man were there with him.

ELLIDA. And nothing has been heard of them since?

LYNGSTRAND. Nothing, Mrs. Wangel. My benefactor told me this in a letter I got from him recently. That's just why I so want to—to commemorate it. His faithless girl and the drowned man coming home from the sea to revenge himself on her. I can see them both so clearly.

ELLIDA. So can I.

She rises.

Come, let's go inside. Or down to Wangel. It's so suffocatingly close here.

She goes out of the arbour.

LYNGSTRAND, *who has also got up.* Yes, well, I must say thank you and be off. I just wanted to pay a little courtesy call, seeing it was your birthday.

ELLIDA. As you wish.

Holds out her hand.

Goodbye. And thank you for the flowers.

LYNGSTRAND *shakes her hand and exits by the garden gate.*

ARNHOLM *gets up and goes over to* ELLIDA. I can see this has touched you deeply, Mrs. Wangel.

ELLIDA. You could put it that way. Except that——

ARNHOLM. Still, it was something you had to be prepared for.

ELLIDA. Prepared for?

ARNHOLM. Yes, surely?

ELLIDA. Prepared for someone to come back? And to come back like that?

ARNHOLM. What on earth——? Is it this business about the dead man which so disturbed you? And I thought——

ELLIDA. What did you think?

ARNHOLM. Why, naturally, I thought you were play-acting all the time he was speaking. I thought you were upset because you'd found out about this secret family celebration. Your husband and his children living a life of memories from which you are excluded.

ELLIDA. Oh, no, no! I have no right to demand of my husband that he shall be wholly and entirely mine.

ARNHOLM. I think you have. You must have.

ELLIDA. Yes. No, no, I haven't. That's the point. I live a life —from which they are excluded.

ARNHOLM. You! Do you mean to say you—you aren't really fond of your husband?

ELLIDA. Yes, yes, I am! I have grown so very fond of him. That's what makes it so dreadful.

ARNHOLM. Now you must tell me what makes you so unhappy. The whole story. Don't you want to tell me, Mrs. Wangel?

ELLIDA. I can't. Not now anyway. Later, perhaps.

BOLETTE *comes out on to the verandah and descends into the garden.*

BOLETTE. Father's just finishing in the surgery. Shall we all go into the garden room?

ELLIDA. Yes, let's.

WANGEL, *who has changed his clothes, appears on the left with* HILDE *from behind the house.*

WANGEL. Well, here I am! Finished for the day! What about a nice glass of something cool, eh?

ELLIDA. Just a moment.

She goes into the arbour and picks up her bouquet.

HILDE. Oh, look! All those lovely flowers! Where did you get them from?

ELLIDA. I got them from young Mr. Lyngstrand, the sculptor.

HILDE. From Lyngstrand?

BOLETTE, *uneasily.* Has Lyngstrand been here again?

ELLIDA. Yes, he came just now with these. For the birthday, you know.

BOLETTE, *nudging* HILDE. Oh!

HILDE *whispers.* The cat!

WANGEL, *in an agony of embarrassment, to* ELLIDA. I—you—Ellida, my dear, I——

ELLIDA, *cutting him short.* Come, children. Let's put my flowers in water with the others.

She goes up to the verandah.

BOLETTE *whispers to* HILDE. She's awfully nice really!

HILDE. Monkey tricks! She's only doing it to please Father!

WANGEL, *up on the verandah, presses* ELLIDA'S *hand.* Thank you, Ellida. Thank you so much, my dear.

ELLIDA, *busying herself with the flowers.* You wouldn't want me to be the only one not celebrating—Mother's birthday, would you?

ARNHOLM. Hm!

He goes up to WANGEL *and* ELLIDA. BOLETTE *and* HILDE *stay down in the garden.*

ACT TWO

*Up on "The Prospect," a wooded height behind the town.
In the background, a cairn of stones with a weathervane.
Large stones arranged as seats stand around the cairn and
in the foreground. Far below to the rear can be seen the
outer part of the fjord, with islets and headlands. The open
sea cannot be seen.*

*It is the half light of a Norwegian summer night. It is red-
dish gold in the air, and above the mountain peaks far
away in the distance. The sound of four-part singing can
be heard faintly from the slopes away down to the right.*

*Young people from the town, of both sexes, come up in
couples from the right, walk, talking intimately, past the
cairn and go out left. A few seconds later* BALLESTED *enters,
acting as guide to a group of foreign tourists and their
ladies. He is weighed down with shawls and bags.*

BALLESTED, *pointing upwards with his stick.* Sehen Sie, meine
Herrschaften—dort there liegt anders hill. Das willen wir
also climb, und so herunter—Mesdames et Messieurs, voila
une autre montaigne. Elle a une vue magnifique—il est
necessaire que nous la monterons aussi——

He leads them out left, continuing in execrable French.

HILDE *comes nimbly up from the right, stops and looks back.
A few moments later,* BOLETTE *follows her.*

BOLETTE. Hilde, why are we running ahead of Lyngstrand like this?

HILDE. Oh, I get bored with going so slowly. Look at the way he crawls along.

BOLETTE. Oh, but you know how ill he is.

HILDE. Do you think it's very serious?

BOLETTE. I do.

HILDE. He came to consult Father this afternoon. I'd like to know what he thinks about it.

BOLETTE. Father told me he's got congestion of the lungs, or something of the kind. He won't live to be old, Father said.

HILDE. No, did he say that? Just as I thought!

BOLETTE. For heaven's sake, don't let him suspect you know anything.

HILDE. What do you take me for?

Half to herself.

Look, Hans has managed to clamber up at last. Hans. He looks as though he ought to be called Hans, doesn't he?

BOLETTE *whispers.* Behave yourself now! Please!

LYNGSTRAND *enters from the right, carrying a parasol.*

LYNGSTRAND. Please forgive me, young ladies, for lagging so far behind you.

HILDE. Have you got yourself a parasol now too?

LYNGSTRAND. It's your mother's. She said I might use it as a stick. I didn't bring one of my own.

BOLETTE. Are they still down there? Father and the rest?

LYNGSTRAND. Yes. Your father went into the refreshment hut. And the others are sitting outside listening to the music. But they're coming up here soon, your mother said.

HILDE *stands staring at him.* You must be very tired.

LYNGSTRAND. Yes, perhaps I am a little tired. I think I'll sit down for a minute.

Sits on a stone in right foreground.

HILDE, *standing in front of him.* Do you know there's going to be dancing down there by the bandstand later?

LYNGSTRAND. Yes, so I heard.

HILDE. Do you think it's fun, dancing?

BOLETTE, *who has gone to pick small flowers in the heather.* Hilde! Give Mr. Lyngstrand a chance to get his breath back!

LYNGSTRAND. Oh, yes, Miss Hilde, I should so love to dance. If only I could.

HILDE. You mean you've never learned?

LYNGSTRAND. No—I have never learned, but that wasn't what I meant. I meant I mustn't, because of my chest.

HILDE. Does it make you very unhappy, having this chest trouble?

LYNGSTRAND. Oh, no, I can't really say that.
Smiles.
I think it's because of that that everyone's so good and kind and—helpful to me.

HILDE. Yes. And it isn't really serious, is it?

LYNGSTRAND. Serious? Good heavens, no, not in the least. Your father made that quite clear to me.

HILDE. It'll be all right as soon as you can get away and travel.

LYNGSTRAND. Yes. It'll be all right, then.

BOLETTE, *with flowers.* Here now, Mr. Lyngstrand. These are to go in your buttonhole.

LYNGSTRAND. Why, thank you, Miss Bolette, thank you. It's really too kind of you.

HILDE, *looking down right.* They're coming now.

BOLETTE, *also looking down.* I hope they know where to turn off. Oh, they've gone wrong.

LYNGSTRAND, *getting up.* I'll run down to the turning and shout to them.

HILDE. You'll have to shout very loud.

BOLETTE. No, don't. It'll make you tired again.

LYNGSTRAND. Nonsense, it's downhill.
Exits right.

HILDE. Downhill—yes.
Watches him.

Now he's jumping! It hasn't occurred to him he's got to climb uphill again on the way back.

BOLETTE. Poor boy!

HILDE. If Lyngstrand asked you to marry him, would you accept him?

BOLETTE. Have you gone mad?

HILDE. I mean if he hadn't got this chest trouble, of course. And if he wasn't going to die so soon. Would you have him then?

BOLETTE. I think he'd suit you better than me.

HILDE. Me?

Laughs.

He hasn't a bean. Not even enough to keep himself alive.

BOLETTE. Why do you always make so much fuss of him, then?

HILDE. Oh, only because of that chest of his.

BOLETTE. I haven't noticed that you feel sorry for him.

HILDE. No, I don't really. I think it's fascinating.

BOLETTE. What?

HILDE. To listen to him saying it's not serious, and that he's going south to become an artist. He believes every word he says, and it makes him so happy. And it'll never come to anything, because he won't live long enough. Oh, I think that's so exciting!

BOLETTE. Exciting?

HILDE. Yes, I think it's exciting. I'm not ashamed to admit it.

BOLETTE. Hilde, you are a cruel little beast!

HILDE. I want to be. So there!

Looks down.

I say! Arnholm's not enjoying all this climbing.

Turns.

It's true, it's true. Do you know what I noticed at dinner?

BOLETTE. No, what?

HILDE. His hair's beginning to fall out. Here in the middle.

BOLETTE. What nonsense! It isn't true.

HILDE. It is! And he's getting wrinkles round both his eyes. Oh, Bolette, how on earth could you have fallen in love with him when he was tutoring you?

BOLETTE *smiles.* Yes, it's strange, isn't it? I remember once I burst into tears because he said he thought Bolette was an ugly name.

HILDE. Not really?

Looks down again.

Oh, come and look! The Lady from the Sea's walking with him. Father's on his own. I wonder if those two are stuck on each other?

BOLETTE. You really ought to be ashamed of yourself! How can you stand there talking like that about her? Just when we're all getting on so well together——

HILDE. Oh yes? That's what you think, my girl! She'll never get on with us. She's not our sort. And we're not hers. God knows why Father ever dragged her into the house! I shouldn't be surprised if she went off her head one of these fine days.

BOLETTE. Off her head? How can you say such a thing?

HILDE. It wouldn't surprise me. Her mother went mad. She died in an asylum. I know.

BOLETTE. Is there anything you don't stick your nose into? Well, don't go round talking about it. Be nice to her—for Father's sake. You hear what I say, Hilde?

WANGEL, ELLIDA, ARNHOLM, *and* LYNGSTRAND *come up from the right.*

ELLIDA, *pointing upstage.* Out there it lies.

ARNHOLM. Yes, that's right. It must be in that direction.

ELLIDA. Out there lies the sea.

BOLETTE, *to* ARNHOLM. Don't you think it's lovely up here?

ARNHOLM. Magnificent. Splendid view.

WANGEL. Yes, I suppose you've never been up here before.

ARNHOLM. No, never. In my time, I don't think you could get up here. There wasn't even a footpath.

WANGEL, *indicating the cairn and stone seats.* None of all this either. It's all new——

BOLETTE. There's an even better view from Lodskollen over there.

WANGEL. Shall we go there, Ellida?

ELLIDA, *sitting on a stone, right.* I won't, thanks. You go on. I'll sit here till you come back.

WANGEL. I'll do the same. The girls can show Dr. Arnholm the way.

BOLETTE. Would you like to come with us, Dr. Arnholm?

ARNHOLM. Thank you, I'd love to. Is there a path up there too?

BOLETTE. Oh, yes. A good broad one.

HILDE. Broad enough for two people to walk arm in arm.

ARNHOLM, *looking at her.* I can well believe it, Miss Hilde.

To BOLETTE.

Shall we two see if she's speaking the truth?

BOLETTE. Yes, let's.

They go out left, arm in arm.

HILDE, *to* LYNGSTRAND. Shall we go too?

LYNGSTRAND. Arm in arm?

HILDE. Why not? I've no objection.

LYNGSTRAND *takes her arm and beams happily.* This is rather a lark, isn't it?

HILDE. A lark?

LYNGSTRAND. Yes, it looks just as though we were engaged.

HILDE. Haven't you ever walked arm in arm with a lady before, Mr. Lyngstrand?

They go out left.

WANGEL, *standing by the cairn.* Well, Ellida, my dear, now we have a moment to ourselves.

ELLIDA. Yes. Come and sit here beside me.

WANGEL, *sitting.* How calm and peaceful it is up here. Now we can talk a little.

ELLIDA. What about?

WANGEL. About you. You and me, Ellida. We can't go on like this.

ELLIDA. What do you want instead?

WANGEL. That we should trust each other—live together as man and wife—the way we used to before.

ELLIDA. If only we could! But it's quite impossible.

WANGEL. I think I know how you feel.

ELLIDA, *passionately*. You don't! Don't say you understand me!

WANGEL. But I do. You are so honest and loyal, Ellida.

ELLIDA. Loyal. Yes.

WANGEL. You couldn't find peace or happiness in any compromise relationship.

ELLIDA. Yes. Go on.

WANGEL. You were not made to be a man's second wife.

ELLIDA. Why do you suddenly say that?

WANGEL. I have often felt it. But today I realised it fully. The children's preparations for the anniversary. You thought I was in the conspiracy, didn't you? One cannot wipe out one's memories. I can't, anyway. I'm not made like that.

ELLIDA. I know that. Oh, I know it so well.

WANGEL. No, no. To you it's almost as though the children's mother were still alive. As though she were invisibly living among us. You think my love is divided between you and her. That thought is the cause of your unrest. You feel as though there were something—indecent in our relationship. That's why you can't—why you don't want to live with me as my wife any longer.

ELLIDA. But you haven't realised it all.

WANGEL *rises*. I know, of course, there is something else too, Ellida.

ELLIDA, *frightened*. Something else?

WANGEL. Yes. You can't stand this place. The mountains oppress you—they weigh you down. There's not enough light for you here. Not enough sky around you. Not enough strong, clean air.

ELLIDA. How right you are! Night and day, winter and summer, it fills me—this homesickness for the sea.

WANGEL. I know.

Puts his hand on her head.

And now my poor, sick child shall go home again.

ELLIDA. What do you mean?

WANGEL. What I say. We are going away.

ELLIDA. Going away?

WANGEL. Yes. Somewhere by the open sea. Somewhere where you can find a real home. The sort of home you long for.

ELLIDA. Oh, no, my dear. You mustn't think of it. You couldn't live anywhere in the world but here.

WANGEL. That's as it may be. Do you suppose I could be happy here without you?

ELLIDA. But I am here. And I shall stay here. I am yours.

WANGEL. Are you mine, Ellida?

ELLIDA. Don't let's talk about leaving. Your life's work lies here.

WANGEL. We are leaving this place. Going away somewhere. That is settled, Ellida.

ELLIDA. But what do you hope we shall gain by it?

WANGEL. Health and peace of mind—for you.

ELLIDA. I wonder. But what about you? Think of yourself too. What do you hope to gain?

WANGEL. You, Ellida. You again.

ELLIDA. But you can't! No, no! You can never do that, Wangel!

WANGEL. We shall have to see. If that's how you feel, there's no other solution. You've got to go! And the sooner the better. That is settled.

ELLIDA. No! Oh no! I'd rather tell you the truth.

WANGEL. Tell me.

ELLIDA. I'm not going to let you make yourself unhappy for my sake. Especially since it can't help us.

WANGEL. You have promised you will tell me the whole truth.

ELLIDA. I will tell you as well as I can. And as truthfully as I can. Come here and sit beside me.

They sit on the stones.

WANGEL. Well, Ellida? Tell me.

ELLIDA. That day you came out to Skjoldviken and asked me to be your wife, you spoke so frankly to me about your first marriage. You told me how happy you had been.

WANGEL. Yes, I was.

ELLIDA. I know. I only want to remind you that I was just as honest with you. I told you quite openly that I had once been in love with someone else. That we had become—in a way—engaged.

WANGEL. In a way?

ELLIDA. Yes. It lasted such a short time. He went away. And I regarded it as finished and done with. I told you all this.

WANGEL. But my dear Ellida, why drag all this up? It had nothing to do with me. I've never even asked who he was.

ELLIDA. No. You're always so considerate towards me.

WANGEL *smiles.* Anyway, I think I could have provided the name myself. Out in Skjoldviken there weren't so many people to choose from. In fact, there was only one.

ELLIDA. You—think it was Arnholm?

WANGEL. Yes. Wasn't it?

ELLIDA. No.

WANGEL. Not he? Well, then you have me baffled.

ELLIDA. Do you remember, late one autumn, a big American ship came in to Skjoldviken for repairs?

WANGEL. Yes. They found the captain one morning murdered in his cabin. I went out myself and did a postmortem.

ELLIDA. Yes, I suppose you did.

WANGEL. It was the mate who killed him.

ELLIDA. You've no right to say that! It was never proved.

WANGEL. There wasn't any room for doubt. Why else should he have gone away and drowned himself?

ELLIDA. He didn't drown himself. He went away with another ship, up into the Arctic.

WANGEL, *surprised.* How do you know that?

ELLIDA, *unwillingly*. Oh, Wangel! That is the man to whom I was engaged.

WANGEL *rises quickly*. What are you saying?

ELLIDA. It was he.

WANGEL. But in heaven's name, Ellida! How could you do such a thing? Go and get engaged to a man like that! A stranger you knew nothing about? What was his name?

ELLIDA. At that time he called himself Freeman. Later, when he wrote to me, he signed himself Alfred Johnston.

WANGEL. Where was he from?

ELLIDA. Finmark, he said. Up in the Arctic Circle. But he was born in Finland. He came to Norway as a child—with his father, I think.

WANGEL. What else do you know about him?

ELLIDA. Only that he went to sea when he was very young. And that he had voyaged all round the world.

WANGEL. Nothing else?

ELLIDA. No. We never talked about him.

WANGEL. What did you talk about then?

ELLIDA. Mostly about the sea.

WANGEL. Ah! The sea!

ELLIDA. Storms and calms. Dark nights at sea. And the sea on sunny days—we talked about that too. But mostly we talked about whales and dolphins, and seals that lie out on the islands. And we spoke of gulls and eagles and all the other sea birds—you know. And—isn't it strange?—when we talked about these things, I had a feeling that these sea beasts and birds were somehow of the same blood as he.

WANGEL. And—you——?

ELLIDA. I felt almost as if I were one of them too.

WANGEL. I see. So—you became engaged to him?

ELLIDA. Yes. Well, he said I should.

WANGEL. Said you should? Had you no will of your own?

ELLIDA. Not when he was with me. Oh, when I look back at it now, it all seems so impossible to understand.

WANGEL. Did you see him often?

ELLIDA. No, not very often. One day he came out to look round the lighthouse. That was how we met. After that we saw each other occasionally. But this thing happened— with the captain—and he had to leave.

WANGEL. Tell me more about that.

ELLIDA. Early one morning—I remember it was scarcely light —I got a note from him. In it he wrote that I was to come out and meet him at Bratthammeren—you remember, that headland between the lighthouse and Skjoldviken.

WANGEL. I remember.

ELLIDA. I was to go out there at once, he wrote, because he wanted to talk to me.

WANGEL. And you went?

ELLIDA. I had to. Well, then he told me that he had killed the captain during the night.

WANGEL. He admitted it!

ELLIDA. But he had only done what had to be done, he said. What was right.

WANGEL. What was right? Why did he kill him, then?

ELLIDA. He said it was nothing for me to know about.

WANGEL. And you believed him? Just like that?

ELLIDA. Yes. It never occurred to me to do otherwise. Well, anyway, he had to leave. But just before he said good-bye——

WANGEL. Yes? Tell me.

ELLIDA. He took out of his pocket a key-chain, and pulled a ring off his finger, a ring he always used to wear. And he took a little ring from my finger too, and put these two rings on to his key-chain. Then he said that we two were going to marry ourselves to the sea.

WANGEL. Marry——?

ELLIDA. Yes, those were the words he used. Then he threw the chain and rings with all his strength, as far as he could, out into the sea.

WANGEL. And you, Ellida—you let him do this?

ELLIDA. It's strange, isn't it? At the time it seemed—ordained. But then, thank God! he went away.

WANGEL. And when he'd gone——?

ELLIDA. Oh, I soon came to my senses, of course. I saw how mad and meaningless the whole thing had been.

WANGEL. But you said something about letters. You have heard from him since, then?

ELLIDA. Yes, I heard from him. First I got a few short lines from Archangel. He just said he was going over to America. And gave an address for me to reply to.

WANGEL. Did you?

ELLIDA. At once. I wrote, of course, that everything was finished between us. And that he was not to think of me any more, just as I would never think of him again.

WANGEL. But he wrote again?

ELLIDA. Yes, he wrote again.

WANGEL. What did he say?

ELLIDA. It was just as though I had never broken with him. He wrote affectionately and—calmly that I was to wait for him. He would let me know when I could come to him. And then I was to come at once.

WANGEL. He wouldn't give you up?

ELLIDA. No. So I wrote again. Almost word for word as I had written before. Even more strongly.

WANGEL. He stopped writing to you then?

ELLIDA. No. No. He wrote as calmly as before. Never a word about my having broken with him. Then I realised it was useless. So I never wrote to him again.

WANGEL. And you never heard from him?

ELLIDA. Yes, I got three more letters. One from California, and then one from China. The last I got from him was from Australia. He wrote that he was going to the gold mines. Since then I've never heard a word.

WANGEL. That man must have had an extraordinary power over you, Ellida.

ELLIDA. Yes. He was a demon.

WANGEL. But you mustn't think about him any more. Only

promise me that, my dearest Ellida. We are going to find a new cure for you now. A fresher air than we have here in the fjords. The cleansing, salt-heavy air of the sea. What do you say?

ELLIDA. I shall never be able to escape from it—there, any more than here.

WANGEL. Escape from it? What—my dear, what exactly do you mean?

ELLIDA. I mean the horrible, unfathomable power he has over my mind.

WANGEL. But you have freed yourself from that. Long ago. When you broke with him. All that is dead and forgotten.

ELLIDA *rises quickly.* No. That's just it. It isn't.

WANGEL. Not forgotten?

ELLIDA. No, Wangel! It isn't forgotten. And I'm afraid it never will be.

WANGEL, *in a choked voice.* You mean, you have never really been able to forget this stranger?

ELLIDA. I did forget him. But he came back to me.

WANGEL. How long ago did this happen?

ELLIDA. About three years ago now. Or perhaps a little longer. It was while I was carrying the child.

WANGEL. Ah! Then! Ellida, now I'm beginning to understand.

ELLIDA. No, my dear, you're wrong. Oh, I don't think anyone will ever be able to understand.

WANGEL. To think that for these three years you have been in love with another man.

ELLIDA. I don't love anyone else. Only you.

WANGEL, *in a subdued voice.* Then why have you refused to live with me as my wife all these years?

ELLIDA. Because I am afraid. Afraid of the stranger.

WANGEL. Afraid?

ELLIDA. Yes, afraid. The sort of fear that only the sea can give you. Oh, Wangel, I——

The young people from the town come back from the left,

wave to ELLIDA *and* WANGEL, *and go out right.* ARNHOLM, BOLETTE, HILDE *and* LYNGSTRAND *come with them.*

BOLETTE, *as they go past.* Hullo, are you still up here?

ELLIDA. Yes. It's so lovely and cool up here on the hill.

ARNHOLM. We're going down to dance.

WANGEL. Fine, fine. We'll be down in a few minutes to join you.

HILDE. Goodbye, then. See you soon.

ELLIDA. Mr. Lyngstrand—would you mind waiting a minute?

LYNGSTRAND *stays.* ARNHOLM, BOLETTE, *and* HILDE *go out right. To* LYNGSTRAND.

Are you going to dance too?

LYNGSTRAND. No, Mrs. Wangel, I don't think I ought to.

ELLIDA. No, better be careful. That chest of yours—it's not quite right yet, is it?

LYNGSTRAND. Not quite, no.

ELLIDA, *slowly.* How long is it now since you were on that voyage when you——?

LYNGSTRAND. When I first got this—trouble?

ELLIDA. Yes, that voyage you were telling us about this morning.

LYNGSTRAND. Oh, it must be about—wait a moment. Yes, about three years ago.

ELLIDA. Three years.

LYNGSTRAND. Perhaps a bit more. We left America in February. Then we got wrecked in March. We ran into the equinoctial gales.

ELLIDA, *looking at* WANGEL. That was the time.

WANGEL. But, dearest Ellida——

ELLIDA. Well, we mustn't keep you, Mr. Lyngstrand. Go on down. But no dancing.

LYNGSTRAND. I won't. I'll just watch.

Exits right.

WANGEL. Ellida, why did you ask him about that voyage?

ELLIDA. Johnston was on board with him. I'm almost sure of it.

WANGEL. What makes you think that?

ELLIDA, *ignoring the question.* He'd heard I'd married some-one else. While he was away. And it was—at that moment that this—came over me.

WANGEL. You mean, this fear?

ELLIDA. Yes. I can see him—in front of me. No, not quite in front—a little to one side. He never looks at me. He's just —there.

WANGEL. How does he look?

ELLIDA. The same as when I saw him last.

WANGEL. Ten years ago?

ELLIDA. Yes. Out at Bratthammeren. I see him so clearly. On his chest there's a pin with a big bluish-white pearl. Like a dead fish's eye. As though it were staring at me.

WANGEL. For heaven's sake! You are sicker than I thought, Ellida. Sicker than you know.

ELLIDA. Help me! If you can. I feel it crowding in on me— more and more.

WANGEL. And you've been in this state for three whole years —suffering in secret—without telling me?

ELLIDA. But—I couldn't! Not till now—when I had to—for your sake, Wangel! If I had told you all this—I should also have had to tell you—something unspeakable.

WANGEL. Unspeakable?

ELLIDA. No, no, no! Don't ask me! Only one thing more. One thing. Wangel—how shall we get to the bottom of—this riddle about the child's eyes?

WANGEL. My dearest Ellida, I promise you that was entirely your own imagination. The child had eyes exactly like any other child's.

ELLIDA. No, he hadn't. Couldn't you see? The child's eyes changed with the sea. When the fjord was calm and sunny, his eyes were the same. And when it was stormy—oh, I saw it clearly enough, even if you didn't.

WANGEL, *humouring her.* Well, suppose you are right? Sup-pose you are? What then?

ELLIDA, *quietly, closer.* I have seen eyes like that before.

WANGEL. When? Where?

ELLIDA. Out at Bratthammeren. Ten years ago.

WANGEL. What do you——?

ELLIDA *whispers*. The child had the stranger's eyes.

WANGEL *cries*. Ellida!

ELLIDA. Now perhaps you understand why I never dare live with you as your wife again!

She turns quickly and runs away down the hill.

WANGEL *runs after her, crying*. Ellida! Ellida! My poor, unhappy Ellida!

ACT THREE

A corner of DR. WANGEL's *garden. The place is damp and marshy, and overshadowed by large old trees. To the right can be seen the edge of a stagnant pond. A low open fence divides the garden from the footpath and the fjord beyond. On the other side of the fjord in the distance can be seen mountain ranges and peaks. It is late afternoon, approaching evening.*

BOLETTE *sits sewing on a stone bench, left. On the bench lie two or three books and a sewing basket.* HILDE *and* LYNGSTRAND *are walking along the edge of the pond, both carrying fishing rods.*

HILDE, *making signs to* LYNGSTRAND. Don't move! I can see a big one.

LYNGSTRAND, *looking.* Where?

HILDE *points.* Can't you see him? Down there! God Almighty, there's another!

Glances away between the trees.

Oh, now he's going to come and frighten them away.

BOLETTE, *looking up.* Who's coming?

HILDE. Your tutor, madame.

BOLETTE. My——?

HILDE. He's never been mine, thank heaven.

ARNHOLM *comes through the trees from the right.*

ARNHOLM. Are there any fish there?

HILDE, *pointing*. Yes, one or two old carp.

ARNHOLM. Those old carp! Are they still alive?

HILDE. Yes, they're tough. But we're going to catch one of them.

ARNHOLM. You'd have a better chance out in the fjord.

LYNGSTRAND. Ah, the pond's more—more mysterious.

HILDE. Yes, it's more exciting here. Have you been in the sea?

ARNHOLM. Yes, I've just come up from the bathhouse.

HILDE. I expect you stayed close to the shore.

ARNHOLM. Yes, I'm not a very good swimmer.

HILDE. Can you swim on your back?

ARNHOLM. No.

HILDE. I can.

To LYNGSTRAND.

Let's try over there on the other bank.

They go along the edge of the pond and out to the right.

ARNHOLM, *going closer to* BOLETTE. Sitting here all by yourself, Bolette?

BOLETTE. Oh, yes. I usually do.

ARNHOLM. Isn't your mother in the garden?

BOLETTE. No. She's taking a walk with Father.

ARNHOLM. How is she this afternoon?

BOLETTE. I don't know. I forgot to ask.

ARNHOLM. What are those books you have there?

BOLETTE. Oh, one's something about plants. And the other's a book about geography.

ARNHOLM. Do you like reading that sort of thing?

BOLETTE. Yes, when I can find the time. But I have to do the housework first.

ARNHOLM. But doesn't your mother—your stepmother—help you with that?

BOLETTE. No, that's my job. I had to see to it during the two years when Father was alone. And I've done it ever since.

ARNHOLM. But I can see you still love reading.

BOLETTE. Yes, I love reading anything I can get—anything useful. I want to know about the world. We live so outside everything here.

ARNHOLM. Don't say that, Bolette.

BOLETTE. Oh, we do. I don't think our life is very different from the life of those carp down there in the pond. The fjord lies so close, with big shoals of wild fish swimming in and out. But the poor tame carp mustn't know anything about what goes on out there. That life is not for them.

ARNHOLM. I don't think they'd be happy if they could get out into the fjord.

BOLETTE. I wonder.

ARNHOLM. Anyway, I don't think you can really say you live outside life here. Not in the summer at any rate. Nowadays your town's become a rendezvous for people from all over the world. They only pass through, of course——

BOLETTE *smiles.* Oh yes. It's easy for you to laugh at us. You're just passing through.

ARNHOLM. Laugh at you?

BOLETTE. What good is it to us that the great strange world glances in here on its way up to see the midnight sun? We can't join them. We shall never see the midnight sun. We just have to go on living here in our pond.

ARNHOLM *sits beside her.* Tell me, Bolette—isn't there something—something special, I mean—that you long for as you sit here?

BOLETTE. Yes—perhaps.

ARNHOLM. What? What do you long for?

BOLETTE. To get away.

ARNHOLM. That most of all?

BOLETTE. Yes. And after that—to learn. I want to know about —oh, about everything!

ARNHOLM. When I used to teach you, your father often said he would send you to the university.

BOLETTE. Oh, yes. Poor Father! He says so many things. But when it comes to the point—he never gets anything done.

ARNHOLM. I'm afraid you're right. But have you ever talked to him about it? Really sat down and talked about it?

BOLETTE. No. I've never done that.

ARNHOLM. But you should! Before it's too late. Why don't you?

BOLETTE. Because I never get anything done, either. I take after Father.

ARNHOLM. Hm. Don't you think you're being unfair to yourself?

BOLETTE. No. Unfortunately, Father has so little time to think about me and my future. And not much inclination either. He avoids thinking about these things as much as he can. He's so occupied with Ellida——

ARNHOLM. With whom?

BOLETTE. I mean—he and my stepmother——
Quickly.
Father and Mother have their own life to live.

ARNHOLM. Well, all the more reason for you to get away from here.

BOLETTE. Yes, I know. I must think of myself too. Try to go somewhere—do something. When Father dies, I've no one else. But, poor Father! I'm afraid to leave him.

ARNHOLM. But, good heavens, your stepmother! He'll still have her.

BOLETTE. Yes, I know. But she can't do all the things Mother used to do so well. There's so much this one doesn't see. Or won't see—or won't bother about. I don't know which it is.

ARNHOLM. Hm. I think I know what you mean.

BOLETTE. Poor Father—he's so hopeless about some things. Perhaps you've noticed that yourself. He hasn't enough work to keep him busy all the time. And she's quite incapable of helping him. Though that's partly his own fault.

ARNHOLM. How do you mean?

BOLETTE. Oh, Father only likes to see happy faces around him. We must have sunshine and happiness in the house, he says. I'm afraid he sometimes gives her medicines which aren't good for her in the long run.

ARNHOLM. Do you really believe that?

BOLETTE. Yes, I can't help it. She's so odd sometimes.

Passionately.

Isn't it unfair that I should have to go on living here? It doesn't do Father any good, really. And I've a duty towards myself, haven't I?

ARNHOLM. Bolette, this is something we two must discuss.

BOLETTE. Oh, what's the use? I was born to stay here in the pond.

ARNHOLM. Perhaps that depends on you.

BOLETTE, *alive.* Do you think so?

ARNHOLM. It lies entirely in your own hands.

BOLETTE. You mean you'd put in a good word for me with Father?

ARNHOLM. That too. But first I'd like to have a serious talk with you.

Glances left.

Ssh! Don't let them notice anything. We'll speak about this later.

ELLIDA *comes in from the left. She is hatless, and wears a large shawl over her head and shoulders.*

ELLIDA, *nervously excited.* Ah it's beautiful here. Beautiful!

ARNHOLM *gets up.* Have you been out walking?

ELLIDA. Yes. A long, long walk over the hills with Wangel. Now we're going out sailing.

BOLETTE. Won't you sit down?

ELLIDA. No, thank you. I don't want to sit.

BOLETTE *moves along the bench.* There's plenty of room here.

ELLIDA, *walking about.* No, no, no. I don't want to sit. I don't want to sit.

ARNHOLM. This walk has done you good. You look so ex-hilarated.

ELLIDA. Oh, yes. I feel so wonderfully well. Happy; and safe.

Looks left.

What's that big steamer coming in there?

BOLETTE *gets up and looks.* That must be the big English ship. Yes. The Englander.

ARNHOLM. Tying up to the buoy. Does she usually stop here?

BOLETTE. Only for half an hour. She's going further up the fjord.

ELLIDA. And then out again tomorrow. Out into the great open sea. And far across the sea. Just imagine if one could sail with her. If one could!

ARNHOLM. Have you never been on a long sea voyage, Mrs. Wangel?

ELLIDA. Never. Only to and fro here in the fjord.

BOLETTE, *with a sigh.* Ah, yes. We have to stick to the land.

ARNHOLM. Well, after all, this is where we belong.

ELLIDA. No, I don't think so. I think if people could only have learned from the beginning to live on the sea—perhaps even in the sea—we should be quite different now from what we are. Better—and happier.

ARNHOLM. Are you serious?

ELLIDA. Yes. I have often talked about it with Wangel.

ARNHOLM. What does he think?

ELLIDA. He thinks I may be right.

ARNHOLM, *jestingly.* Well, perhaps you are right. But what's done is done. We've taken the wrong turning and become land animals instead of sea animals, and must remain so. It's too late to alter things now.

ELLIDA. I'm afraid you're right. And I think people sense it. They endure it, as one endures a secret sorrow. I'm sure that's the real reason why people are melancholy. I'm sure of it.

BOLETTE. You mustn't brood like that. A few moments ago you were so happy.

ELLIDA. Yes, yes, I know. Oh, I'm just being stupid.

Looks uneasily round.

Why doesn't Wangel come? He promised me he would. But he's forgotten. Oh, dear Dr. Arnholm, would you go and look for him?

ARNHOLM. Of course. Gladly.

ELLIDA. Tell him he must come at once. I can't—see him.

ARNHOLM. Can't see him?

ELLIDA. You don't understand what I mean. When he's not with me, I can't remember how he looks. Then it's as though I'd lost him. It's horrible. Please go!

She walks restlessly up and down by the pond.

BOLETTE, *to* ARNHOLM. I'll go with you. You won't know where to look.

ARNHOLM. Never mind, I can manage.

BOLETTE, *half aloud.* No, I'm worried. I'm afraid he may be aboard the ship.

ARNHOLM. Afraid?

BOLETTE. Yes. He usually goes aboard to see if there's anyone he knows among the passengers. And the bar will be open——

ARNHOLM. Ah! Well, come along, then.

ARNHOLM *and* BOLETTE *go out left.* ELLIDA *stands for a moment staring down into the pond. Now and then she talks quietly and in snatches to herself. Then, outside, beyond the garden fence, a* STRANGER *comes down the path from the left. He is dressed as though for a journey, with a travelling bag slung on a strap from his shoulder, and a Scottish cap on his head. He has bushy, reddish hair and beard.*

THE STRANGER *walks slowly along by the fence and looks into the garden. Then he sees* ELLIDA, *stops, looks hard and searchingly at her, and says softly.* Good evening, Ellida.

ELLIDA *turns and cries.* Oh, my love! Have you come at last?

STRANGER. Yes, at last.

ELLIDA *stares at him, surprised and uneasy.* Who are you? Are you looking for someone here?

STRANGER. You know who I am.

ELLIDA. What do you mean? Whom have you come to see?

STRANGER. I have come to see you.

ELLIDA. Ah!

Stares at him, staggers backwards and cries.

The eyes! The eyes!

STRANGER. You know me at last! I knew you at once, Ellida.

ELLIDA. The eyes! Don't stare at me like that. I'll shout for help.

STRANGER. Ssh! Don't be afraid! I shan't hurt you.

ELLIDA *puts her hand over her eyes.* Don't look at me!

STRANGER *leans his arms on the fence.* I came with the Englander.

ELLIDA *looks timidly at him.* What do you want with me?

STRANGER. I promised I'd come back to you, as soon as I could.

ELLIDA. Go! Go away! Don't come back! Never come back again! I wrote to you that everything was finished between us. For ever. You know that.

STRANGER. I wanted to come before. But I couldn't. This was the first chance I got. Now I am yours again, Ellida.

ELLIDA. What do you want with me? Why have you come here?

STRANGER. You know I've come here to fetch you.

ELLIDA. But you know I'm married.

STRANGER. Yes, I know.

ELLIDA. And yet you have come to fetch me?

STRANGER. Yes.

ELLIDA *clasps her head in her hands.* Oh, this is horrible!

STRANGER. Don't you want to come?

ELLIDA. Don't look at me like that!

STRANGER. I am asking you: "Don't you want to come?"

ELLIDA. No, no. I don't want to! I can't. I won't!

More quietly.

Besides, I daren't.

STRANGER *climbs over the fence and comes into the garden.* Very well, Ellida. Just let me say one thing before I go.

ELLIDA *wants to run away but cannot. She stands as though paralysed by fear and supports herself against a tree by the pond.* Don't touch me! Don't come near me! Stay where you are! Don't touch me!

STRANGER *goes carefully a few paces towards her.* You mustn't be afraid of me, Ellida.

ELLIDA *puts her hand over her eyes.* Don't look at me.

STRANGER. Don't be afraid. Don't be afraid.

DR. WANGEL *comes through the garden from the left.*

WANGEL, *as he comes through the trees.* I'm afraid I've kept you waiting a long time.

ELLIDA *rushes to him, clings tightly to his arm, and cries.* Oh, Wangel, save me! Save me—if you can!

WANGEL. Ellida, what in heaven's name——!

ELLIDA. Save me, Wangel! Can't you see him? Over there!

WANGEL *looks.* That man?

Goes towards him.

May I ask who you are? And what you are doing in this garden?

STRANGER, *nodding towards* ELLIDA. I want to talk to her.

WANGEL. What do you want with my wife?

Turns.

Do you know him, Ellida?

ELLIDA, *quietly.* Yes, yes!

WANGEL, *quickly.* What?

ELLIDA. It's he, Wangel! It's he! You know. The one who——

WANGEL. What? What are you saying?

Turns.

Are you that—Johnston, who once——?

STRANGER. You can call me Johnston if you like. It's not my name.

WANGEL. Not your name?

STRANGER. Not any more.

WANGEL. Well, what do you want with my wife? You know that—the lighthouse keeper's daughter married long ago. And perhaps you also know who is her husband.

STRANGER. Yes. I've known that for more than three years.

ELLIDA. How did you find out?

STRANGER. I was on my way home to you. I saw an old newspaper. It contained the news of the wedding.

ELLIDA, *to herself*. The wedding!

STRANGER. I thought it strange. Because when we buried the rings in the sea—that was a wedding too, Ellida.

ELLIDA *covers her face with her hands*. Ah——!

WANGEL. How dare you?

STRANGER. Had you forgotten?

ELLIDA *feels his eyes on her*. Don't stand there looking at me!

WANGEL *stands in front of the* STRANGER. Speak to me, not to her. Since you know the situation, what is your business here? Why have you come here to see my wife?

STRANGER. I promised Ellida I'd come back to her as soon as I could.

WANGEL. Ellida! How dare you call my wife——?

STRANGER. And Ellida promised to wait for me until I came.

WANGEL. Kindly do not address my wife by her first name. I don't allow such familiarities here.

STRANGER. She belongs to me.

WANGEL. To you!

ELLIDA, *moving behind* WANGEL. He will never let me go.

STRANGER. Did she ever tell you about the two rings? Mine and Ellida's?

WANGEL. Yes. What of it? All that is finished. You got her letters. You know it is finished.

STRANGER. Ellida and I agreed that those rings should bind us as surely as any priest.

ELLIDA. But I don't want you. I never want to see you again! Don't look at me like that!

WANGEL. You must be out of your mind if you think you can come here and claim any rights because of such childish tricks.

STRANGER. Certainly I have no rights—the way you mean.

WANGEL. Then what do you want here? You surely don't

think you can take her from me by force? Against her own will!

STRANGER. No. What would be the good of that? If Ellida wants to come with me, she must come of her own free will.

ELLIDA. Of my own free will!

WANGEL. And you suppose—?

ELLIDA, *to herself*. Of my own free will!

WANGEL. You must be out of your mind. Be off with you! We have nothing further to discuss with you.

STRANGER *looks at his watch*. It's almost time for me to go aboard again.

Takes a step towards ELLIDA.

Well, Ellida. I have fulfilled my half of our pledge.

Another step towards her.

I have kept the promise I made you.

ELLIDA. Don't touch me! Please!

STRANGER. Think it over before tomorrow night!

WANGEL. There is nothing to think over. Get out!

STRANGER, *still addressing* ELLIDA. I'm going up the fjord now with the ship. Tomorrow night I shall be here again, on my way back. I shall come to you. Wait for me here in the garden. You and I will decide this matter alone.

ELLIDA, *quietly, trembling*. Oh, Wangel, do you hear what he says?

WANGEL. Don't worry. We know a way to prevent any such visit.

STRANGER. Goodbye then, Ellida. Till tomorrow night.

ELLIDA, *beseechingly*. No, no! Don't come tomorrow night! Don't ever come back here again!

STRANGER. If you decide to come with me—across the sea——

ELLIDA. Don't look at me like that.

STRANGER. I only meant—be ready for the journey, Ellida.

WANGEL. Go into the house, Ellida.

ELLIDA. I can't. Help me! Save me, Wangel!

STRANGER. Think hard, Ellida. If you don't come with me to-morrow, you will never see me again.

ELLIDA. Never again?

STRANGER *nods*. Never again, Ellida. I shall never come to you. You will never see me. Nor hear from me, either. I shall be dead and gone from you for ever.

ELLIDA. Ah!

STRANGER. So think carefully before you decide. Goodbye.

Turns, climbs over the fence, stops, and says

Yes, Ellida. Be ready for the journey tomorrow night. I shall be here to fetch you.

Goes slowly and calmly out down the footpath to the right.

ELLIDA, *looking after him*. Of my own free will. He said I should go with him—of my own free will!

WANGEL. Don't worry. He has gone now. You will never see him again.

ELLIDA. How can you say that? He is coming back tomorrow night.

WANGEL. Let him come. He won't see you.

ELLIDA *shakes her head*. Oh, Wangel. Don't think you can stop him.

WANGEL. Yes, my dear, I can. Trust me.

ELLIDA, *not listening*. After he's come here tomorrow night—and gone away with his ship across the sea——

WANGEL. Yes?

ELLIDA. I wonder—will he—ever come back?

WANGEL. No, Ellida, you need never fear that. What point would there be in his coming? After hearing from your own lips that you want no more of him? The whole thing's finished and done with.

ELLIDA, *to herself*. Tomorrow then. Or never.

WANGEL. And even if he should come back here——

ELLIDA. Yes?

WANGEL. We know how to clip his wings.

ELLIDA. We could never do that.

WANGEL. Oh, yes, we could. If we can't keep him away from

you by any other means, we shall report him for the murder of his captain.

ELLIDA, *passionately.* No! We know nothing about the captain's death. Nothing.

WANGEL. Nothing? But he confessed to you himself.

ELLIDA. We shall say nothing about that! If you say anything, I shall deny the whole story. Don't lock him up in a prison! He belongs out there, on the open sea.

WANGEL *looks at her and sighs slowly.* Oh, Ellida! Ellida!

ELLIDA *throws herself into his arms.* Oh, my dear, my dearest! Save me from that man!

WANGEL *frees himself gently.* Come, Ellida. Come with me.

LYNGSTRAND *and* HILDE, *both with fishing tackle, come along the pond from the right.*

LYNGSTRAND, *going eagerly to* ELLIDA. I say, Mrs. Wangel, I've got some news for you!

WANGEL. What?

LYNGSTRAND. Just imagine! We've seen the American.

WANGEL. The American!

HILDE. Yes, I saw him too.

LYNGSTRAND. He walked up past the garden and went on board the big steamer.

WANGEL. How did you know that man?

LYNGSTRAND. I went to sea with him once. I was sure he'd been drowned. But here he is, alive and kicking.

WANGEL. Do you know anything else about him?

LYNGSTRAND. No. But I'm sure he must have come to revenge himself on that faithless girl of his.

WANGEL. What did you say?

HILDE. Lyngstrand wants to make a masterpiece out of him.

WANGEL. I don't understand a word——

ELLIDA. I'll explain to you later.

ARNHOLM *and* BOLETTE *come from the left down the path outside the fence.*

BOLETTE, *to the others in the garden.* Come and look! The English steamer's starting off up the fjord!

A large ship glides slowly past in the distance.

LYNGSTRAND, *to* HILDE *by the fence.* He'll visit her tonight.

HILDE *nods.* The faithless wife. Yes.

LYNGSTRAND. At midnight. I say!

HILDE. How exciting!

ELLIDA, *looking after the ship.* Tomorrow then——

WANGEL. For the last time.

ELLIDA. Oh, Wangel! Save me from myself!

WANGEL. Ellida! I feel it—there is something behind him.

ELLIDA. The tide is behind him.

WANGEL. The tide?

ELLIDA. That man is like the sea.

She goes slowly and heavily through the garden out to the left. WANGEL *walks uneasily beside her, watching her closely.*

ACT FOUR

DR. WANGEL's *garden room. Doors right and left. In the background, between the two windows, is an open glass door giving on to the verandah. Beyond can be seen a part of the garden. Sofa with table, downstage. Right, a piano; further back, a large arrangement of flowers. In the middle of the room is a round table, surrounded by chairs. On the table, a flowering rose-tree, and other plants in pots. It is morning.*

At the table on the left, BOLETTE *is seated on the sofa, embroidering.* LYNGSTRAND *is on a chair at the upstage side of the table. Down in the garden* BALLESTED *is seated, painting.* HILDE *is standing beside him, watching him work.*

LYNGSTRAND, *his arms on the table, sits for a moment in silence, watching* BOLETTE. That bit round the edge. It must be jolly difficult to do that bit, Miss Wangel.

BOLETTE. Oh, no, it's not so difficult. It's just a matter of counting right.

LYNGSTRAND. Counting? Do you have to count too?

BOLETTE. Yes, the stitches. Like this.

LYNGSTRAND. I say. By Jove! It's, why, it's almost like a kind of art! Can you draw too?

BOLETTE. Yes, when I have a pattern to copy.

LYNGSTRAND. Not otherwise?

BOLETTE. No, not otherwise.

LYNGSTRAND. Oh, then it isn't really an art after all.

BOLETTE. No. It's just a knack.

LYNGSTRAND. But you know, I believe you could become an artist.

BOLETTE. But I haven't any talent.

LYNGSTRAND. No, but if you could be with a real artist all the time——

BOLETTE. You think I could learn from him?

LYNGSTRAND. I don't mean through lessons. I think it would just happen little by little. Like a miracle, Miss Wangel.

BOLETTE. How very strange.

LYNGSTRAND, *after a moment.* Have you ever considered—I mean—have you ever thought seriously about marriage, Miss Wangel?

BOLETTE, *with a quick glance at him.* About——? No.

LYNGSTRAND. I have.

BOLETTE. Have you? Really?

LYNGSTRAND. Oh, yes, I think a lot about such things. Marriage especially. I've read a lot about it in books too. I think marriage must be a kind of miracle. The way a woman gradually changes her personality so as to become like her husband.

BOLETTE. Share his interests, you mean?

LYNGSTRAND. Yes, exactly.

BOLETTE. What about his ability, his talent? Could she share them too?

LYNGSTRAND. Mm? Oh, yes. I should think she could.

BOLETTE. Then you think that what a man has made himself through thought and study, all that could somehow be communicated to his wife too?

LYNGSTRAND. Yes, that too. Little by little. Through a kind of miracle. But I know that can only happen to people who really love each other and tell each other everything.

BOLETTE. Has it never struck you that a man might be

brought over to his wife's way of thinking? Become like her, I mean?

LYNGSTRAND. A man? No, I'd never imagined that.

BOLETTE. Why not?

LYNGSTRAND. Ah, a man's got a vocation to live for. It's that that gives a man strength and purpose, Miss Wangel. He has a calling in life, a man has.

BOLETTE. All men?

LYNGSTRAND. Oh, no. I was thinking of the artist.

BOLETTE. Do you think an artist ought to get married?

LYNGSTRAND. Yes, I think so. When he finds someone he really loves——

BOLETTE. Even then, I think he ought to live just for his art.

LYNGSTRAND. Of course he must. But he can do that just as well when he's married.

BOLETTE. What about her?

LYNGSTRAND. Her?

BOLETTE. The woman he marries. What is she to live for?

LYNGSTRAND. She must live for his art, too.

BOLETTE. I'm not sure——

LYNGSTRAND. Yes, Miss Wangel, honestly, believe me. Not only because of all the honour and respect she'll get through him. But to be able to help him to create—to make his work easy for him by being with him and looking after him and keeping him happy and comfortable. I think that must be a wonderful life for a woman.

BOLETTE. Oh you don't know how conceited you are!

LYNGSTRAND. Conceited—me? Good heavens, if only you knew me a little better!

Leans closer to her.

Miss Wangel—when I am gone—which I soon will be——

BOLETTE, *compassionately.* You mustn't say such dreadful things.

LYNGSTRAND. Dreadful? What's dreadful about that?

BOLETTE. I don't understand.

LYNGSTRAND. Why, I'm going away in a month. And then in a short while I'll be going south, to the Mediterranean.

BOLETTE. That. Oh, yes, of course.

LYNGSTRAND. Will you sometimes think of me after I've gone, Miss Bolette?

BOLETTE. Yes, of course.

LYNGSTRAND, *joyfully.* Promise?

BOLETTE. Yes, I promise.

LYNGSTRAND. Cross your heart?

BOLETTE. Cross my heart.

In a changed voice.

Oh, but what's the point of all this? It can't lead to anything.

LYNGSTRAND. How can you say that? It would be wonderful for me to know that you were sitting here thinking of me.

BOLETTE. And then what?

LYNGSTRAND. Then? Why, I don't know——

BOLETTE. Neither do I. So much stands in the way. The whole world stands in our way, I think.

LYNGSTRAND. Well, a miracle might happen. You see, I believe I'm lucky.

BOLETTE, *warmly.* Yes! You believe that, don't you!

LYNGSTRAND. Oh, yes, I do believe it. In a year or two, when I come home again, a famous sculptor, healthy and successful——

BOLETTE. Oh, yes, we all hope you will.

LYNGSTRAND. You can be sure I shall. If you think fondly of me while I am away in the south. And now I have your word that you will.

BOLETTE. Yes, you have my word.

Shakes her head.

But it can't lead to anything, all the same.

LYNGSTRAND. Yes, Miss Bolette, it will mean I shall be able to work more confidently at my composition.

BOLETTE. Do you believe that?

LYNGSTRAND. Yes, I feel it inside me. And I think it would be so inspiring for you too—sitting up here—to know that you were, so to speak, helping me to create.

BOLETTE *looks at him.* And you?

LYNGSTRAND. I?

BOLETTE *looks out towards the garden.* Ssh! Let's talk about something else, Dr. Arnholm's coming.

DR. ARNHOLM *appears down in the garden left. He stops and talks with* BALLESTED *and* HILDE.

LYNGSTRAND. Are you fond of your old teacher, Miss Bolette?

BOLETTE. Fond of him?

LYNGSTRAND. I mean, do you like him?

BOLETTE. Oh, yes. He's a fine person to have as a friend and adviser. And he's always so helpful.

LYNGSTRAND. Isn't it odd that he should never have married?

BOLETTE. Do you think it's odd?

LYNGSTRAND. Yes. Since he's said to be well off.

BOLETTE. He is well off. I suppose it hasn't been so easy for him to find someone willing to have him.

LYNGSTRAND. Why?

BOLETTE. Oh, almost all the girls he knows are old pupils of his. He says so himself.

LYNGSTRAND. Well, what's wrong with that?

BOLETTE. Good heavens, one doesn't marry a man who's been one's teacher!

LYNGSTRAND. Don't you think it's possible for a young girl to love her teacher?

BOLETTE. Not once one's grown up.

LYNGSTRAND. I say!

BOLETTE, *warningly.* Ssh!

BALLESTED *has meanwhile gathered his things together and is taking them away to the right in the garden.* HILDE *is helping him.* ARNHOLM *goes up on to the verandah and comes into the garden room.*

ARNHOLM. Good morning, Bolette, my dear. Good morning, Mr.—Mr.—hm.

He gives LYNGSTRAND *an annoyed look and nods coldly to him.* LYNGSTRAND *gets to his feet and bows.*

BOLETTE *gets up and comes over to* ARNHOLM. Good morning, Dr. Arnholm.

ARNHOLM. How are you today?

BOLETTE. Oh, quite well, thank you.

ARNHOLM. Is your stepmother down bathing today, too?

BOLETTE. No, she's up in her room.

ARNHOLM. Not feeling well?

BOLETTE. I don't know. She's locked herself in.

ARNHOLM. Hm. Has she?

LYNGSTRAND. Mrs. Wangel was very shaken by seeing that American yesterday.

ARNHOLM. What do you know about that?

LYNGSTRAND. I told Mrs. Wangel I'd seen him walking alive past the garden.

ARNHOLM. Oh, I see.

BOLETTE, *to* ARNHOLM. You and Father were sitting up late together last night.

ARNHOLM. Quite late, yes. We got on to something rather important.

BOLETTE. Did you get a chance to say anything to him about me?

ARNHOLM. No, Bolette, I wasn't able to get on to that. He was —preoccupied.

BOLETTE *sighs.* Ah, yes. He always is.

ARNHOLM, *looking meaningly at her.* But later today you and I will have a serious talk about this. Where is your father now? Isn't he at home?

BOLETTE. Yes, he's probably in the surgery. I'll go and fetch him.

ARNHOLM. No, don't bother. I'll find him.

BOLETTE, *listening left.* Wait a moment, Dr. Arnholm. I think that's Father coming downstairs. Yes. He must have been upstairs with her.

DR. WANGEL *comes in through the door on the left.*

WANGEL, *holding out his hand.* Arnholm, my dear fellow, are you here already? I'm delighted you've come so early. There's something more I want to talk to you about.

BOLETTE, *to* LYNGSTRAND. Shall we go down into the garden and join Hilde?

LYNGSTRAND. Yes, what a good idea. I'd love to.

He and BOLETTE *go down into the garden and out through the trees in the background.*

ARNHOLM, *who has watched them leave, turns to* WANGEL. Do you know that young man well?

WANGEL. No, not at all.

ARNHOLM. Do you approve of him seeing so much of your girls?

WANGEL. Does he? I hadn't noticed.

ARNHOLM. I think you ought to keep an eye open.

WANGEL. Yes, you're perfectly right. But, good heavens, what's a fellow to do? The girls have grown so used to looking after themselves. They won't listen to what I say, or Ellida.

ARNHOLM. Not to her either?

WANGEL. No. Besides, I can't ask her to bother about such matters. These things bore her. But this isn't what I wanted to talk to you about. Tell me—have you thought any more about this business? What I was telling you last night?

ARNHOLM. I haven't been able to think of anything else since I left you.

WANGEL. What do you think I ought to do?

ARNHOLM. My dear doctor, I think you, as a medical man, ought to know the answer better than I.

WANGEL. Ah, if you only knew how difficult it is for a doctor to diagnose for a patient who means a lot to him! Besides, this isn't any ordinary illness. No ordinary doctor can do anything in this case—nor any ordinary medicines, either.

ARNHOLM. How is she today?

WANGEL. I was up with her just now, and she seemed quite calm. But behind all her moods there's something hidden which I cannot fathom. And she's so changeable—so unpredictable. She alters so suddenly.

ARNHOLM. I suppose that's because of her mental state.

WANGEL. Not only that. She was born like that. Ellida is one of the sea people. That is really what it is.

ARNHOLM. What exactly do you mean, my dear doctor?

WANGEL. Haven't you noticed that the people who live out there by the open sea are a different race? It's almost as though they lived the same life as the sea does. Their way of thinking, feeling—they're like the tide, they ebb and flow. And they can never uproot themselves and settle anywhere else. Oh, I should have thought of all this before. I sinned against Ellida when I tried to take her away and bring her inland to this place.

ARNHOLM. Is that how you feel now?

WANGEL. More and more. But I ought to have known it from the first. In my heart I did know it. But I wouldn't let myself believe it. I loved her so much. So I put myself first. I was unforgivably selfish.

ARNHOLM. Hm—well, everyone is a little selfish in such circumstances. Though I've never noticed that fault in you, Dr. Wangel.

WANGEL, *pacing uneasily up and down.* Oh, yes, yes! And I've been selfish since, too. I am so much older than she is. I ought to have been a father to her, and a guide. I ought to have developed her mind, taught her to think clearly. But no. I never got down to it. I wanted her as she was. But then things went from bad to worse with her. And I sat here not knowing what to do.

More quietly.

That was why, in my—distress, I wrote to you and asked you to come and see us.

ARNHOLM *looks at him amazed.* What? Was that why you wrote?

WANGEL. Please don't tell anyone.

ARNHOLM. But, my dear doctor, what help did you suppose I could give you? I don't understand.

WANGEL. No, I—I suppose not. I was completely on the wrong track. I thought Ellida had been in love with you, once. That she was perhaps a little fond of you still. I thought it might possibly do her good to see you again, and talk to you about her home and the old days.

ARNHOLM. Then it was your wife you were referring to when you wrote that someone here was waiting for me—longing to see me again?

WANGEL. Yes. Who else?

ARNHOLM, *quickly*. No, of course you're right. But I didn't realise.

WANGEL. Quite understandably. I was on the wrong track.

ARNHOLM. And you call yourself a selfish man?

WANGEL. Oh, I have so much to atone for. I didn't think I had the right to neglect any—anything that might possibly ease her mind a little.

ARNHOLM. How do you explain the power which this stranger has over her?

WANGEL. My dear friend, there are aspects of this case which cannot be explained.

ARNHOLM. You mean it's something that's beyond rational explanation?

WANGEL. Yes. For the time being, anyway.

ARNHOLM. Do you believe in such things?

WANGEL. I neither believe nor disbelieve. I just don't know. So I leave it at that.

ARNHOLM. Yes, but tell me one thing. This curious, horrible notion she has about the child's eyes——

WANGEL. That business about the eyes is rubbish! Rubbish! Pure imagination. Nothing else.

ARNHOLM. Did you notice the man's eyes when you saw him yesterday?

WANGEL. Certainly I did.

ARNHOLM. And you saw no likeness?

WANGEL, *evasively*. Good heavens, what do you want me to say? It was quite dark when I saw him. And Ellida had talked so much about this likeness—I couldn't look at him objectively.

ARNHOLM. No, I suppose not. But—this other matter—I mean, what she says about all this anxiety and unrest that came over her just at the time when this stranger had started on his journey home?

WANGEL. That's also something she must have made herself believe since the day before yesterday. It didn't come over her as suddenly as she pretends now. Ever since she heard from this young Lyngstrand that Johnston—Freeman— whatever he calls himself—was on his way here three years ago—in March—she's persuaded herself that these disturbances of hers started just in that month.

ARNHOLM. Isn't that true, then?

WANGEL. Not at all. The first signs came much earlier. I admit it did happen to be in March three years ago that she had a particularly bad time of it——

ARNHOLM. Then——!

WANGEL. Yes, but that's easily explained by the circumstances. The condition she was in at the time.

ARNHOLM. What is one to believe?

WANGEL, *clasping his hands.* To be unable to help her—to be unable to think of any way out——

ARNHOLM. If you could go away? Move somewhere else. So that she could live somewhere where she'd feel more at home.

WANGEL. Don't you suppose I've thought of that? I suggested to her that we should move out to Skjoldviken. But she doesn't want to.

ARNHOLM. She doesn't want to?

WANGEL. No. She doesn't think it would do any good. Perhaps she's right.

ARNHOLM. Hm. Do you think so?

WANGEL. Yes. Besides, when I think about it I don't know if I really ought to go and settle there. The children, I mean —it'd be so awful for them to have to live in such a backwater. They must live somewhere where they'll have some chance of finding a husband.

ARNHOLM. A husband? Are you beginning to think about that already?

WANGEL. Good Lord, I must consider them too. But then on the other hand, Ellida—my poor sick Ellida—oh, my dear Arnholm, which of them am I to put first?

ARNHOLM. I don't think you need worry about Bolette——

Breaks off.

I wonder where she—where they've gone to?

Goes to the open door and looks out.

WANGEL, *over by the piano.* I'd make any sacrifice—for all three of them. If only I knew what to do.

ELLIDA *comes in through the door on the left.*

ELLIDA, *as she enters, to* WANGEL. Don't go out this morning, my dear.

WANGEL. No, of course I won't. I'll stay at home with you.

Indicates ARNHOLM, *as the latter comes over to them.*

But aren't you going to say good morning to our friend?

ELLIDA *turns.* Oh, it's you, Dr. Arnholm?

Holds out her hand.

Good morning.

ARNHOLM. Good morning, Mrs. Wangel. Not swimming today as usual?

ELLIDA. No, no, no! Don't talk about that today. But won't you sit down for a moment?

ARNHOLM. No, thank you so much, not now.

Looks at WANGEL.

I promised the girls I'd join them in the garden.

ELLIDA. Heaven knows if you'll find them there. I never know where they are.

WANGEL. I think you'll find them down there by the pond.

ARNHOLM. I'll track them down somewhere.

Nods and passes through the verandah out into the garden, right.

ELLIDA. What time is it, Wangel?

WANGEL *looks at his watch.* Just past eleven.

ELLIDA. And at eleven o'clock tonight—half-past eleven—the steamer will come. Oh, if only it were all over!

WANGEL *goes nearer to her.* Ellida, my dear—there's one thing I should like to ask you.

ELLIDA. What's that?

WANGEL. The night before last—up there on the Prospect—you said that often during these last three years you had seen him clearly, standing alive before you.

ELLIDA. Yes, I have.

WANGEL. What did he look like?

ELLIDA. What did he look like?

WANGEL. I mean how did he look when you thought you saw him?

ELLIDA. But, Wangel, you know yourself what he looks like now.

WANGEL. Did he look the same then?

ELLIDA. Yes.

WANGEL. Just the same as when you saw him yesterday evening?

ELLIDA. Yes. Just the same.

WANGEL. Then, how was it that you didn't immediately recognise him?

ELLIDA. Didn't I?

WANGEL. No. You said yourself that to begin with you had no idea who this stranger could be.

ELLIDA. Yes, of course—you're right! That was strange, wasn't it? To think I didn't recognise him at once.

WANGEL. It was only the eyes, you said——

ELLIDA. Yes—the eyes!

WANGEL. But—up on the Prospect the night before last, you said he always appeared to you looking just the same as when you last saw him. Out there ten years ago——

ELLIDA. Did I say that?

WANGEL. Yes.

ELLIDA. Then he must have looked the same then as he does now.

WANGEL. No. You painted quite a different picture of him the night before last on the way home. Ten years ago, he had no beard, you said. And different clothes. And his tie-pin with the pearl—the man yesterday wore no such thing.

ELLIDA. No, that's true.

WANGEL *looks closely at her.* Think a little harder, Ellida. Or perhaps—perhaps you can't remember any longer how he looked when he stood with you at Bratthammeren.

ELLIDA *closes her eyes, trying to remember.* Not—clearly. No —today I can't. Isn't that strange?

WANGEL. Not so strange. You've got a new image of him in your mind—the real one. And that shadows the old image, so that you can't see it any longer.

ELLIDA. Do you think so, Wangel?

WANGEL. Yes. And it shadows your sick imaginings too. That's why I think it is good that reality has come at last.

ELLIDA. Good? You call it good?

WANGEL. Yes. His coming may be what you need to bring you back to health.

ELLIDA *sits on the sofa.* Wangel—come and sit here beside me. I want to try to tell you what's in my mind.

WANGEL. Yes, my dear. Do.
Sits on a chair on the other side of the table.

ELLIDA. It was a great misfortune—for both of us—that you and I ever met.

WANGEL. What?

ELLIDA. Oh, yes. It was. It had to end in tragedy. After the way we came together.

WANGEL. What was wrong with that?

ELLIDA. Wangel, it's no use our going on lying to ourselves.

WANGEL. Lying?

ELLIDA. Yes. Or hiding the truth. The real truth of the matter is that you came out there and bought me.

WANGEL. Bought! Did you say bought?

ELLIDA. Oh, I wasn't any better than you. I agreed to the bargain. Left home and sold myself to you.

WANGEL. Ellida!

ELLIDA. Is there any other word for it? You couldn't stand the emptiness of your house any longer. You looked round for a new wife——

WANGEL. And a new mother for my children, Ellida.

ELLIDA. You didn't know if I was at all suited for that. You'd only spoken to me two or three times. Then you—wanted me, and——

WANGEL. Call it what you like.

ELLIDA. And I—I stood there, helpless. So when you came and offered to—support me for life, I—agreed.

WANGEL. I asked you quite frankly if you would like to share with me and the children the little I could call mine.

ELLIDA. But I shouldn't have accepted. I shouldn't have sold myself. I wish now I'd done anything—starved—so long as I'd chosen to do so—chosen freely.

WANGEL *gets up.* Then have these five or six years we have lived together meant nothing to you at all?

ELLIDA. Oh, no, Wangel, no! I have had everything here that anyone could wish for. But I didn't come to your home of my own free will.

WANGEL *stares at her.* Not of your own free will? I remember. I heard that phrase yesterday.

ELLIDA. In that phrase lies everything. It opened my eyes. Now I see it all.

WANGEL. What do you see?

ELLIDA. I see that the life we two are living together is not really a marriage.

WANGEL, *bitterly.* God knows that is true. The life we are living together now is no marriage.

ELLIDA. It never has been. Not even in those first weeks. *Stares ahead of her.*

My first—that could have been a real marriage.

WANGEL. Your first?

ELLIDA. My marriage with him.

WANGEL. I simply don't understand you.

ELLIDA. Oh, Wangel, don't let's lie to each other. And to ourselves.

WANGEL. I don't want to lie.

ELLIDA. Don't you see? We can never escape from that fact —that a promise given freely is just as binding as any marriage.

WANGEL. But, what in heaven's name——?

ELLIDA *rises*. Let me go. Let me leave you, Wangel.

WANGEL. Ellida!

ELLIDA. Please let me go! You must believe me—it will never be any different between you and me, even if I stay. Not after the way we came together.

WANGEL. So it's come to that.

ELLIDA. It had to.

WANGEL. Then our life together has not made you mine. You have never really belonged to me.

ELLIDA. Oh, Wangel—if only I could love you as you deserve to be loved. I do so want to. But I can't and I shall never be able to.

WANGEL. Divorce, then? Is that what you want? A full, legal divorce?

ELLIDA. How little you understand me. I don't care about the formalities. All I want is that we two should freely agree to release each other.

WANGEL *nods bitterly*. Cancel the bargain, you mean?

ELLIDA, *alive*. Exactly! Cancel the bargain.

WANGEL. And then, Ellida? What then? Afterwards? Have you thought how all this will seem to us then? How life will shape itself for you and me?

ELLIDA. That can't be helped. It will have to shape itself, as best it can. I beg you, I pray you, Wangel—give me my freedom. Give me my full freedom again. That's all that matters now.

WANGEL. Ellida, this is a dreadful thing you are asking me to do. Let me have time to think. Let us talk about it again. Give yourself time.

ELLIDA. We have no time. I must have my freedom again today.

WANGEL. Why today?

ELLIDA. Because he is coming here tonight.

WANGEL. He? What has this stranger to do with this?

ELLIDA. I want to be free when I meet him. Free to choose for myself.

WANGEL. And then—what do you intend to do?

ELLIDA. I don't want to hide behind the fact of being another man's wife. To hide behind the pretext that I am not free to choose. Otherwise there would be no choice to make.

WANGEL. You speak of choice. Choice, Ellida? In this?

ELLIDA. Yes, I must be free to choose. To let him go—or to go with him.

WANGEL. Do you realise what you're saying? Go with him? Give your whole future into his hands?

ELLIDA. Didn't I put my whole future into your hands?

WANGEL. But he! He! An utter stranger. A man you know practically nothing about.

ELLIDA. I knew even less about you. But I went with you.

WANGEL. At least you knew what kind of life you were going to. But he! He! Think, Ellida. What do you know about him? Nothing. Not even who he is—or what he is.

ELLIDA, *to herself.* I know. It's just that that is so—demonic.

WANGEL. It certainly is.

ELLIDA. That's why I think I must go to meet it.

WANGEL, *looking at her.* Because it is demonic?

ELLIDA. Yes.

WANGEL *comes closer to her.* Ellida, what exactly do you mean by demonic?

ELLIDA *pauses.* The demonic—is something that appals—and attracts.

WANGEL. Attractive, too?

ELLIDA. More than anything, I think.

WANGEL, *slowly*. You are like the sea, Ellida.

ELLIDA. So is this demon.

WANGEL. I have never really known you. I am beginning to realise it now.

ELLIDA. That's why you must give me my freedom! I am not the woman you wanted to marry. Now you see it yourself. Now we can part freely, with understanding.

WANGEL, *bitterly*. Perhaps it would be best for us both to part. No, I can't! You are to me—what he is to you.

Pause.

If only we can get through today. We mustn't lose our heads. I dare not let you go—give you your freedom—today. I haven't the right to do that. For your own sake, Ellida, I assert my right—my duty—to protect you.

ELLIDA. Protect me? What is there to protect me against? There is no power or force outside me that threatens me. The root of that fascination lies in my own mind. What can you do against that?

WANGEL. I can help you to fight it.

ELLIDA. Perhaps—if I wanted to fight it.

WANGEL. You mean you don't?

ELLIDA. I don't know.

WANGEL. Tonight it will all be settled, Ellida.

ELLIDA. Yes! The moment of decision is so near! I must decide. For all my life.

WANGEL. And tomorrow?

ELLIDA. Tomorrow? Perhaps by then I shall have thrown away my life.

WANGEL. Your life?

ELLIDA. A whole, full life thrown away. A life of freedom. My life—perhaps his too.

WANGEL, *more quietly, takes her wrist*. Ellida, do you love this stranger?

ELLIDA. Do I? I can't tell. I only know that for me he is— the demon—and——

WANGEL. Yes?

ELLIDA, *tearing herself free.* It's to him I feel I belong!

WANGEL *bows his head.* I am beginning to understand.

ELLIDA. Can you help me? Can you advise me?

WANGEL, *heavily.* Tomorrow he will be gone. Then the danger will be past, and I shall be willing to give you your freedom—and let you go. Then we will cancel the bargain, Ellida.

ELLIDA. Oh, Wangel! Tomorrow it will be too late.

WANGEL *looks out towards the garden.* The children! Let us at least keep the children out of this—while we can.

ARNHOLM, BOLETTE, HILDE *and* LYNGSTRAND *appear in the garden.* LYNGSTRAND *takes his leave of the others there and exits right. The others come into the garden room.*

ARNHOLM. Well, we've been making great plans——

HILDE. We want to go out on the fjord tonight, and——

BOLETTE. No, don't tell them.

WANGEL. We two have also been making plans.

ARNHOLM. Indeed?

WANGEL. Tomorrow, Ellida will be going away to Skjoldviken —for a while.

BOLETTE. Going?

ARNHOLM. What a good idea, Mrs. Wangel.

WANGEL. Ellida wants to go home to the sea again.

HILDE *moves impulsively towards* ELLIDA. Are you going away? Are you leaving us?

ELLIDA, *startled.* But, Hilde! What is the matter with you?

HILDE. Oh, nothing.

Half aloud, turning away.

Go, go. By all means.

BOLETTE, *frightened.* Father, I see it in your face. You will be going away, too, to Skjoldviken.

WANGEL. I? Not at all. I shall be going out there now and then to see her——

BOLETTE. But you'll come back to us?

WANGEL. Why, of course.

BOLETTE. Now and then.

WANGEL. Dear child, it's got to be.

Goes across the room.

ARNHOLM *whispers.* I'll have a word with him, now, Bolette. In private.

Goes over to WANGEL. *They talk quietly together near the door.*

ELLIDA, *half aloud to* BOLETTE. What's the matter with Hilde? She looks quite upset.

BOLETTE. Haven't you ever noticed what Hilde has been yearning for, day after day?

ELLIDA. Yearning for?

BOLETTE. Ever since you entered this house.

ELLIDA. No, no. What?

BOLETTE. One single loving word from you.

ELLIDA. Ah! Could there be a place for me in this house? *She clasps her hands to her head and stares ahead of her, motionless, as though torn by conflicting thoughts and emotions.* WANGEL *and* ARNHOLM, *whispering, come back across the room.* BOLETTE *goes and looks into the adjoining room, then opens the door wide.*

BOLETTE. Father dear, the food's on the table.

WANGEL, *with forced composure.* Is it, child? Good, good! Dr. Arnholm, please! Let us go in and drink a farewell cup to—to the Lady from the Sea.

They go towards the door on the right.

ACT FIVE

DR. WANGEL's *garden, by the pond. The deepening twilight of a summer night.* ARNHOLM, BOLETTE, LYNGSTRAND *and* HILDE, *in a boat, punt from the left along the bank.*

HILDE. Look, we can easily jump ashore here.

ARNHOLM. No, no, don't do that!

LYNGSTRAND. I can't jump, Miss Hilde.

HILDE. Dr. Arnholm, can't you jump either?

ARNHOLM. I'd like to avoid it if possible.

BOLETTE. Let's tie her up to the steps by the bathhouse, then.

They punt out to the right. As they do so, BALLESTED *comes down the footpath from the right carrying sheets of music and a French horn. He waves to them in their boat, turns and talks to them. Their replies are heard more and more distantly, offstage.*

BALLESTED. What's that you say? Yes, of course it's because of the English steamer. It's the last time she'll be here this year. If you want to hear the concert, you mustn't play around too long in that punt.

Shouts.

What?

Shakes his head.

I can't hear you.

ELLIDA, *her shawl over her head, comes in from the left, followed by* WANGEL.

WANGEL. But, dear Ellida, I assure you—there's plenty of time yet.

ELLIDA. No, no, there isn't! He may be here any moment.

BALLESTED, *outside the garden fence.* Why, good evening, Doctor! Good evening, Mrs. Wangel.

WANGEL. Oh, it's you? Is there going to be a concert here tonight?

BALLESTED. Yes. The Horn Society will—ah—hold forth. There is no shortage of festive occasions nowadays. Tonight we are playing in honour of the Englander.

ELLIDA. The Englander? Is he in sight already?

BALLESTED. Not yet. But he's coming down the fjord through the islands. We shan't get any warning. Suddenly—poof! He'll be upon us.

ELLIDA. Yes.

WANGEL. Tonight will be the last time. He will not come again.

BALLESTED. A grievous thought, Doctor. However, that is all the more reason why we wish to honour him.
Sighs.
Ah dear! As it says in the tragedy: "Summer's joys will soon be past and gone, and every way to the sea be locked with ice."

ELLIDA. "Every way to the sea be locked."

BALLESTED. A melancholy reflection. For these few months we have been merry children of summer. It will be hard to accept the season of darkness. For the first few weeks, I mean. Men and women can acclai—acclimatise themselves, Mrs. Wangel. Yes, indeed they can.
He bows and exits left.

ELLIDA, *looking out over the fjord.* Oh, God, this torture! This unbearable hour before the moment of decision!

WANGEL. You are still determined to speak with him, then?

ELLIDA. I must speak with him myself. I must choose freely.

WANGEL. You have no choice, Ellida. I won't let you choose.

ELLIDA. You can't stop me. You or anyone. You can forbid me to go with him—if that is what I choose to do. You can keep me here by force. Against my will. But you cannot stop me from choosing—him and not you—if I should want to—if I should have to choose that way.

WANGEL. No. That I cannot stop.

ELLIDA. Don't you see? In this house I have nothing to keep me. I have no roots here, Wangel. The children are not mine. They don't love me. They never have loved me. When I go—if I go—with him, tonight—or out to Skjoldviken tomorrow—I haven't even a key to give up, or any instructions to leave behind. I have been—outside—outside everything. From the first day I came here.

WANGEL. You wanted it that way.

ELLIDA. No, I didn't. I simply let everything stay the way it was on the day I arrived. It is you who wanted it to be like this.

WANGEL. I only wanted to do what I thought would make you happy.

ELLIDA. Oh, yes, Wangel, I know. But there is retribution in this. For now there is nothing to bind me here—nothing to give me strength. I feel nothing for you. You, our home, the children—nothing.

WANGEL. Yes, I realise that now, Ellida. Tomorrow you shall have your freedom again. You shall live your own life.

ELLIDA. My own life? Oh, no. The life I was born to lead ended when I came to live with you.

Clasps her hands in anguish.

And now—in half an hour—he will come—the man I should have remained faithful to. He is coming to ask me—for the last time—to start my life afresh.

WANGEL. That's why you must let me, as your husband—and as your doctor—choose for you.

ELLIDA. Yes, Wangel, I realise that. There are moments when I think the only escape, the only peace I could find would be to give myself wholly to you—and turn my back on all this. But I can't. No, I can't!

WANGEL. Come, Ellida. Let us take a little walk together.

ELLIDA. I should like to. But I daren't. He told me to wait for him here.

WANGEL. You have plenty of time yet.

ELLIDA. Have I?

WANGEL. Plenty of time.

ELLIDA. Let us go then. For a few minutes.

They go out downstage right, as ARNHOLM *and* BOLETTE *come along the upper bank of the pond.*

BOLETTE, *noticing the others as they go out.* Look!

ARNHOLM, *quietly.* Ssh! Let them go.

BOLETTE. Can you make out what has been the matter with them these last few days?

ARNHOLM. Have you noticed anything?

BOLETTE. Have I——? Of course.

ARNHOLM. Something—in particular?

BOLETTE. Yes. Lots of things. Haven't you?

ARNHOLM. Why, I don't think so——

BOLETTE. Of course you have. You just don't want to admit it.

ARNHOLM. I think it will be a good thing for your stepmother to go away for a while.

BOLETTE. Do you?

ARNHOLM. Mightn't it be a good thing for you all if she could get away now and then?

BOLETTE. If she goes to Skjoldviken tomorrow, she will never come back to us again.

ARNHOLM. What on earth makes you say that?

BOLETTE. I know it. You'll see. She will never come back here again. Not as long as I and Hilde are here, anyway.

ARNHOLM. Hilde too?

BOLETTE. Not so much her, perhaps. She's still almost a child. And she worships Ellida, in her heart, I think. But with me, it's different. A stepmother who isn't so much older than oneself——

ARNHOLM. My dear, it may not be so long before you have a chance to get away.

BOLETTE, *alive*. You really think so? Have you spoken to Father?

ARNHOLM. Yes, I spoke to him, too.

BOLETTE. Well, what did he say?

ARNHOLM. Er—well, he's so occupied with other things just now, you know——

BOLETTE. What did I tell you?

ARNHOLM. I did get one thing out of him, though. You can't count on any help from him.

BOLETTE. No help?

ARNHOLM. He spoke to me quite openly about his—about how things are with him. He made it clear it would be quite impossible for him to help you financially.

BOLETTE. Why did you have to raise my hopes? Just to make a fool of me?

ARNHOLM. Dear Bolette, it depends entirely on you whether you leave or stay.

BOLETTE. Depends on me? What depends on me?

ARNHOLM. Whether you get out into the world. Get the chance to learn everything you want to learn. Live a full life. What do you say, Bolette?

BOLETTE *clasps her hands*. Oh, dear God! But all this is impossible. If Father won't—can't—then there is no-one I could turn to.

ARNHOLM. Would you be prepared to accept a helping hand from your old—I mean, your former teacher?

BOLETTE. From you, Dr. Arnholm? You mean you would be willing to——?

ARNHOLM. To help you? Yes. Gladly. And not only with words. Do you agree, then? Well? Do you agree?

BOLETTE. Do I agree? To be able to go away—to see the world—to learn something—something real and worth while!

ARNHOLM. Yes. You have only to say the word.

BOLETTE. And you, you are prepared to help me to achieve all this? But how can I accept such an offer from—from a stranger?

ARNHOLM. You can accept it from me, Bolette.

BOLETTE *takes his hands.* Yes, I think—I think I can! I don't know why—but—oh, I could laugh and cry for joy. I'm so happy! I am to live after all! I was beginning to fear that life was slipping away from me.

ARNHOLM. You don't have to worry about that any longer, Bolette. But first you must tell me frankly. Is there any-thing—anything—which binds you here?

BOLETTE. Binds me? No. Nothing. That is—Father, in a way of course—and Hilde too. But——

ARNHOLM. Well, you'll have to leave your father sooner or later. And Hilde will have to go her own way some time too. But otherwise there's nothing, Bolette? No tie of any kind?

BOLETTE. No, none at all. I can leave here any time.

ARNHOLM. Then, Bolette, my dear—come away. With me.

BOLETTE *clasps her hands.* Oh, dear God! If that could only be.

ARNHOLM. You trust me, don't you?

BOLETTE. Yes, of course.

ARNHOLM. Then you are prepared to give yourself unreserv-edly into my hands, Bolette? You are ready to do that, aren't you?

BOLETTE. Yes, yes, of course! You are my old teacher—I mean, you used to be my teacher in the old days.

ARNHOLM. I—didn't mean because of that. But—I—you are free, then, Bolette. I therefore ask you—if you could—if you could be willing to bind yourself to me—for life.

BOLETTE, *horrified.* What are you saying?

ARNHOLM. For all your life, Bolette. Will you be my wife?

BOLETTE, *half to herself.* No, no. This is impossible. Quite impossible.

ARNHOLM. Would it be so impossible for you to——?

BOLETTE. Dr. Arnholm, you can't mean what you are saying. *Looks at him.*

Was that what you meant when—when you offered to do so much for me?

ARNHOLM. Listen a minute, Bolette. I see I have surprised you.

BOLETTE. Such a thing—from you—how could it but surprise me.

ARNHOLM. Perhaps you are right. You couldn't know that it was because of you I came here.

BOLETTE. You came here because of me?

ARNHOLM. Yes, Bolette. Last spring I got a letter from your father. It contained a sentence, which led me to believe that your memories of—of your former tutor were tinged with more than affection.

BOLETTE. How could Father write that?

ARNHOLM. He didn't mean that. But I allowed myself to imagine that in this house a young girl was sitting and waiting for the day when I should come back. No, don't interrupt me, Bolette. When a man is no longer in his first youth, such a belief—illusion, if you like—affects him deeply. At first, I felt—merely grateful—but then—I felt I must come to see you—to tell you I shared the feelings which I—deluded myself into supposing that you cherished towards me.

BOLETTE. But now—when you know that I didn't?

ARNHOLM. That doesn't help, Bolette. My feelings towards you will always be coloured by that illusion I once had. You find this difficult to understand perhaps. But that is how it is.

BOLETTE. I had never dreamed that anything like this could happen.

ARNHOLM. But now that you know it can, what do you say? Could you not agree to—yes, to become my wife?

BOLETTE. You used to be my tutor. I can't imagine ever standing in any other relationship towards you.

ARNHOLM. No, no. Well, if you feel you can't, then, let our relationship remain as it was.

BOLETTE. What do you mean?

ARNHOLM. My offer stands. I shall enable you to get away from here and see the world. To learn something. To be secure and independent. And I shall secure your future too, Bolette. In me you will always have someone you can trust. I want you to know that.

BOLETTE. But, good heavens, Dr. Arnholm, all that is impossible now.

ARNHOLM. Is that impossible, too?

BOLETTE. Of course it is. After what you have said to me—and my reply—surely you must understand that I can't accept anything from you, ever. Now.

ARNHOLM. Would you rather go on sitting here, watching life slip away?

BOLETTE. I can't bear to think about it.

ARNHOLM. Do you want to turn your back on everything you dream of? To know there's so much more in life—and never experience it? Think, Bolette. Think hard.

BOLETTE. Yes. Yes, Dr. Arnholm. That is perfectly true.

ARNHOLM. Then, later—when your father is no longer here—perhaps to stand alone and helpless in the world? Or to have to give yourself to another man for whom you might not be able to feel any affection either?

BOLETTE. Oh, yes. I see clearly enough how true all that is. Everything you say. And yet—perhaps——

ARNHOLM, *tensely.* Yes?

BOLETTE, *in two minds.* Perhaps it's not so impossible after all.

ARNHOLM. What, Bolette?

BOLETTE. That it might work. That I might—what you suggested just now——

ARNHOLM. You mean, you might perhaps be willing to grant me the happiness of being allowed to help you as a loyal friend?

BOLETTE. No, no, no! That would be quite impossible now. No, Dr. Arnholm. Rather take me——

ARNHOLM. Bolette! You mean——?

BOLETTE. Yes—I think—I do.

ARNHOLM. You mean, you want—to be my wife?

BOLETTE. Yes. If you still want to have me.

ARNHOLM. If I still——!

Seizes her hand.

Thank you! Thank you, Bolette. If I have not won your heart yet, I shall find a way to win it. Oh, Bolette! I will—carry you through life—on my hands.

BOLETTE. I shall be able to see the world. To live. You promised me that.

ARNHOLM. I will keep my promise.

BOLETTE. And learn anything I want?

ARNHOLM. I myself shall be your teacher. As I used to be, Bolette.

BOLETTE, *quietly, deep in her own thoughts.* To be free. To come out into—all that's strange. Not to have to worry about the future. Not to have to pinch and scrape——

ARNHOLM. You need never worry about such things again. That's good, isn't it, Bolette?

BOLETTE. Yes. It is good. Yes.

ARNHOLM *puts his arm round her waist.* You will see how happy we shall be together. How calm and trusting. It will be a good life, Bolette.

BOLETTE. Yes. I begin to think—— Oh yes! It must work!

Looks out right, and frees herself sharply from his grip.

Ssh! Don't say anything.

ARNHOLM. What is it, my dear?

BOLETTE. It's that poor——

Points.

Look over there.

ARNHOLM. Your father?

BOLETTE. No, the young sculptor. He's walking there with Hilde.

ARNHOLM. Oh, Lyngstrand. What's the matter with him?

BOLETTE. You know how ill he is.

ARNHOLM. If he isn't just imagining it.

BOLETTE. No. He isn't just imagining it. He hasn't got very long. Well, perhaps it's for the best.

ARNHOLM. For the best?

BOLETTE. Yes, nothing would come of his art even if—let's go before they come.

ARNHOLM. With all my heart, Bolette.

HILDE *and* LYNGSTRAND *appear by the pond.*

HILDE. Hullo! Aren't you going to wait for us?

ARNHOLM. Bolette and I will go on ahead.

They go out left.

LYNGSTRAND *laughs quietly.* It's lovely here just at this time. Everybody going in couples. Hand in hand.

HILDE, *looking after them.* Do you know, I think he's courting her.

LYNGSTRAND. Really? Have you noticed something?

HILDE. Oh, yes. It's not difficult. When one keeps one's eyes open.

LYNGSTRAND. Miss Bolette will never accept him. I'm sure of that.

HILDE. No. She thinks he's begun to look so old. She says he'll be bald soon, too.

LYNGSTRAND. I didn't only mean that. She wouldn't have him anyway.

HILDE. Why do you think that?

LYNGSTRAND. There's someone else she's promised to wait for. And think about.

HILDE. Think about?

LYNGSTRAND. Yes, while he's away.

HILDE. You mean you?

LYNGSTRAND. Perhaps.

HILDE. Has she promised to do that?

LYNGSTRAND. Yes. She promised me. But you mustn't tell her you know.

HILDE. Cross my heart! I'll be as silent as the grave.

LYNGSTRAND. I think it was—good of her to say that.

HILDE. And then when you come back home—will you get engaged to her? And marry her?

LYNGSTRAND. Oh, no. I daren't think of that for the first few years. And when—if—I should ever be in a position to—she'll be too old for me then.

HILDE. But you want her to sit here and think of you?

LYNGSTRAND. Yes. It'll mean so much to me, don't you see? As an artist, I mean. And it wouldn't be difficult for her, as she hasn't really any particular vocation. But it's nice of her to say she'll do it.

HILDE. Do you think you'll be able to work better if you know Bolette is sitting here thinking of you?

LYNGSTRAND. Yes, I think so. To know that somewhere in the world there's a lovely, silent young woman sitting quietly and dreaming of me. I think it must be so—so—I don't know how to describe it.

HILDE. Exciting?

LYNGSTRAND. Exciting? Yes! Just that! Exciting! More or less. *Looks at her for a moment.*

You're so wise, Miss Hilde. Amazingly wise. When I come home again, you'll be about the same age as your sister is now. Perhaps you will look like her too. Perhaps you'll have the same mind as she has now. You and she will have become—one person, so to speak.

HILDE. Would you like that to happen?

LYNGSTRAND. I don't know. Yes, I think so. But now—this summer—I want you to stay just as you are—not like anyone else. Just yourself.

HILDE. Do you like me best as I am?

LYNGSTRAND. Yes. I like you very much as you are.

HILDE. Hm. Tell me, as an artist, do you think I'm right always to wear these light summer clothes?

LYNGSTRAND. Yes. I think they suit you very well.

HILDE. You think these light colours suit me?

LYNGSTRAND. Yes. I think they suit you—beautifully. I think.

HILDE. But, tell me, speaking as an artist—how do you think I would look in black?

LYNGSTRAND. In black, Miss Hilde?

HILDE. Yes, all in black. Do you think I would look good in that?

LYNGSTRAND. Black is no colour to wear in the summertime. Though I think you would look very beautiful in black, too. Yes. Your looks would suit black perfectly.

HILDE, *to herself.* Black—up to the neck—black crepe all round —black gloves—and a long black veil hanging down behind.

LYNGSTRAND. If you dressed like that, Miss Hilde, I should wish myself a painter, so that I might paint you—as a beautiful young widow in mourning.

HILDE. Or as a young bride in mourning?

LYNGSTRAND. Yes, that would be even better. But surely you couldn't want to dress like that?

HILDE. I don't know really. But I think it's exciting.

LYNGSTRAND. Exciting?

HILDE. Exciting to think of. Yes.

Suddenly points left.

Oh look!

LYNGSTRAND, *looking.* The big English steamer! She's right alongside.

WANGEL *and* ELLIDA *appear by the pond.*

WANGEL. No, Ellida, my dear—you're wrong, I promise you. *Sees the others.*

Are you two here? That's right, isn't it, Mr. Lyngstrand— she's not in sight yet, is she?

LYNGSTRAND. The English ship?

WANGEL. Yes.

LYNGSTRAND, *pointing.* There she is, Doctor!

ELLIDA. Ah! I knew it!

WANGEL. You mean she's come?

LYNGSTRAND. Come like a thief in the night, as one might say. Softly—soundlessly——

WANGEL. You must take Hilde down to the jetty. Hurry! She'll want to hear the music.

LYNGSTRAND. Yes, we were just going, Doctor.

WANGEL. We'll come on in a few minutes.

HILDE *whispers to* LYNGSTRAND. Hand in hand! What did I say?

She and LYNGSTRAND *go out through the garden, left. Horn music is audible from far out on the fjord during the following dialogue.*

ELLIDA. He's come, then. He's here. Yes, yes. I feel it.

WANGEL. You'd better go indoors, Ellida. Let me talk to him alone.

ELLIDA. Oh, it's impossible. Impossible, I tell you.

Cries.

There he is!

THE STRANGER *enters from the left and stands on the path outside the garden fence.*

STRANGER. Good evening. Well, Ellida. Here I am again.

ELLIDA. Yes, yes. The hour has come.

STRANGER. Are you ready to go with me? Or not?

WANGEL. You can see for yourself that she is not.

STRANGER. I don't mean is she dressed for travelling? Or has she packed her bags? All she needs on the journey I have on board. I've got her a cabin too.

To ELLIDA.

I am asking you if you are ready to come with me. Of your own free will.

ELLIDA, *weakly.* Don't ask me. Don't tempt me.

A ship's bell is heard in the distance.

STRANGER. That is the first warning. You must say yes or no.

ELLIDA. To decide. To decide for one's whole life! And never to be able to undo it!

STRANGER. In half an hour it will be too late.

ELLIDA, *shyly and searchingly.* What makes you hold on to me so relentlessly?

STRANGER. Don't you feel, as I do, that we two belong together?

ELLIDA. You mean, because of the promise I gave you?

STRANGER. Promises bind no-one. No man, no woman. I hold on to you because I cannot do otherwise.

ELLIDA, *quiet and trembling.* Why didn't you come before?

WANGEL. Ellida!

ELLIDA. Oh, this man tempts me and draws me into the unknown! All the power of the sea is gathered in this man!

THE STRANGER *climbs over the garden fence.*

ELLIDA *takes refuge behind* WANGEL. What is it? What do you want?

STRANGER. I see it in your face, Ellida. I hear it in your voice. You will choose me in the end.

WANGEL *takes a step towards him.* The choice does not lie with my wife. It is my duty to choose for her—and to protect her. Yes, protect her! If you don't leave the country, and swear never to return, do you know what will happen to you?

ELLIDA. No, Wangel, no! You mustn't!

STRANGER. What will you do to me?

WANGEL. I will have you arrested as a common criminal. Now, at once, before you board the ship. I know the truth about that murder out at Skjoldviken.

ELLIDA. Wangel! How can you——?

STRANGER. I was prepared for that.

Draws a revolver from his breast pocket.

So I took the precaution of bringing this.

ELLIDA *throws herself in front of* WANGEL. No, no! Don't kill him. If you must kill anyone, kill me!

STRANGER. Don't worry. I don't want to kill either of you. This is for myself. I mean to live and die a free man.

ELLIDA. Wangel! Let me say this—and say it so that he hears it too! Of course you can keep me here. You have the power and the means to do so. And that is what you want to do. But my mind—my thoughts—my dreams and longings—those you cannot imprison. They strain to roam and hunt—out into the unknown—which I was born for—and which you have locked me away from.

WANGEL, *quietly, in pain.* I see it, Ellida! Little by little you are slipping away from me. Your longing for the boundless, the infinite, will end by driving your mind into darkness.

ELLIDA. Oh, yes, yes! I feel it! Like—black soundless wings—beating over me.

WANGEL. It mustn't come to that. There's no other way to save you. None that I can see. Therefore—I agree to—to cancel the bargain. Now—at once. Now you can make your choice, Ellida. In freedom.

ELLIDA *looks at him for a moment.* Do you mean that? Do you really mean it? With all your heart?

WANGEL. Yes. I mean it—with all my heart.

ELLIDA. But, can you—can you—let me go?

WANGEL. Yes. I can. I can—because I love you so much—so very much.

ELLIDA, *quiet and trembling.* Am I so close—so very close to you, then?

WANGEL. You have become a part of me, Ellida. Through the years we have lived together.

ELLIDA. And I have been blind to all this!

WANGEL. Your thoughts were directed elsewhere. But now—now you are free for ever from me and from everything that belongs to me. Now you can go back to the life that is really yours. Now you can choose—freely—on your own responsibility.

ELLIDA *stares unseeingly at him.* Free—but responsible!

To herself.

Responsible?

The ship's bell sounds again.

STRANGER. Do you hear, Ellida? She is sounding for the last time. Come.

ELLIDA *turns, gazes at him, and says in a clear voice.* I cannot go with you.

STRANGER. You're not coming?

ELLIDA, *putting her arm round* WANGEL. I can never go with you now.

WANGEL. Ellida! Ellida!

STRANGER. Then it is finished?

ELLIDA. Yes. Finished for ever.

STRANGER. Yes. I see. There is something here stronger than my will.

ELLIDA. Your will has no power over me any longer. For me you are a dead man washed up by the sea, whom the sea will soon claim again for her own. I no longer fear you. I no longer want you.

STRANGER. Goodbye, then.

He vaults over the fence.

Henceforth you are no more to me than a lost ship.

He goes out left.

WANGEL *looks at her for a moment.* Ellida, your mind is like the sea. It flows and ebbs. What changed you?

ELLIDA. Don't you understand? The change came when you let me choose freely.

WANGEL. And the unknown attracts you no longer?

ELLIDA. I no longer yearn for it, nor fear it. I have seen into the heart of it—I could have entered it—if I had chosen to do so. I was free to choose the unknown. So—I was free to reject it.

WANGEL. I begin to understand you, little by little. You think and feel in pictures and visual images. Your restless yearning for the sea—your yearning for this stranger—all that was nothing but an expression of your longing for freedom. Nothing more.

ELLIDA. Perhaps. I don't know. But you have been a good doctor to me. You discovered, and dared to prescribe, the right remedy—the only one that could have cured me.

WANGEL. When things are desperate, we doctors have to take desperate measures. But now—will you come back to me, Ellida?

ELLIDA. Yes, Wangel—my dear, faithful Wangel. Now I come to you freely, of my own choice.

WANGEL. Ellida! Ellida! We have found each other at last. Now we can live—for each other——

ELLIDA. And with our memories. Yours as well as mine.

WANGEL. Yes! Yes.

ELLIDA. And with our children, Wangel. Our two children.

WANGEL. *Our* children?

ELLIDA. They are not yet mine. But I shall win them.

WANGEL. Our children!

He kisses her hands.

Thank you, Ellida! Thank you!

HILDE, BALLESTED, LYNGSTRAND, ARNHOLM, *and* BOLETTE *come into the garden from the left. At the same time, a number of young people from the town and summer visitors appear on the footpath outside.*

HILDE, *half aloud to* LYNGSTRAND. Look at her and Father! Why, they look as though they'd just got engaged!

BALLESTED, *overhearing her.* It is summertime, little lady.

ARNHOLM, *looking at* ELLIDA *and* WANGEL. The Englander is sailing now.

BOLETTE, *going to the fence.* Here's the best place to watch from.

LYNGSTRAND. The last trip of the year.

BALLESTED. Every way to the sea will soon be locked, as the poet says. A sad thought, Mrs. Wangel. And now we shall lose you, too, for a while. You will be off to Skjoldviken tomorrow, they tell me.

WANGEL. No. This evening we two have changed our plans.

ARNHOLM, *looking from one to the other.* You have!

BOLETTE *comes over to them.* Father, is this true?

HILDE, *to* ELLIDA. Then you'll be staying with us after all?

ELLIDA. Yes, Hilde dear—if you want me to.

HILDE, *torn between joy and tears.* If—oh!

ARNHOLM, *to* ELLIDA. Well, this is certainly a surprise!

ELLIDA *smiles.* Why, Dr. Arnholm, don't you remember what we two were saying yesterday? Once one has become a landsman, one can never find one's way back to the sea. Or to the way of life—that belongs to the sea.

BALLESTED. Why, that's just like my mermaid!

ELLIDA. Yes, more or less.

BALLESTED. With one big difference. The mermaid died. But men and women—they can acclaim—acclimatise themselves. Yes, I assure you, Mrs. Wangel! They can acc—li—matise—themselves.

ELLIDA. If they are free, Mr. Ballested.

WANGEL. Free and responsible, Ellida.

ELLIDA, *quickly, gives him her hand.* Yes!

The big steamer glides silently out across the fjord. The music grows louder.

The Master Builder

INTRODUCTION

Ibsen wrote THE MASTER BUILDER in Christiania in 1892, at the age of sixty-four. It was the first play he had written in Norway since *The Pretenders* in 1863.

The previous summer, he had left his home in Munich for a holiday to the North Cape. While he was there, he decided to stay in Christiania over the winter; and in fact he stayed for the remaining fifteen years of his life.

There were several reasons for this decision to settle again in his native country after twenty-seven years abroad. He told Georg Brandes that it would be more convenient for him financially, but Fru Ibsen later said she thought it was because he wanted to die in Norway. During his visit in 1885 he had been unwell, and had then spoken of settling there; and in the beginning of 1890 he had a severe attack of influenza, which may have helped to remind him that he was no longer young. Moreover, he still had the obsessive longing for the sea which had twice recently driven him northwards (in 1885 and 1887), and a further factor was that his son Sigurd was now very active in Norwegian politics, and was being spoken of as a likely Foreign Minister as soon as Norway should obtain her independence from Sweden. Ibsen was very devoted to his son, and although he himself did not nowadays take much interest in politics he found himself acclaimed by both the right and the left wing parties. Life in Norway had seemed insufferable to him when he had been impoverished and unsuccessful; now that he was a national hero, it held certain attractions. So he stayed.

Departing from his usual routine of writing only during the summer and autumn, he began work on a new play that March (1892). Before the spring was over, however, he appears to have scrapped everything he had written and started afresh. He finished his new draft some time in October, and THE MASTER BUILDER was published by Gyldendals of Copenhagen on December 12, 1892. People everywhere were puzzled by it, as they had been puzzled by his two preceding plays, *The Lady from the Sea* and *Hedda Gabler,* but for a different reason. Some new element had entered into Ibsen's work; it had been perceptible in *Hedda Gabler,* but in THE MASTER BUILDER it was more than perceptible; it stuck out for all to see. Put bluntly, THE MASTER BUILDER seemed primarily to be a play about sex; one did not need to wait for Freud to be made uneasy by all that talk about the beauty of towers and spires. People speculated as to what new influence could have entered into the old man's life to turn his thoughts so sharply in this direction, and not until after Ibsen's death in 1906 was the answer given.

In that year, Georg Brandes published a series of letters which Ibsen had written between October 1889 and December 1890 (i.e., twenty-nine to fifteen months before he began THE MASTER BUILDER) to a young Austrian girl named Emilie Bardach. These revealed that, in the summer of 1889, when Ibsen was sixty-one and Emilie was eighteen, they had met at Gossensass in the Austrian Tyrol and that some kind of infatuation had resulted; whether mutual or one-sided was not quite clear. They had corresponded for over a year, and then Ibsen, gently but firmly, had told her not to write to him any more.

At about the time these letters appeared, a friend of Ibsen's, the German literary historian Julius Elias, published an account of a conversation he had had with Ibsen about Emilie Bardach which seemed to put the incident into proportion. This conversation had taken place in Berlin in February 1891, over lunch, while Ibsen was waiting for a train:

"An expansive mood came over Ibsen and, chuckling over his champagne glass, he said: 'Do you know, my next play is already hovering before me—in general outline, of course. One thing I can see clearly, though—an experience I once had myself—a female character. Very interesting—very interesting.' Then he related how he had met in the Tyrol a Viennese girl of very remarkable character, who had at once made him her confidant. The gist of it was that she was not interested in the idea of marrying some decently brought up young man; most likely she would never marry. What tempted, fascinated, and delighted her was to lure other women's husbands away from them. She was a demonic little wrecker; she often seemed to him like a little bird of prey, who would gladly have included him among her victims. He had studied her very, very closely. But she had had no great success with him. 'She did not get hold of me, but I got hold of her—for my play. Then I fancy she consoled herself with someone else.' "

This seemed to settle the matter. Ibsen's version of Emilie's character, or Elias's report of it, received general acceptance, and Emilie Bardach went down to history, while she was still a young woman (she lived until November 1, 1955), as a predatory little monster, more or less identical with the character of Hilde Wangel which Ibsen based on her. In 1923, however, two remarkable articles entitled "Ibsen and Emilie Bardach" were published in the American *Century Magazine*. The author was Basil King, an Ibsen enthusiast; in 1908, he had met Emilie, then a woman of thirty-seven, "gentle of manner, soft of voice, dressed with the distinction of which Viennese women have long possessed the art . . . going to Paris for the spring, to London for the season, and often to Scotland for country-house gatherings." She allowed King to see, and later to quote from, the diary she had kept during the time she had known and corresponded with Ibsen. These articles caused no particular sensation at the time, interest in Ibsen being rather low during the early twenties; there seems, however, no reason to doubt the authenticity of the diary extracts, and they go much further than Ibsen's account of the incident to explain the stormy and dynamic quality of his last five plays, after the comparative optimism of *The Lady from the Sea*.

Ibsen had come to Gossensass in July of 1889. He had

holidayed there on several previous occasions, but this was
his first visit for five years, and the town had decided to celebrate his return by naming his old lookout on the hill the
Ibsenplatz. There was a festal procession, and Ibsen, despite
the steep ascent, climbed at the head of it and "received
with friendliness and dignity all the homage that was accorded him." Emilie Bardach wrote in her diary (August 5,
1889):

"The weather is very bad and we cannot make any excur-
sions. The day of the Ibsen fete has been the only fine one;
but I washed my hair and could not go. After the concert,
however, I made his acquaintance in a way quite delightful."

There was a valley on the outskirts of the town named the
Pflerschthal, with a stream flowing through it, and a view of
mountains and glaciers. While walking here, Ibsen saw a girl
seated on a bench with a book. He came and sat beside her,
and learned her name, her parentage, her home residence,
and the fact that in Gossensass they lived so near together
that his windows looked into hers. A few days later she ran
into him at a dull birthday party. "It is a pity," she noted,
"that German gives him so much difficulty, as apart from that
we understand each other so well."

She fell ill and, a few days later, Ibsen came to see her,
climbing over the garden gate to do so. "He remained with
me a long while, and was both kind and sympathetic." A little later: "We talk a great deal together. His ardour ought
to make me feel proud." Then:

"Ibsen has begun to talk to me quite seriously about myself. He stayed a long time with me on Saturday, and also
again this evening. Our being so much together cannot but
have some powerful influence over me. He puts such strong
feeling into what he says to me. His words often give me a
sensation of terror and cold. He talks about the most serious
things in life, and believes in me so much. He expects from
me much, much more than, I am afraid, he will ever find.
Never in his whole life, he says, has he felt so much joy in
knowing anyone. He never admired anyone as he admires
me. But all in him is truly good and noble. What a pity it is
that I cannot remember all his words! He begs me so intensely

to talk freely to him, to be absolutely frank with him, so that we may become fellow-workers together."

Next she writes: "Mama has just gone out, so that I have the room to myself. At last I am free to put down the incredible things of these recent days. How poor and insufficient are the words! Tears say these things better. Passion has come when it cannot lead to anything, when both of us are bound by so many ties. Eternal obstacles! Are they in my will? Or are they in the circumstances? . . . How could I compare anything else that has happened to an outpouring like this? It could never go so far, and yet . . . !" She swings off on to Baron A., the only lover who afforded a standard of comparison. "But how much calmer *he* was!—how inarticulate!—beside this volcano, so terribly beautiful! Yesterday afternoon, we were alone together at last. Oh, the words!—if only they could have stamped themselves on my heart more deeply and distinctly! All that has been offered me before was only the pretense at love. This is the true love, the ideal, he says, to which without knowing it he gave himself in his art. At last he is a real poet through pain and renunciation. And yet he is glad of having known me—the most beautiful! the most wonderful! Too late! How small I seem to myself that I cannot spring to him!"

Neither Ibsen's wife nor Emilie's mother suspected what was afoot. But:

"The obstacles!—how they grow more numerous, the more I think of them! The difference of age!—his wife!—his son!—all that there is to keep us apart! Was it inevitable? Could I have foreseen it? Could I have prevented it? When he talks to me as he does, I often feel that I must go far away from here—far away!—and yet I suffer at the thought of leaving him. I suffer most from his impatience, his restlessness. I begin to feel it now even when we are in the salon, quite apart from each other.

"It all came to me so suddenly! I noticed first how he began to change his regular ways of life, but I didn't know what it meant. Of course—I was flattered at his sympathy, and at being distinguished among the many who surround him, eager for a word."

An early snowstorm came, and the guests at Gossensass

began to leave. Emilie realised they would soon have to part. "And I have nothing to give him, not even my picture, when he is giving me so much. But we both feel it is best to remain outwardly as strangers. His wife shows me much attention. Yesterday I had a long talk with his son.

"I am reading Ibsen's *Love's Comedy*, but if anyone comes I am seen holding Beaconsfield's *Endymion* in my hands. Nearly everyone has gone. The days we have still to spend here can now be counted. I don't think about the future. The present is too much. We had a long talk together in the forenoon, and after lunch he came again and sat with me. What am I to think? He says it is to be my life's aim to work with him. We are to write to each other often; but what am I to write?"

Ibsen confided his feelings to two ladies. One fainted; another described the scene to Emilie as "beautiful and terrible as an Alpine thunderstorm. She wonders that I do not lose my head. She says that she herself would have been absolutely overcome. This consoles me. I do not seem so weak."

Did something happen between Ibsen and Emilie on September 19, and if so was it anything like what Hilde Wangel describes as having happened between her and Solness on another September 19? Nearly forty years later, in 1927, Emilie told A. E. Zucker that Ibsen had never kissed her; perhaps, with Ibsen as with Solness, these things only happened in his mind. Next day, September 20, he wrote in Emilie's album: *"Hohes, schmerzliches Glück—um das Unerreichbare zu ringen!"*—— "High and painful joy—to struggle for the unattainable!"

A week later, on September 27, Emilie noted in her diary: "Our last day at Gossensass. Then nothing but memory will remain. Two weeks ago, memory seemed to Ibsen so beautiful, and now—— He says that tomorrow he will stand on the ruins of his happiness. These last two months are more important in his life than everything that has gone before. Am I unnatural in being so terribly quiet and normal? . . . Last evening when Mama went to talk to his wife he came over and sat at our table. We were quite alone. He talked about his plans. I alone am in them—I, and I again. I feel quieter because he is quieter, though yesterday he was terrible."

That night, at 3 A.M., the express from Verona to Vienna passed through Gossensass, and Emilie left on it. The same night, she wrote in her diary:

"He means to possess me. This is his absolute will. He intends to overcome all obstacles. I do what I can to keep him from feeling this, and yet I listen as he describes what is to lie before us—going from one country to another—I with him —enjoying his triumphs together . . . Our parting was easier than I had feared."

Emilie told Zucker in 1927 that Ibsen had, in Gossensass, "spoken to her of the possibility of a divorce and of a subsequent union with her, in the course of which they were to travel widely and see the world." The last entry in her diary would seem to bear this out. Once back in Munich, however, Ibsen seemed to resign himself to the impossibility of going through with such a plan. Perhaps he feared the scandal; perhaps he felt a duty towards his sickly and ageing wife, who had stood so firmly by him during the long years of failure; perhaps he reflected that the difference of forty-three years between their ages was too great; perhaps, away from Gossensass, he felt old. Probably he felt all these things. At any rate, his letters from Munich to her in Vienna are no more than those of an affectionate old man to a charming schoolgirl (though we must bear in mind that he is writing in a foreign language which "gives him much difficulty," that he was always an extremely inhibited letter-writer, and that he must have been very careful not to commit himself on paper).

> *München, Maximilianstrasse 32.*
> *October 7, 1889.*

With my whole heart I thank you, my beloved Fräulein, for the dear and delightful letter which I received on the last day of my stay at Gossensass, and have read over and over again.

There the last autumn week was a very sad one, or it was so to me. No more sunshine. Everything—gone. The few remaining guests could give me no compensation for the brief and beautiful end-of-summer life. I went to walk in the Pflerschthal. There there is a bench where two can commune together. But the bench was empty, and I went by without sitting down. So, too, the big salon was waste and desolate . . . Do you remember the big, deep bay-window on the right from the verandah? What a charming niche! The flowers and plants are still there, smelling so sweetly—but how empty—how lonely—how forsaken!

We are back here at home—and you in Vienna. You write that you feel surer of yourself, more independent, happier. How glad I am of these words! I shall say no more.

A new poem begins to dawn in me. I want to work on it this winter, transmuting into it the glowing inspiration of the summer. But the end may be disappointment. I feel it. It is my way. I told you once that I only corresponded by telegraph. So take this letter as it is. You will know what it means. A thousand greetings from your devoted—H.I.

The "poem" may have been *Hedda Gabler,* which he was to write the following year, or it may have been THE MASTER BUILDER itself. He did not in fact write the latter until three years later, but he may have conceived it at this early stage and then, deliberately, put it aside until he could consider it with more detachment.

Emilie's diary, October 8, 1889:

"A few words before I go to bed. I have good news. To-day, at last, came Ibsen's long-expected letter. He wants me to read between the lines. But do not the lines themselves say enough? This evening I paid grandmama a quite unpleasant visit. The weather is hot and stuffy and so is papa's mood. In other days, this would have depressed me; but now I have something to keep me up."

We do not know how she replied to Ibsen, for he did not preserve her letter. On October 15, however, he writes again:

I receive your letter with a thousand thanks—and have read it, and read it again. Here I sit as usual at my desk, and would gladly work, but cannot do so.

My imagination is ragingly at work, but always straying to where in working hours it should not. I cannot keep down the memories of the summer, neither do I want to. The things we have lived through I live again and again—and still again. To make of them a poem is for the time being impossible.

For the time being?

Shall I ever succeed in the future? And do I really wish that I could and would so succeed?

For the moment, at any rate, I cannot—or so I believe. That I feel—that I know.

And yet it must come. Decidedly it must come. But will it? or can it?

Ah, dear Fräulein!—but forgive me!—you wrote so charmingly in your last—no, no! God forbid!—in your previous letter you wrote so charmingly: "I am not Fräulein for you"—— So, dear Child—for that you surely are for me—tell me—do you remember that once we talked about Stupidity and Madness —or, more correctly, I talked about it; and you took up the role of teacher, and remarked, in your soft, musical voice, and with your far-away look, that there is always a difference between Stupidity and Madness . . . Well, then, I keep thinking over and over again: Was it Stupidity or was it Madness that we should have come together? Or was it both Stupidity and Madness? Or was it neither?

I believe the last is the only supposition that would stand the test. It was a simple necessity of nature. It was equally our fate . . . Your always devoted H. I.

On receipt of this letter, Emilie wrote in her diary: "I left it unopened till I had finished everything, and could read it quietly. But I was not quiet after reading it. Why does he not tell me of something to read which would feed my mind, instead of writing in a way to inflame my already excited imagination? I shall answer very soberly."

Ibsen to Emilie, October 29, 1889:

I have been meaning every day to write you a few words, but I wanted to enclose the photograph. This is still unfinished, and my letter must go off without it . . .

How charmingly you write! Please keep sending me a few lines, whenever you have a half hour not good for anything else.

So you leave my letters unopened till you are alone and quite undisturbed! Dear Child! I shall not try to thank you. That would be superfluous. You know what I mean.

Don't be uneasy because just now I cannot work. In the

*back of my mind, I am working all the time. I am dreaming
over something which, when it has ripened, will become a
poem.*

*Someone is coming. Can write no further. Next time a
longer letter. Your truly devoted H. I.*

Emilie's diary: "I wrote to him on Monday, very late at
night. Though I was tired, I did not want to put off doing
so, because I had to thank him for the books I received on
Sunday. The same evening I had read *Rosmersholm*, parts
of which are very fine. I have to make so many duty calls,
but this and a great many other things I can stand better
than I used to. They are only the outward things; my inner
world is something very different. Oh, the terror and beauty
of having him care about me as he never cared about anyone
else! But when he is suffering he calls it *hohes, schmerzliches
Glück*—high, and painful joy!"

Ibsen to Emilie, November 19, 1889:

*At last I can send you the new picture. I hope you may
find it a better likeness than the one you have already. A
German sketch of my life will appear within a few days, and
you will receive it at once. Read it when you have the time.
It will tell you my story up to the end of last year.*

*Heartfelt thanks for your dear letter; but what do you
think of me for not having answered it earlier? And yet—you
know it well—you are always in my thoughts, and will remain
there. An active exchange of letters is on my side an impossibility. I have already said so. Take me as I am. . . .*

*I am greatly preoccupied with the preparations for my
new work. Sit tight at my desk the whole day. Go out only
toward evening. I dream and remember and write. To dream
is fine; but the reality at times can be still finer. Your most
devoted H. I.*

On the back of the photograph stood the inscription: *"An
die Maisonne eines Septemberlebens"* [To the May sun of a
September life]."

Ibsen to Emilie, December 6, 1889:

*Two dear, dear letters have I had from you, and answered
neither till now. What do you think of me? But I cannot find*

the quiet necessary to writing you anything orderly or straightforward. This evening I must go to the theatre to see An Enemy of the People. *The mere thought of it is a torture. Then, too, I must give up for the time being the hope of getting your photograph. But better so than to have an unfavourable picture. Besides, how vividly your dear, serene features remain with me in my memory! The same enigmatic princess stands behind them. But the enigma itself? One can dream of it, and write about it—and that I do. It is some little compensation for the unattainable—for the unfathomable reality. In my imagination I always see you wearing the pearls you love so much. In this taste for pearls I see something deeper, something hidden. I often think of it. Sometimes I think I have found the interpretation—and then again not. Next time I shall try to answer some of your questions; but I myself have so many questions to ask you. I am always doing it—inwardly—inaudibly. Your devoted H.I.*

In her diary, Emilie repeats his words: "It is some little compensation for the unattainable, for the impenetrable reality."

Ibsen to Emilie, December 22, 1889:

How shall I thank you for your dear and delightful letter? I simply am not able to, not at least as I should like. The writing of letters is always hard for me. I think I have told you so already, and you will in any case have noticed it for yourself.

I read your letter over and over, for through it the voice of the summer awakens so clearly. I see—I go through again —the things we lived together. As a lovely creature of the summer, dear Princess, I have known you, as a being of the season of butterflies and wild flowers. How I should like to see you as you are in winter! I am always with you in spirit. I see you in the Ring Strasse, light, quick, poised like a bird, gracious in velvet and furs. In soirées, in society, I also see you, and especially at the theatre, leaning back, a tired look in your mysterious eyes. I should like, too, to see you at home, but here I don't succeed, as I haven't the data. You have told me so little of your home-life—almost nothing defi-

nite. As a matter of fact, dear Princess, in many important details we are strangers to each other . . .

More than anything I should like to see you at home on Christmas night, where I suppose you will be. As to what happens to you there, I have no clear idea. I only imagine—to myself.

And then I have a strange feeling that you and Christmas don't go well together. But who knows? Perhaps you do. In any case accept my heartfelt wishes and a thousand greetings. Your always devoted H.I.

Ibsen to Emilie, December 30, 1889:

Your lovely and charming picture, so speakingly like, has given me a wholly indescribable joy. I thank you for it a thousand times, and straight from the heart. How you have brought back, now in midwinter, those brief sunny summer days!

So, too, I thank you from the heart for your dear, dear letter. From me you must expect no more than a few words. I lack the time, and the necessary quiet and solitude, to write to you as I should like . . .

Ibsen to Emilie, January 16, 1890:

How sorry I am to learn that you, too, have been ill. But what do you think? I had a strong presentiment that it was so. In my imagination I saw you lying in bed, pale, feverish, but sweet and lovely as ever . . . How thankful I am that I have your charming picture!

Ibsen to Emilie, February 6, 1890:

Long, very long, have I left your last, dear letter—read and read again—without an answer. Take today my heartfelt thanks for it, but given in very few words. Henceforth, till we see each other face to face, you will hear little from me, and very seldom. Believe me, it is better so. It is the only right thing. It is a matter of conscience with me to end our correspondence, or at least to limit it. You yourself should have as little to do with me as possible. With your young life you have other aims to follow, other tasks to fulfil. And I—I have

told you so already—can never be content with a mere ex-
change of letters. For me it is only half the thing; it is a false
situation. Not to give myself wholly and without reserve
makes me unhappy. It is my nature. I cannot change it. You
are so delicately subtle, so instinctively penetrating, that you
will easily see what I mean. When we are again together, I
shall be able to explain it all more fully. Till then, and always,
you will be in my thoughts. You will be so even more when
we no longer have to stop at this wearisome halfway-house of
correspondence. A thousand greetings. Your H.I.

For four days after the reception of this letter, there is no
entry in Emilie's diary. Then she writes of balls, singing lessons, domestic duties; then suddenly: "What is my inner life
after Ibsen's letter? I wrote at once and henceforth will be
silent, silent." Ten days later: "Will he never write any more?
I cannot think about it. Who could? And yet, not to do so is
in his nature. In his very kindness there is often cruelty."

For seven months he did not write to her. During this time
he was struggling with *Hedda Gabler*. On June 29, he wrote
to the Swedish poet, Carl Snoilsky, that he had been hoping
to spend the summer in the Tyrol but had encountered difficulties in the writing of his new play and did not want to
leave Munich until he had overcome them. He had in fact
been planning to return to Gossensass, and from the references in his letters to "when we are together again" I think
it is fair to assume that he hoped to meet Emilie there (we
must remember that her parents knew nothing of her feelings
for Ibsen). It is interesting to note that, in the first draft of
Hedda Gabler, in the scene where Hedda is showing Løv-
borg the photographs from her honeymoon, the dialogue runs
as follows:

HEDDA. What was this little country town called?
TESMAN. What? Let me think. Oh, that's Gossensass, on the
    Brenner Pass. We stayed a day there——
HEDDA. Yes, and met all those amusing people.

In his final draft, Ibsen struck out all mention of Gossensass, and the dialogue reads:

HEDDA. Do you remember that little country town?

TESMAN. Oh, that one below the Brenner Pass? That was where we stayed the night.

King observes: "Though in that play [i.e., *Hedda Gabler*] there is no outward trace of Emilie Bardach or Gossensass, both must be present as vital forces . . . It is safe to say that to the girl in Vienna *Hedda Gabler* owes much of its marvellous *élan*. She was not in it, but she was behind it, as, according to her English biographer [Edmund Gosse] she was to be behind everything else for the rest of the poet's life."

In September, Ibsen broke his silence to write Emilie a letter of sympathy on the bereavement of her father, with some news of himself and his family, but no more. On December 30, he writes briefly to thank her for a Christmas present:

I have duly received your dear letter, as well as the bell with the beautiful picture. I thank you for them, straight from the heart. My wife finds the picture very pretty. But I beg you, for the time being, not to write to me again. When conditions have changed, I will let you know. I shall soon send you my new play. Accept it in friendship—but in silence. How I should love to see you and talk with you again! A Happy New Year to you and to Madame your mother. Your always devoted H. I.

She did not write to him again, nor did the meeting to which they had both looked forward so eagerly ever take place. For seven years there was no contact between them. Then, on his seventieth birthday, an occasion of great celebration in Scandinavia, she sent him a telegram of congratulation. His letter of reply was the last message that passed between them:

Christiania, March 15, 1898.
Herzlich liebes Fräulein!
Accept my most deeply felt thanks for your message. The summer in Gossensass was the happiest, the most lovely, in my whole life.

I scarcely dare to think of it—and yet I must think of it always—— Always!
Your truly devoted H. I.

It is against this background that we must read THE MAS-
TER BUILDER. Other elements, of course, intrude into it. He
had returned to Norway by the time he began to write it,
and he took pains to make Hilde almost ostentatiously Norwegian in her speech and manners. He had by this time struck
up a friendship with a young Norwegian pianist, Hildur Andersen, the daughter of old friends from his Bergen days.
She seems to have had many of the qualities which he admired in Emilie, notably the combination of eagerness and
sensitivity, and it may be that her name, Hildur, caused him
to remember the Hilde whom he had created as a minor
character in *The Lady from the Sea* and whom he now resurrected, ten years older, to play a more important role. Aline
Solness is plainly based on Ibsen's wife, and the relationship
between the Solnesses bears an uncomfortable resemblance
to that which appears to have existed at this time in the
Ibsen household. Shortly after their return to Norway, Ibsen's
mother-in-law, Magdalene Thoresen, wrote in a letter: "They
live splendidly, and have an elegant home, though all is
pretty much in philistine style. They are two lonely people—
each for himself—each absolutely for himself."

A few months before Ibsen began THE MASTER BUILDER,
the young novelist Knut Hamsun had delivered three lectures
in Christiania on the decadence of modern literature. In
them, he had particularly attacked the "Big Four" of Norwegian literature, Ibsen, Bjørnson, Lie, and Kielland. An in-
vitation was sent to Ibsen and, to the consternation of those
present, he attended all three lectures, sitting in seat number
one in the front row. He is reported to have sat "quiet and
serious, with unmoved countenance . . . His strong blue eyes
did not leave the speaker for a minute." It may well have
been the memory of Hamsun's invective that suggested Solness's fear of "youth banging on the door." In passing, one
may note that in the course of his lectures Hamsun had insisted on the necessity of probing into the dark and unconscious corners of the human mind, and that Ibsen, in THE
MASTER BUILDER and the three plays which followed, was
to do just this—he had already begun to do so in *The Lady
from the Sea*.

The character of Solness was the closest thing to a self-

portrait that Ibsen had yet attempted, though he was to follow it with two more in *John Gabriel Borkman* and *When
We Dead Awaken*. He admitted in a speech a few years
later that Solness "is a man who is somewhat related to me."
Ibsen had long regarded himself as a builder, and his plays
as works of architecture. As early as 1858, in a poem entitled "Building Plans," he had compared the artist to a master builder, and when Erik Werenskiold, seeing him looking
at some new buildings in Christiania, asked him: "You are
interested in architecture?" Ibsen replied: "Yes; it is, as you
know, my own trade." Ibsen, like Solness, had always had a
fear of looking down from a great height, or into a deep
chasm, and this had become worse as he had grown older.
Solness's ruthlessness, his readiness to sacrifice the happiness
of those nearest him for the sake of his ambition, his longing
for and fear of youth, and the conflict in him between aes-
thetic and ethical demands—all these were Ibsen's too. Moreover, during Ibsen's last years in Munich, we are told that he
continually raised the subject of hypnotism, of how one human being could gain power over the mind of another, and
how unexpressed wishes sometimes translated themselves into
actions. This curiosity, too, had already manifested itself in
The Lady from the Sea.

A word about trolls. Solness's repeated references to them
are meaningless unless one has a clear understanding of what
the word means. The great Norwegian scholar, Professor
Francis Bull, defined them admirably in a lecture delivered
at Oxford in 1954:

*Trolls—what are they? The word cannot be translated at
all! The trolls are supernatural beings, akin to the enemies of
the gods in the heathen world, and very well known in Norwegian fairy tales and folklore. They are supposed to live in
the woods and mountains, and you must not imagine them in
the shape of little goblins; they look more like Polyphemus
and Cyclops in the* Odyssey—*huge, clumsy and ugly . . .
[They] may be said to represent the evil forces in Nature,
at first only as incarnations of frightening sounds and visions
from without, but in more recent literature gradually taken
in a wider sense, embodying or symbolizing those powers of*

evil, hidden in the soul of man, which may at times suddenly suppress his conscious will and dominate his actions. A great Norwegian novelist and friend of Ibsen has written two volumes of short stories and fairy tales, simply called Trolls, *starting with this declaration: "That there are trolls in Man, everybody knows who has any insight into such things" . . . In . . .* The Master Builder, *which is very much the author's personal confession, Solness, half in joke and half in earnest and remorse, tells about his devils or trolls; in a way they serve him, but by ever pandering to his evil instincts and desires they have come to be really his rulers—mysterious powers that make him afraid of himself.*

Ever since childhood, Ibsen had been fascinated by towers. In the memoirs of his childhood and youth which he had compiled a few years previously, to help Henrik Jæger in the writing of his authorised biography, Ibsen had mentioned that the house in which he was born "stood exactly opposite the front of the church, with its high flight of steps and its conspicuous tower, from which the watchman used to proclaim the hour at night." A poodle also lived in the tower; it "had fiery red eyes, but was rarely visible. Indeed, so far as I know, he was never seen but once." One New Year's morning, just as the watchman shouted "One" through the opening in the front of the tower, the poodle appeared behind him and looked at him with his fiery eyes, whereupon the watchman fell down into the market place and was killed. "From that night, the watchman never calls 'One' from the church tower at Skien." It was from the opening in this tower, Ibsen continues, that he received "the first conscious and permanent impression on my mind. My nurse one day took me up the tower and allowed me to sit on the ledge outside . . . I perfectly recollect how amazed I was at looking down on the tops of the hats of the people below." His mother happened to look up from her window, saw him there, shrieked, and fainted "as people used to do in those days . . . As a boy, I never went across the market place without looking up at the tower window. I always felt as though the opening and the church poodle were some special concern of mine."

In a letter written to his sister Hedvig on March 13, 1891

(when he was already planning THE MASTER BUILDER), Ibsen recalled that "the house where I was born and lived the first years of my childhood, and the church, the old church with its christening-angel under the roof, are now burned down. All that my earliest memories are associated with—it was all burned." These feelings are strongly echoed in Solness's account of the burning of his wife's family home; and the christening-angel (which was lowered when a child was to be christened) may be the original of Aline's dolls.

Shortly before he left Munich that summer, Ibsen heard from Helene Raff the legend of the master builder who had built St. Michael's Church there, and had thrown himself down from the tower of the church because he was afraid the roof would not hold. Ibsen said he thought the legend must have arisen in Scandinavia, and when Helene observed that every famous cathedral in Germany had the same legend, he replied that this must be because people felt instinctively that a man could not build so high without paying the penalty for his hubris.

The publication of THE MASTER BUILDER was eagerly awaited throughout Europe. English, French, and German translations appeared almost simultaneously with the original, the German translation being by Ibsen's son, Sigurd. Translations into Russian, Dutch, Polish, and Bohemian followed shortly afterwards. Great arguments developed as to the meaning of the play. As one contemporary put it: "While one person sees Solness as Ibsen himself, another sees him as Bjørnson, a third as a symbol of the right wing party, a fourth as a symbol of the left and its leader; a fifth sees Solness as a symbol of Man rising in rebellion against God; a sixth sees the play as a conflict between youth and the older generation." Some sought to identify Solness with Bismarck, while the *Saturday Review* in London decided that he was meant as a portrait of Mr. Gladstone, and that the play was full of references to the Irish question. Ibsen, when asked which of these interpretations was true, answered that the play merely portrayed people whom he had known and that he could not understand what everyone was arguing about.

THE MASTER BUILDER received its first performance at

Trondheim in January 1893, after the usual public reading in London to secure performing copyright. Before the end of the month, it had also been staged in Bergen, Copenhagen, Gothenburg, Stockholm, Åbo, Helsingfors, and Berlin. London and Chicago saw it in February, and Rome in April. It has remained one of Ibsen's most admired and most frequently performed plays.

In 1908, in Munich, Emilie Bradach saw THE MASTER BUILDER for the first time. After the performance, she commented: "I didn't see myself, but I saw him. There is something of me in Hilde; but in Solness, there is little that is not Ibsen."

M. M.

CHARACTERS

HALVARD SOLNESS, master builder
ALINE SOLNESS, his wife
DR. HERDAL, a family physician
KNUT BROVIK, sometime architect, now assistant to SOLNESS
RAGNAR BROVIK, his son, a draughtsman
KAJA FOSLI, bookkeeper, niece to KNUT BROVIK
HILDE WANGEL
LADIES
PEOPLE IN THE STREET

The action takes place in SOLNESS'S *house.*

ACT ONE

A plainly furnished office in SOLNESS's *house. In the left-hand wall, double doors lead out to the hall. To the right is a door leading to the inner rooms of the house. In the rear wall is an open door leading to the drawing office. Downstage left, a high desk with books, papers, and writing materials. Upstage of the door, a stove. In the right-hand corner, a sofa, with a table and two or three chairs. On the table, a water carafe and glasses. A smaller table, with a rocking chair and an armchair, downstage right. Lighted lamps are on the table in the drawing office, and also on the table in the corner, and on the desk.*

Inside the drawing office sit KNUT BROVIK *and his son,* RAGNAR, *occupied with plans and calculations.* KAJA FOSLI *stands at the desk in the office, writing in the ledger.* KNUT BROVIK *is a thin old man with white hair and beard, dressed in a somewhat worn but carefully preserved black tail coat. He wears spectacles and a white cravat, which has turned rather yellow.* RAGNAR BROVIK *is in his thirties; well dressed, fair haired, with a slight stoop.* KAJA FOSLI *is a slender girl, in her early twenties, neatly dressed, but of sickly appearance. She wears a green shade over her eyes. For a while, all three work in silence.*

KNUT BROVIK *gets up suddenly from the drawing table, as though in distress, and breathes heavily and with diffi-*

culty as he comes forward into the doorway. No, I can't go on with this much longer.

KAJA *goes over to him.* It's really bad tonight, isn't it, Uncle?

BROVIK. Yes, it seems to grow worse every day.

RAGNAR *has got up, and comes closer.* You'd better go home, Father. Try to get a little sleep——

BROVIK, *impatiently.* Go to bed? Do you want me to suffocate?

KAJA. Take a little walk, anyway.

RAGNAR. Yes, do that. I'll come with you.

BROVIK. I'm not going before he comes! This evening I'm going to have it out with—
Bitterly.
—with him. The master builder!

KAJA, *anxiously.* Oh, no, Uncle, let that wait.

RAGNAR. Yes, better wait, Father.

BROVIK *laughs with difficulty.* I can't afford to wait very long.

KAJA *listens.* Ssh! I can hear him coming up the steps.

All three go back to their work again. Short pause. HAL-VARD SOLNESS, *master builder, enters through the hall door. He is an oldish man, strong and vigorous, with close-cut, curly hair, dark moustache, and dark, thick eyebrows. He is dressed in a grey-green jacket, buttoned up, with high collar and broad lapels. He has a soft grey felt hat on his head, and two or three portfolios under his arm.*

SOLNESS, *in the doorway, points towards the drawing office and asks in a whisper.* Have they gone?

KAJA, *softly, shakes her head.* No.

She takes off her eyeshade. SOLNESS *walks across the room, throws his hat on a chair, puts the portfolios on the table by the sofa, and comes back towards the desk.* KAJA *continues writing, but seems nervous and ill at ease.*

SOLNESS, *aloud.* What's that you're entering there, Miss Fosli?

KAJA *starts.* Oh, just something that——

SOLNESS. Let me see.

Leans over her, pretending to look at the ledger, and whispers.

Kaja?

KAJA, *softly, as she writes.* Yes?

SOLNESS. Why do you always take off that eyeshade when I come in?

KAJA. It makes me look so ugly.

SOLNESS *smiles.* And you don't want to look ugly, Kaja?

KAJA *half glances up at him.* Not for anything. Not to you!

SOLNESS *strokes her hair gently.* Poor, poor little Kaja!

KAJA *moves her head away.* Ssh! They can hear you!

SOLNESS *strolls across the room to the right, turns, and stands by the door to the drawing office.*

SOLNESS. Has anyone been asking for me?

RAGNAR *gets up.* Yes, that young couple who want the villa built out at Løvstrand.

SOLNESS *growls.* Oh, them? Well, they'll have to wait. The plan's not come clear in my mind yet.

RAGNAR *comes closer, a little diffidently.* They were very anxious to get the drawings as soon as possible.

SOLNESS. Yes, that's what they all say.

BROVIK *looks up.* They're longing to get into a place of their own.

SOLNESS. Oh, yes, yes. I know that sort. They'll take anything with four walls and a roof over it. Anywhere to lay their heads. That's not what I call a home. If that's what they want, let them go to someone else. Tell them that next time they come.

BROVIK *pushes his spectacles up on to his forehead, and stares amazed.* Someone else? Would you let the contract go?

SOLNESS, *impatiently.* Yes, damn it, yes! If it comes to the point. I'd rather that than build rubbish. Anyway I don't know these people.

BROVIK. Oh they're sound enough. Ragnar knows them. He's a friend of the family. Very sound people.

SOLNESS. Oh, sound, sound! That's not what I mean. Great God, don't you understand me either?

Angrily.

I don't want to have anything to do with people I don't know. As far as I'm concerned, they can go to anyone they like.

BROVIK *gets up.* Are you serious?

SOLNESS. Yes. For once.

He walks across the room. BROVIK *glances at* RAGNAR, *who makes a warning gesture, then goes into the other room.*

BROVIK. May I have a few words with you?

SOLNESS. Certainly.

BROVIK. Go inside for a moment, Kaja.

KAJA, *uneasy.* But, Uncle——

BROVIK. Do as I say, child. And close the door after you.

KAJA *goes unwillingly into the drawing office, glances anxiously and pleadingly at* SOLNESS, *and closes the door.*

BROVIK *lowers his voice.* I don't want the children to know how seriously ill I am.

SOLNESS. Yes, you look rather poorly these days.

BROVIK. I haven't much longer. My strength gets less every day.

SOLNESS. Sit down for a moment.

BROVIK. Thank you, may I?

SOLNESS *moves the armchair a little.* Here. Well?

BROVIK *sits down with difficulty.* It's this question of Ragnar. That's what weighs most on my mind. What's to become of him?

SOLNESS. Your son? He'll stay here with me, for as long as he wants to.

BROVIK. But that's just it. He doesn't want to. He doesn't feel he can—now.

SOLNESS. Well, he's doing quite well for himself, I should have thought. Still, if he wants a little more, I wouldn't be un-willing to——

BROVIK. No, no, that's not it.

Impatiently.

It's time he was given the chance to do something on his own.

SOLNESS, *not looking at him.* Do you think he's got the ability?

BROVIK. That's what's so dreadful. I've begun to have doubts about the boy. In all these years you've never uttered so much as a single word of encouragement about him. But it must be there. I can't believe he hasn't got the ability.

SOLNESS. But he doesn't know anything. Not really. Except how to draw.

BROVIK, *with suppressed hatred.* You didn't know much either, when you were working for me. But you managed to get started all right.

Breathes heavily.

Fought your way up. Put me out of business—and plenty of others.

SOLNESS. Yes—things worked out for me.

BROVIK. That's right. Everything worked out nicely for you. But surely you won't let me die without seeing what Ragnar can do. And I would like to see them married before I go.

SOLNESS, *sharply.* Does she want that?

BROVIK. Not Kaja so much. It's Ragnar—he talks about it every day.

Pleadingly.

You must—you *must* help him to stand on his own feet now! I must see the lad do something on his own. Do you hear?

SOLNESS, *angrily.* But, damn it, I can't conjure contracts out of the air for him.

BROVIK. He could get a commission right away. A nice big job.

SOLNESS, *startled, uneasy.* Could he?

BROVIK. If you agree.

SOLNESS. What kind of a job would that be?

BROVIK, *a little diffidently.* He could build that villa out at Løvstrand.

SOLNESS. That! But I'm going to build that myself.

BROVIK. Oh, you don't really want to do that.

SOLNESS. Don't want to? Who dared to say that?

BROVIK. You said so yourself, just now.

SOLNESS. Oh, never mind what I *say*. Could Ragnar get that contract?

BROVIK. Yes. He knows the family, you see. And then, he's— just for the fun of it, you know—he's made drawings and estimates and so on——

SOLNESS. And these drawings—are they satisfied with them? These people who are going to live there?

BROVIK. Yes. If only you'd just look through them and approve them, they——

SOLNESS. They'd like Ragnar to build their home for them?

BROVIK. They were very taken with his idea. They thought it was so new and original.

SOLNESS. Oh! New! Not the old-fashioned junk I build?

BROVIK. They thought this was—different.

SOLNESS. So it was Ragnar they came to see—while I was out.

BROVIK. They came to talk to you. And to ask if you'd be willing to give way——

SOLNESS. I? Give way for your son!

BROVIK. Rescind the contract, they meant.

SOLNESS. What's the difference?

Laughs bitterly.

So that's it! Halvard Solness is to retire! Retire to make way for younger men! or apprentices! Make way for the young! Make way! Make way!

BROVIK. Good heavens, there's room in this town for more than one——

SOLNESS. Oh, there's not so much room round here either. But that's not the point. I shall never give way! I shall never make way for anyone! Not of my own free will. Never, never!

BROVIK *gets up with difficulty.* Won't you let me die in

peace? Happy—believing in my son? Won't you let me see him do one thing on his own?

SOLNESS *turns half aside and mutters.* Don't ask me that now.

BROVIK. Yes, answer me! Must I die so poor?

SOLNESS *seems to fight with himself, then says, quietly but firmly.* You must die as best you can.

BROVIK. So be it.

Walks away.

SOLNESS *follows him, almost desperately.* I can't do otherwise, don't you understand? I am what I am. And I can't create myself anew.

BROVIK. No, no. You can't do that.

Stumbles and stops by the sofa table.

May I have a glass of water?

SOLNESS. Of course.

Pours one out and hands it to him.

BROVIK. Thank you.

Drinks and puts the glass down. SOLNESS *goes over to the door of the drawing office and opens it.*

SOLNESS. Ragnar, you'd better take your father home.

RAGNAR *gets up quickly. He and* KAJA *come into the office.*

RAGNAR. What is it, Father?

BROVIK. Take my arm. Let's go.

RAGNAR. All right. Put your coat on, Kaja.

SOLNESS. Miss Fosli must stay. For a few minutes. I have a letter to write.

BROVIK *looks at* SOLNESS. Good night. Sleep well—if you can.

SOLNESS. Good night.

BROVIK *and* RAGNAR *go out through the front door.* KAJA *goes across to her desk.* SOLNESS *stands with bowed head near the armchair on the right.*

KAJA, *uncertainly.* Have you got a letter——?

SOLNESS, *curtly.* No, no, of course not.

Looks sharply at her.

Kaja!

KAJA, *quietly, frightened.* Yes?

SOLNESS *points commandingly with a finger towards the floor.*
Come here. At once!

KAJA, *unwillingly.* Yes.

SOLNESS, *still in the same tone.* Closer!

KAJA, *obeying him.* What do you want me to do?

SOLNESS *looks at her for a moment.* Is it you I have to thank
for this?

KAJA. No, no, please don't think that.

SOLNESS. So you want to get married now.

KAJA, *quietly.* Ragnar and I have been engaged for nearly
five years, so——

SOLNESS. So you think it's time something happened. That's
it, isn't it?

KAJA. Ragnar and Uncle say I must. So I suppose I shall.

SOLNESS, *more gently.* You're quite fond of Ragnar, too, aren't
you, Kaja?

KAJA. I was very fond of Ragnar. Before I came here.

SOLNESS. But not any longer?

KAJA, *passionately.* Oh, you know there's only one person
now. There's no-one else in all the world. I'll never be fond
of anyone else.

SOLNESS. Yes, you say that. But you're going to leave me, all
the same. Leave me here to put up with everything alone.

KAJA. But couldn't I stay here with you even if Ragnar——?

SOLNESS. No, no, that's quite impossible. If Ragnar leaves me
and sets up on his own account, he'll want to have you
with him.

KAJA. Oh, I don't feel I can leave you! I can't, possibly—I
can't!

SOLNESS. Then try to get Ragnar to put these foolish ideas
out of his head. Marry him as much as you like—
Changes his tone.
Yes, yes, I mean, persuade him to stay on in this good posi-
tion he's got with me. Because then I can keep you, too,
Kaja dear.

KAJA. Oh, yes, how wonderful! If only it could work out like that!

SOLNESS *takes her face between his hands and whispers.* I can't be without you, you see. I must have you here with me, every day.

KAJA. God! Oh God!

SOLNESS *kisses her hair.* Kaja, Kaja!

KAJA *drops on her knees.* Oh, you're so kind to me! So wonderfully kind!

SOLNESS, *sharply.* Get up! Get up, for heaven's sake! I think I can hear someone.

He helps her up. She falters over towards the desk. MRS. SOLNESS *comes in through the door on the right. She looks thin and haggard, but retains traces of former beauty. Fair hair hanging in ringlets. She is elegantly dressed, all in black. She speaks rather slowly and plaintively.*

MRS. SOLNESS, *in the doorway.* Halvard!

SOLNESS *turns.* Oh, is it you, my dear?

MRS. SOLNESS *glances at* KAJA. I've come at an inconvenient moment, I see.

SOLNESS. Not at all. Miss Fosli is just writing a short letter for me.

MRS. SOLNESS. So I see.

SOLNESS. What was it you wanted, Aline?

MRS. SOLNESS. I only wanted to tell you that Dr. Herdal is in the drawing room. Would you like to come in and join us, Halvard?

SOLNESS *looks at her suspiciously.* H'm. Has he something special to say to me?

MRS. SOLNESS. No, nothing special. He came to visit me, and he'd like to see you while he's here.

SOLNESS *laughs quietly.* Yes, I'm sure he would. Well, ask him to wait a moment.

MRS. SOLNESS. You'll come and talk to him later, then?

SOLNESS. Perhaps. Later, my dear—later. In a little while.

MRS. SOLNESS, *with another look at* KAJA. Yes, well, don't forget now, Halvard.

Goes out, closing the door behind her.

KAJA, *quietly*. Oh, God, oh, God—I'm sure she thinks something dreadful about me!

SOLNESS. Well, not more than usual, anyway. I think you'd better go now, though, Kaja.

KAJA. Yes, yes, I *must* go now.

SOLNESS, *sternly*. And get this other thing settled for me. Do you hear?

KAJA. Oh God, if it were only up to me——

SOLNESS. I want it settled, do you hear? And by tomorrow.

KAJA. If there's no other way, I'll break it off with him.

SOLNESS. Break it off? Have you gone mad? Do you want to break it off?

KAJA. Yes—I'd rather that than——! I must—I must stay here with you! I can't leave you! I can't—possibly!

SOLNESS. But, for Christ's sake, what about Ragnar?

KAJA. Is it Ragnar you——?

SOLNESS. Oh no, no, of course not. You don't understand me.

Gently, quietly.

Of course it's you I want, Kaja. Above all else. And it's just because of that that you must persuade Ragnar to stay. Now then, run along home.

KAJA. Yes, yes. Good night, then.

SOLNESS. Good night.

As she turns to go.

Oh, by the way—are Ragnar's drawings in there?

KAJA. Yes, I didn't see him take them.

SOLNESS. Go in and find them for me. I might have a glance at them after all.

KAJA, *happily*. Oh, yes, please do!

SOLNESS. I'll do it for your sake, Kaja. Well, hurry up and find them for me, then!

KAJA *runs into the drawing office, searches anxiously in the drawer of the desk, finds a portfolio, and brings it out.*

KAJA. All the drawings are here.

SOLNESS. Good. Put them over there on the table.

KAJA *puts down the portfolio.* Good night, then.

Pleadingly.

Think kindly of me, won't you?

SOLNESS. Oh, I always do. Good night, my dear little Kaja.

Glances right.

Hurry up, now, run off.

MRS. SOLNESS *and* DR. HERDAL *enter through the door on the right. He is a stout, elderly man with a round, genial face, clean-shaven, with sparse, fair hair and gold-rimmed spectacles.*

MRS. SOLNESS, *in the doorway.* Halvard, I couldn't keep the doctor waiting any longer.

SOLNESS. Well, come in, then.

MRS. SOLNESS, *to* KAJA, *who is turning down the lamp on the desk.* Quite finished your letter, Miss Fosli?

KAJA, *confused.* Letter?

SOLNESS. Yes, it was just a short one.

MRS. SOLNESS. It must have been very short.

SOLNESS. You may go, Miss Fosli. Be sure you're here punctually tomorrow.

KAJA. Why, of course. Good night, Mrs. Solness.

Goes out through hall door.

MRS. SOLNESS. You must be very pleased, Halvard, to have got hold of this young lady.

SOLNESS. Yes, indeed. She's useful in all sorts of ways.

MRS. SOLNESS. I'm sure she is.

HERDAL. Good at bookkeeping, too?

SOLNESS. Well—she's picked up a little in these two years. And she's always cheerful and willing, whatever one asks her to do.

MRS. SOLNESS. Yes, that must be a great advantage——

SOLNESS. It is. Especially when one isn't used to that kind of thing.

MRS. SOLNESS, *gently reproachful.* Halvard, how can you say that?

SOLNESS. Oh, no, no, Aline dear. I apologize.

MRS. SOLNESS. There's no need. Well, Doctor, you'll come back later and take tea with us?

HERDAL. As soon as I've seen that patient, I'll be back.

MRS. SOLNESS. Good.

Goes out through door, right.

SOLNESS. Are you in a hurry, Doctor?

HERDAL. No, not at all.

SOLNESS. May I have a word with you?

HERDAL. By all means.

SOLNESS. Let us sit down, then.

He indicates the rocking chair to the doctor, and seats himself in the armchair.

SOLNESS *looks searchingly at him.* Tell me—did you notice anything about Aline?

HERDAL. Just now, you mean?

SOLNESS. Yes. In her attitude towards me. Did you notice anything?

HERDAL *smiles.* Yes, well, damn it—one couldn't very well help noticing that your wife—er——

SOLNESS. Yes?

HERDAL. That your wife doesn't altogether approve of this Miss Fosli.

SOLNESS. Oh, that? I'd noticed that myself.

HERDAL. Well, it's not really surprising, is it?

SOLNESS. What isn't?

HERDAL. That she doesn't exactly like your having another woman with you in the house every day.

SOLNESS. No, no, you may be right. But there's nothing to be done about that.

HERDAL. Couldn't you get yourself a male clerk?

SOLNESS. The first man jack who put his head through the door? No, thank you, that's not the way I work.

HERDAL. But if your wife——? She's very frail, you know. If she can't stand this arrangement——

SOLNESS. Well, she'll have to put up with it. I don't mean it like that, but I have to keep Kaja Fosli. She's the only one who'll do.

HERDAL. The only one?

SOLNESS, *curtly.* Yes, the only one.

HERDAL *pushes his chair closer.* Listen, Mr. Solness. May I ask you a question—in strict confidence?

SOLNESS. By all means.

HERDAL. Women, you know—they've a damnably sharp nose for some things——

SOLNESS. They have. That's quite true. But——

HERDAL. Well, now, listen a moment. If your wife can't stand the sight of this Kaja Fosli——

SOLNESS. Yes, what then?

HERDAL. Isn't it possible that she may have some—some grounds for this instinctive dislike?

SOLNESS *looks at him, and gets up.* Oh-ho!

HERDAL. Please don't take this amiss. But am I right?

SOLNESS, *curtly, firmly.* No.

HERDAL. No grounds whatever?

SOLNESS. None other than her own suspiciousness.

HERDAL. You've—known a few women in your time.

SOLNESS. I have.

HERDAL. And been fairly fond of one or two of them?

SOLNESS. Oh, yes, that too.

HERDAL. But this Miss Fosli—there's nothing like that between you?

SOLNESS. Nothing whatever. As far as I'm concerned.

HERDAL. And what about her?

SOLNESS. I don't think you have a right to ask that, Doctor.

HERDAL. We were talking about your wife's instinct, remember.

SOLNESS. So we were. Well, as a matter of fact—

Lowers his voice.

—that sharp nose of Aline's that you were talking about hasn't altogether misled her.

HERDAL. Well—there we are!

SOLNESS *sits.* Dr. Herdal—I'm going to tell you a strange story. If you care to listen to it.

HERDAL. I like listening to strange stories.

SOLNESS. Good. Well, you remember, I dare say, some time ago I took Knut Brovik and his son into my employ—when things were going badly for the old man.

HERDAL. Yes, I know something about that.

SOLNESS. They're clever fellows, you know, those two. They've both got ability, in different ways. But then the son went and got himself engaged; and then, of course, he wanted to marry the girl, and start out on his own. That's what they all want nowadays, these young people.

HERDAL *laughs.* Yes, they've all got this bad habit of wanting to get married.

SOLNESS. Mm. Well, I didn't like it. I needed Ragnar. And the old man, too. He's so damned clever at working out stresses and cubic content and all that bloody nonsense, you know.

HERDAL. Ah, well, that's part of the job, I suppose.

SOLNESS. So it is. But Ragnar—he wanted to go off and start on his own. He wouldn't listen to me.

HERDAL. But he has stayed with you.

SOLNESS. Well, that's just it. One day this girl, Kaja Fosli, came to see them on some errand or other. She'd never been here before. Well, when I saw how infatuated they were with each other, the idea struck me that if I could get her to come and work here in the office, Ragnar might stay too.

HERDAL. A reasonable supposition.

SOLNESS. Yes, but I didn't mention a word of all this. I just stood and looked at her—and kept wishing from the bottom of my heart that I had her here. Well, I chatted to her in a friendly way about one thing and another. And then she went.

HERDAL. Well?

SOLNESS. But then next day, in the evening, after old Brovik and Ragnar had gone home, she came back and acted just as though we'd come to some kind of an agreement.

HERDAL. What kind of agreement?

SOLNESS. The very one I'd been wanting to suggest. But which I hadn't mentioned a word about.

HERDAL. That was very strange.

SOLNESS. Yes. And now she wanted to know what kind of work she'd be doing. Whether she could begin at once the next morning. And so on.

HERDAL. Don't you think she did this to be near her young man?

SOLNESS. That was what I thought at first. But no, that wasn't it. She seemed to drift away from him—once she was here with me.

HERDAL. Drifted—over to you?

SOLNESS. Yes, completely. I've noticed that she knows I'm looking at her, even when her back's turned. She trembles and shivers if I even go near her. What do you make of that?

HERDAL. I suppose that could be explained.

SOLNESS. But what about this other business—that she thought I'd told her what I'd only wished for? Silently; inwardly, secretly. What do you make of that? Can you explain such a thing to me, Dr. Herdal?

HERDAL. No, that's outside my field.

SOLNESS. That's what I thought; and that's why I haven't wanted to talk to you about it before. But in the long run, it's been a confounded nuisance to me, you know. I have to walk round here day after day pretending I—— And it's not fair to her, poor girl.

Violently.

But what else can I do? If she leaves me, Ragnar will go too.

HERDAL. And you haven't told your wife all this?

SOLNESS. No.

HERDAL. Why on earth don't you, then?

SOLNESS. Because somehow I feel it does me good to suffer Aline to do me an injustice.

HERDAL *shakes his head*. I'm damned if I understand a word of that.

SOLNESS. Oh, yes—you see it's like paying a minute instalment on a great debt—a debt so vast it can never be settled.

HERDAL. A debt to your wife?

SOLNESS. Yes. And that—eases my mind a little. I can breathe more freely—for a while, you understand.

HERDAL. No, I'm damned if I understand a word——

SOLNESS *breaks off and gets up again*. No, no—well, we won't talk about it any more.

Wanders across the room, comes back and stops beside the table. He looks at the doctor with a quiet smile.

I suppose you think you're drawing me out pretty successfully, eh, Doctor?

HERDAL, *somewhat vexed*. Drawing you out? I really don't know what you mean, Mr. Solness.

SOLNESS. Oh, stop pretending. I've noticed it clearly enough.

HERDAL. Noticed what?

SOLNESS. That you come here to keep an eye on me.

HERDAL. I? Why on earth should I do that?

SOLNESS. Because you think I'm——

Flares up.

Damn it—you think the same about me as Aline does!

HERDAL. And what does she think about you?

SOLNESS, *in control of himself again*. She's begun to think I'm —well—you know—ill.

HERDAL. Ill? You? She's never mentioned a word about this to me. What could be the matter with you, my dear fellow?

SOLNESS *leans over the back of the chair, and whispers*. Aline thinks I'm mad. Oh, yes, she does.

HERDAL *gets up.* But, my dear Mr. Solness——

SOLNESS. Yes, by God, she does! That's what she thinks; and she's got you to believe it too! Oh, I know it, Doctor, I can see it in your behaviour. I'm not that easily deceived, I promise you.

HERDAL *stares, amazed.* Never, Mr. Solness—never has such a thought entered my head.

SOLNESS, *with a distrustful smile.* Indeed? Hasn't it really?

HERDAL. Never. Nor your wife's either—I think I could swear to that.

SOLNESS. Well, I wouldn't if I were you. In a way, you see, she might not be altogether wrong.

HERDAL. No, really, this is going too far!

SOLNESS. Well, well, my dear doctor—let's not pursue the matter. It's better left as it is.

Quietly gleeful.

But now, listen, Doctor—hm——

HERDAL. Yes?

SOLNESS. As you don't think I'm—hm—ill—deranged—mad—or anything like that——

HERDAL. Well? What do you mean?

SOLNESS. Then you must be labouring under the illusion that I am an exceedingly lucky man.

HERDAL. Would that be an illusion?

SOLNESS *laughs.* No, no—of course not! God forbid! Just think of it—to be a master builder, *the* master builder, Halvard Solness! Oh, yes, that's not to be sniffed at.

HERDAL. Yes, I really must say you seem to have been unbelievably lucky all your life.

SOLNESS *represses an ironic smile.* That's right. I can't complain.

HERDAL. First of all that crazy old castle of yours burned down. And you'll admit that was a great stroke of luck.

SOLNESS. It was Aline's ancestral home. Remember that.

HERDAL. Yes, it must have been a terrible blow to her.

SOLNESS. She has never got over it, to this day. Not in all these twelve—thirteen—years.

HERDAL. What followed must have been the heaviest blow for her.

SOLNESS. The one with the other.

HERDAL. But it was that that gave you your start. You began as a poor country lad, and here you are, the top man in your profession. Oh, yes, Mr. Solness, you've had the luck on your side all right.

SOLNESS *glances nervously at him.* I know. That's what makes me so afraid.

HERDAL. Afraid? Because you've been lucky?

SOLNESS. Day and night—I'm afraid. Because some time my luck must change.

HERDAL. Nonsense. What should make it change?

SOLNESS, *swiftly, with conviction.* Youth.

HERDAL. Rubbish! Youth? You're not past it yet. Oh, no—your position's stronger now than it's ever been.

SOLNESS. My luck will change. I know it. And I feel it will happen soon. Someone will stand up and demand: "Make way for me!" And then all the others will storm after him shaking their fists and shouting: "Make way! Make way!" Just you wait, Doctor. One fine day, youth will come and bang on that door——

HERDAL *laughs.* Well, for heaven's sake, what of it?

SOLNESS. What of it? Why, that will be the end for master builder Solness.

There is a banging on the door to the left.

SOLNESS *starts.* What was that? Did you hear something?

HERDAL. It's someone banging on the door.

SOLNESS, *loudly.* Come in!

HILDE WANGEL *comes in through the hall door. She is of medium height, and slender and supple build. A little sun-tanned. She is wearing walking clothes, with a caught-up skirt, a sailor collar, and a small sailor hat on her head. She has a rucksack on her back, a plaid in a strap, and a long alpenstock.*

HILDE *goes over to* SOLNESS, *her eyes alight and happy.* Good evening!

SOLNESS *looks at her uncertainly.* Good evening.

HILDE *laughs.* I believe you don't recognize me.

SOLNESS. No—to be honest, just for the moment I——

HERDAL *goes closer to her.* But I recognize you, Miss——

HILDE, *delighted.* Oh, no! Is it you——?

HERDAL. Indeed it's me.

To SOLNESS.

We met up in one of the mountain huts this summer.

To HILDE.

What happened to the other ladies?

HILDE. Oh, they went on to the west coast.

HERDAL. They didn't like all that noise in the evenings.

HILDE. No, they didn't.

HERDAL *wags his finger.* And you must confess you flirted a little with us!

HILDE. Well, it was more fun than knitting socks with all those old ladies.

HERDAL *laughs.* I couldn't agree with you more.

SOLNESS. Did you come to town this evening?

HILDE. Yes, I've just arrived.

HERDAL. All alone, Miss Wangel?

HILDE. Why, yes!

SOLNESS. Wangel? Is your name Wangel?

HILDE *looks at him in merry surprise.* Yes, of course.

SOLNESS. Then—could it be that you are the daughter of the district physician up at Lysanger?

HILDE, *in the same tone as before.* Yes, who else would I be the daughter of?

SOLNESS. Ah, then we must have met up there. That summer when I went up to build the tower on the old church.

HILDE, *more earnestly.* Yes, that was it.

SOLNESS. Well, that's a long time ago.

HILDE *gazes hard at him.* It was exactly ten years ago.

SOLNESS. You can only have been a child at the time.

HILDE, *carelessly.* I was nearly thirteen.

HERDAL. Is this the first time you've visited this town, Miss Wangel?

HILDE. Yes.

SOLNESS. So you—don't know anyone here, I suppose?

HILDE. No-one except you. Oh, and your wife.

SOLNESS. Really? You know her too?

HILDE. Only slightly. We stayed at the same place up in the mountains. For a few days.

SOLNESS. Oh, up there.

HILDE. She said I might visit her if I ever came this way. *Smiles.*

Not that there was any need.

SOLNESS. I wonder why she didn't mention it to me——

HILDE puts down her alpenstock by the stove, takes off her rucksack, and puts it and her plaid on the sofa. DR. HERDAL *tries to help her;* SOLNESS *stands looking at her.*

HILDE *goes towards him.* Can I stay the night here?

SOLNESS. I think that could be arranged.

HILDE. I haven't any clothes apart from what I'm wearing, you see. Oh, and a set of underclothes in my rucksack. I'll have to get them washed, though. They're filthy.

SOLNESS. Oh, well that can be taken care of. I'd better tell my wife——

HERDAL. And I'll go and see my patient.

SOLNESS. Yes, do. And come back when you've finished.

HERDAL, *merrily, with a glance at* HILDE. Yes, you can be damn sure I will!

Laughs.

Well, you are a true prophet after all, Mr. Solness.

SOLNESS. How do you mean?

HERDAL. Why, youth *has* come and banged upon your door.

SOLNESS, *cheerfully.* Yes, but not quite the way I meant!

HERDAL. I should say not.

He goes out through the hall door. SOLNESS *opens the door to the right and speaks into the side room.*

SOLNESS. Aline! Will you come in here, please? There's a Miss Wangel here, whom you know.

MRS. SOLNESS *appears in the doorway.* Who is it, do you say?

Sees HILDE.

Oh, is it you, my dear?

Goes over to her and holds out her hand.

So you came this way after all?

SOLNESS. Miss Wangel has just arrived. She asks if she may stay the night.

MRS. SOLNESS. With us? Yes, with pleasure.

SOLNESS. You know, to get her clothes in order.

MRS. SOLNESS. I'll look after you as well as I can. It's my simple duty. Your luggage will be coming on later, of course?

HILDE. I haven't any.

MRS. SOLNESS. Oh; well, I'm sure you'll manage. Just make yourself at home with my husband while I get a room ready for you.

SOLNESS. Can't we use one of the nurseries? They're all ready.

MRS. SOLNESS. Oh, yes. We've plenty of room *there.*

To HILDE.

Sit down, now, and rest a little.

She goes out to the right. HILDE *wanders round the room with her hands behind her back, looking at this and that.* SOLNESS *stands by the table downstage, also with his hands behind his back, watching her.*

HILDE *stops and looks at him.* Have you got more than one nursery, then?

SOLNESS. There are three nurseries in this house.

HILDE. That's a lot. You must have heaps of children.

SOLNESS. No. We have no children. But now you can be the child here for a while.

HILDE. For tonight, yes. I won't cry. I intend to sleep like a log.

SOLNESS. Yes, I suppose you must be very tired.

HILDE. Not me! I'll sleep all right, though. I think it's absolutely marvellous to lie in bed and dream.

SOLNESS. Do you often dream at night?

HILDE. Gosh, yes. Nearly every night.

SOLNESS. What do you mostly dream about?

HILDE. I shan't tell you this tonight. Some other time—perhaps.
She wanders across the room again, stops by the desk, and fingers among the books and papers.

SOLNESS *goes over to her.* Are you looking for something?

HILDE. No, I'm just looking around.
Turns.
Perhaps I mustn't?

SOLNESS. No, please do.

HILDE. Do you write in this big ledger?

SOLNESS. No, my bookkeeper does. I leave that to her.

HILDE. A woman?

SOLNESS *smiles.* Yes.

HILDE. And she works here with you?

SOLNESS. Yes.

HILDE. Is it a married woman?

SOLNESS. No, it isn't.

HILDE. I see.

SOLNESS. But she's going to get married soon.

HILDE. How very nice for her.

SOLNESS. But not so nice for me. Because then I'll have no-one to help me.

HILDE. Can't you find another one who'd do as well?

SOLNESS. Perhaps you'd like to stay here and—and write in the ledger?

HILDE *looks at him scornfully.* What an idea! No, thank you. None of that.
She wanders across the room again and sits in the rocking chair. SOLNESS *comes to the table beside her.*

HILDE, *as though continuing.* There are better things here for me to do than that.

Looks at him with a smile.

Don't you think so?

SOLNESS. I understand. You want to go shopping and get something smart to wear.

HILDE, *gaily.* No, I think I'll give that a miss.

SOLNESS. Oh?

HILDE. I've spent all my money, you see.

SOLNESS *laughs.* No luggage, and no money!

HILDE. No. Oh, hell, what do I care?

SOLNESS. You know, I like you for that!

HILDE. Just for that?

SOLNESS. Among other things.

Sits in the armchair.

Is your father still alive?

HILDE. Yes, he's alive.

SOLNESS. And now you're thinking of studying here, perhaps?

HILDE. No, I hadn't thought of that.

SOLNESS. But you'll be staying for some time?

HILDE. That depends.

She sits for a few moments, rocking herself and looking at him with a half smile. Then she takes off her hat and puts it on the table in front of her.

Mr. Solness?

SOLNESS. Yes?

HILDE. Have you a bad memory?

SOLNESS. A bad memory? No, not that I'm aware of.

HILDE. Don't you want to talk to me about what happened up there?

SOLNESS *starts momentarily.* Up at Lysanger?

Casually.

Well, there isn't much to talk about, is there?

HILDE *looks at him reproachfully.* How can you say such a thing?

SOLNESS. All right, you talk to me about it, then.

HILDE. The day the tower was ready was a great day for our little town.

SOLNESS. Yes, I shan't forget that day in a hurry.

HILDE *smiles*. Won't you? That's nice of you.

SOLNESS. Nice——?

HILDE. There was music in the churchyard. And hundreds and hundreds of people. We schoolgirls were dressed in white. And we all had flags.

SOLNESS. Ah, yes. Those flags! I remember them.

HILDE. Then you climbed up the scaffolding. Up to the very top. You carried a big wreath with you. And you hung that wreath right up on the weathercock.

SOLNESS, *curtly, interrupts her*. I used to do that in those days. It's an old custom.

HILDE. It was so marvellously exciting to stand down there and stare up at you. Think—if he should fall now! The great master builder himself!

SOLNESS, *as though trying to deflect her*. Yes, yes, yes, and it could very easily have happened. One of those little white devils suddenly waved and shouted up at me——

HILDE, *glowing and excited*. "Hurrah for Solness! Hurrah for the master builder!" Yes!

SOLNESS. And waved her flag and swung it about so that I— I almost turned giddy watching it.

HILDE, *quiet, serious*. That little devil was me.

SOLNESS *stares hard at her*. Of course. It must have been you.

HILDE, *full of life again*. It was so frightfully exciting and marvellous! I'd never imagined there could be a master builder anywhere in the world who could build such an enormously high tower! And then to see you standing there yourself, right up at the top! And you weren't at all giddy! That was the thing that—that made me feel giddy!

SOLNESS. What made you so sure I wasn't——?

HILDE. Don't be silly! I knew it—in here. Otherwise, how could you have stood up there singing?

SOLNESS *stares at her, amazed*. Singing? Did I sing?

HILDE. You certainly did.

SOLNESS *shakes his head.* I've never sung a note in my life.

HILDE. Well, you sang then. It sounded like harps in the air.

SOLNESS, *thoughtfully.* This is most extraordinary.

HILDE *looks at him silently for a moment, then says softly.* But it was afterwards—that the real thing happened.

SOLNESS. The real thing?

HILDE. Yes. I don't have to remind you about that?

SOLNESS. Yes, remind me a little about that, too.

HILDE. Don't you remember they gave a great banquet for you at the Club?

SOLNESS. Oh, yes. That must have been the same evening. I left next morning.

HILDE. When it ended we invited you home for supper.

SOLNESS. You're quite right, Miss Wangel. It's remarkable how clearly you remember all these little details.

HILDE. Little details! You're a fine one! Was it just a little detail that I happened to be alone in the room when you came in?

SOLNESS. Were you?

HILDE. You didn't call me a little devil then.

SOLNESS. No, I don't suppose I did.

HILDE. You said I looked beautiful in my white dress. Like a little princess.

SOLNESS. So you did, Miss Wangel. And besides—I felt so happy and free that evening——

HILDE. And then you said that when I grew up, I would be *your* princess.

SOLNESS, *with a short laugh.* Well, well! Did I say that, too?

HILDE. Yes, you did. And then, when I asked how long I should have to wait, you said you'd come back in ten years —like a troll—and carry me off. To Spain or somewhere like that. And you promised that when we got there, you'd buy me a kingdom.

SOLNESS, *in the same tone as before.* Yes, after a good dinner one doesn't count the shillings. But did I really say all this?

HILDE *laughs quietly.* Yes. And you told me what this kingdom was to be called, too.

SOLNESS. Oh, what?

HILDE. You said it was to be called Orangia.

SOLNESS. Well, that's a nice appetizing name.

HILDE. I didn't like it. It sounded as though you were making fun of me.

SOLNESS. I'm sure I didn't mean that.

HILDE. I can well believe you didn't. Considering what you did next——

SOLNESS. And what on earth did I do next?

HILDE. No, that's the last straw! Have you forgotten that, too? I really think you might have remembered that!

SOLNESS. Well, give me a hint, and perhaps—— Well?

HILDE. You took me in your arms and kissed me, Mr. Solness.

SOLNESS *gets up from his chair, his mouth open.* I did?

HILDE. Yes, you did. You took me in both your arms and bent me backwards and kissed me. Many, many times.

SOLNESS. Oh, but my dear, good Miss Wangel——

HILDE *gets up.* You're not going to deny it?

SOLNESS. I certainly am!

HILDE *looks at him scornfully.* Oh. I see.

She turns and walks slowly across to near the stove, where she stands motionless with her back towards him and her hands behind her. Short pause.

SOLNESS *goes diffidently up behind her.* Miss Wangel——!

She remains silent and motionless.

Don't stand there like a statue. All this that you've just told me must have been something you've dreamed.

He touches her arm.

Now, listen——

She makes an impatient gesture with her arm. Then, as a thought strikes him.

Or—wait a moment! No, there's more to it than that.

She does not move. He speaks softly, but with emphasis.

I must have thought all this. I must have wanted it—wished it—desired it. So that—— Couldn't that be an explanation? *She remains silent. He bursts out impatiently.*

Oh, damn it! Have it your own way—say I *did* it!

HILDE *turns her head slightly, but does not look at him.* You confess?

SOLNESS. Yes. Anything you say.

HILDE. That you put your arms round me?

SOLNESS. Yes, yes.

HILDE. And bent me over backwards?

SOLNESS. Yes, right back.

HILDE. And kissed me?

SOLNESS. Yes, I kissed you.

HILDE. Many times?

SOLNESS. As many as you like.

HILDE *turns quickly towards him, her eyes again glowing and excited.* You see! I wormed it out of you in the end!

SOLNESS *smiles wryly.* Yes, just fancy—that I could forget a thing like that!

HILDE *walks away from him, a little sulky again.* Oh, you've kissed so many women in your time, I suppose.

SOLNESS. No, you mustn't think I'm that sort.

HILDE *sits in the armchair.* SOLNESS *stands, leaning against the rocking chair.*

SOLNESS *looks searchingly at her.* Miss Wangel?

HILDE. Yes?

SOLNESS. What happened? What more happened between you and me?

HILDE. Nothing more happened. You know that. The other guests arrived, and then—well——

SOLNESS. Yes, of course! The others arrived, and—fancy my forgetting that too!

HILDE. Oh, you haven't forgotten anything. You're just a bit ashamed. One doesn't forget things like that. I know.

SOLNESS. No, one would think not.

HILDE, *alive again, looks at him.* Perhaps you've also forgotten what day it was?

SOLNESS. What day?

HILDE. Yes, what day was it when you hung the wreath on the tower? Well? Tell me at once!

SOLNESS. Hm—I've forgotten the actual day, I must confess. I know it was ten years ago. Some time in the autumn.

HILDE *nods slowly several times.* It was ten years ago. The nineteenth of September.

SOLNESS. Yes, about then, I suppose. So you remember that, too!

Pauses.

But wait a moment! Today is the nineteenth of September!

HILDE. Exactly. And the ten years are up. And you didn't come—as you'd promised you would.

SOLNESS. Promised? I only said it to frighten you.

HILDE. I didn't find it frightening.

SOLNESS. Well, to tease you.

HILDE. Was that all you wanted to do? Tease me?

SOLNESS. Oh, I don't remember—for fun, if you like. It can't have been anything else, you were only a child at the time.

HILDE. Oh, maybe I wasn't such a child. Not such a little innocent as you think.

SOLNESS *looks searchingly at her.* Did you really and seriously think I'd come back?

HILDE, *suppressing a half-teasing smile.* Oh, yes! I'd expected no less of you!

SOLNESS. That I'd come to your home and take you away with me?

HILDE. Yes, like a troll.

SOLNESS. And make you a princess?

HILDE. That's what you promised.

SOLNESS. And give you a kingdom, too?

HILDE *looks up at the ceiling.* Why not? It didn't have to be an ordinary kingdom.

SOLNESS. But—something else, just as good?

HILDE. Yes, at least as good.

Looks at him for a moment.

If you could build the highest church tower in the world, I thought you would be able to find your way to a kingdom too. Of some kind.

SOLNESS *shakes his head.* I can't quite make you out, Miss Wangel.

HILDE. You can't? To me it's all so simple.

SOLNESS. No, I can't make out whether you mean what you say. Or whether you're simply having me on—

HILDE *smiles.* Making fun of you?

SOLNESS. Yes, exactly. Making fun of me. Of us both.

Looks at her.

Have you known for long that I'm married?

HILDE. I've known all along. Why do you ask that?

SOLNESS, *casually.* No, no, I just wondered.

Looks earnestly at her and says quietly.

Why have you come?

HILDE. Because I want my kingdom. The time's up now.

SOLNESS *laughs involuntarily.* That's a good one!

HILDE, *merrily.* Stump up my kingdom, master builder!

Taps with her finger.

On the table!

SOLNESS *pushes the rocking chair closer and sits down.* Seriously, why have you come? What do you want here?

HILDE. Well, to begin with, I want to go round and look at everything you've built.

SOLNESS. Then you'll have a lot of walking to do.

HILDE. Yes, you've built such a frightful lot.

SOLNESS. I have. Especially these last years.

HILDE. Lots of church spires, too? As high as the sky?

SOLNESS. No. I don't build church spires any more. Nor churches, neither.

HILDE. What do you build now, then?

SOLNESS. Homes for people to live in.

HILDE, *thoughtfully.* Couldn't you put little spires on them, too?

SOLNESS *starts.* What do you mean?

HILDE. I mean—something that points—straight up in the air. With a weathercock high up at the top—so high it makes you giddy!

SOLNESS, *musingly.* It's strange you should say that. That's just what I'd like to do—most of all.

HILDE, *impatiently.* Why don't you, then?

SOLNESS *shakes his head.* No, people don't want that.

HILDE. Really? They don't want that?

SOLNESS, *more lightly.* But now I'm building a new home for myself. Here, just opposite.

HILDE. For yourself?

SOLNESS. Yes. It's almost ready. And on that there's a spire.

HILDE. A high spire?

SOLNESS. Yes.

HILDE. Very high?

SOLNESS. People are sure to say it's too high. For a home.

HILDE. I'm going out to see that spire first thing tomorrow morning.

SOLNESS *sits leaning his cheek on his hand, staring at her.* Tell me, Miss Wangel, what's your name? Your first name, I mean?

HILDE. Hilde, of course.

SOLNESS, *as before.* Hilde? Really?

HILDE. Don't you remember? You called me Hilde. The day you misbehaved.

SOLNESS. I called you Hilde?

HILDE. Yes, but then you said "little Hilde." And I didn't like that.

SOLNESS. So you didn't like that, Miss Hilde?

HILDE. No. Not just then. But—Princess Hilde—that'll sound quite nice, I think.

SOLNESS. Yes, indeed. Princess Hilde of—what was our kingdom to be called?

HILDE. Ugh! I don't want any of that stupid kingdom. I want quite a different kind of kingdom.

SOLNESS *has leaned back in his chair, still staring at her.* Isn't it strange——? The more I think about it now—the more it seems to me as though for years I've been torturing myself —hm——

HILDE. Go on.

SOLNESS. Trying to remember something—something that had happened to me and that I must have forgotten. But I could never discover what it was.

HILDE. You ought to have tied a knot in your handkerchief, master builder.

SOLNESS. Then I'd only have gone round wondering what the knot stood for.

HILDE. Oh, well, I suppose it takes trolls like you to make a world.

SOLNESS *gets up slowly.* I'm glad you've come to me just at this time.

HILDE *looks into his eyes.* Are you glad?

SOLNESS. I've been so alone. Staring at it all. So helpless.

Lowers his voice.

You see—I've begun to be so afraid—so terribly afraid—of youth.

HILDE, *scornfully.* Youth? Is youth something to be afraid of?

SOLNESS. Yes, it is. That's why I've shut myself up here.

Secretively.

Some day, youth will come here and thunder on my door, and force its way in to me!

HILDE. Then I think you ought to go out and open the door.

SOLNESS. Open the door?

HILDE. Yes. And let youth in. As a friend.

SOLNESS. No, no! Youth means retribution. It marches at the head of a rebel army. Under a new banner.

HILDE *gets up, looks at him, and says with a tremble round her mouth.* Can you use me, master builder?

SOLNESS. Yes! Yes, now I can use you! For you, too, march under a new banner. Youth against youth——

DR. HERDAL *comes in through the hall door.*

HERDAL. Hullo—are you and our young friend still here?

SOLNESS. Yes. We two have found many things to talk about.

HILDE. Both old and new.

HERDAL. Oh, have you, indeed?

HILDE. It's been great fun. The master builder has a quite in-credible memory. Every little detail—just like that!

MRS. SOLNESS *enters through the door on the right.*

MRS. SOLNESS. Well, Miss Wangel, your room's ready now.

HILDE. Oh, how kind you are!

SOLNESS, *to* MRS. SOLNESS. The nursery?

MRS. SOLNESS. Yes. The middle one. But let's have supper first.

SOLNESS *nods to* HILDE. Hilde shall sleep in the nursery to-night.

MRS. SOLNESS *looks at him.* Hilde?

SOLNESS. Yes, Miss Wangel's name is Hilde. I used to know her when she was a child.

MRS. SOLNESS. No, did you really, Halvard? Well, please come in. Supper's on the table.

She takes DR. HERDAL's *arm and goes out with him to the right. Meanwhile,* HILDE *has gathered her things together.*

HILDE, *swiftly, quietly, to* SOLNESS. Was it true, what you said? Can you find some use for me?

SOLNESS *takes her things from her.* You are the one I've been wanting.

HILDE *looks at him in joyful amazement and clasps her hands.* Oh, master builder——!

SOLNESS, *tensely.* Yes——?

HILDE. Then I have my kingdom!

SOLNESS, *involuntarily.* Hilde!

HILDE, *the tremble round her mouth again. Almost*—I was go-ing to say.

She goes out to the right. SOLNESS *follows her.*

ACT TWO

A pleasantly furnished little sitting room in SOLNESS's *house. In the rear wall is a glass door leading to the verandah and garden. The right-hand corner is broken by a bay, containing stands for plants and a large window. A similar bay in the left-hand corner contains a small door covered with wallpaper. In each of the side walls is an ordinary door. Downstage right, a console table with a large mirror.*

A rich profusion of flowers and plants. Downstage left, a sofa, with a table and chairs. Further back, a bookcase. In the middle of the room, in front of the bay, a small table and one or two chairs. It is early morning.

SOLNESS *is seated at the small table, with* RAGNAR BROVIK's *portfolio open in front of him. He leafs through the drawings, examining some of them closely.* MRS. SOLNESS *is going round silently with a small can, watering the flowers. She is dressed in black, as before. Her hat, overcoat, and parasol lie on a chair by the mirror.* SOLNESS *looks at her once or twice, without her noticing. Neither of them speaks.* KAJA FOSLI *comes quietly in through the door on the left.*

SOLNESS *turns his head and says casually.* Oh, it's you?

KAJA. I just wanted to tell you I'm here.

SOLNESS. Yes, good. Is Ragnar there, too?

KAJA. No, not yet. He had to stay behind to wait for the

doctor. He won't be long, he wants to come and ask you how you feel about the——

SOLNESS. How's the old man feeling today?

KAJA. Bad. He says will you please excuse him, but he'll have to stay in bed today.

SOLNESS. By all means let him. You go along and start work, though.

KAJA. Yes.

Stops at the door.

Perhaps you'd like to speak to Ragnar when he comes?

SOLNESS. No, not particularly.

KAJA *goes out again to the left.* SOLNESS *continues to look through the drawings.*

MRS. SOLNESS, *over by the plants.* It wouldn't surprise me if he died too.

SOLNESS *looks at her.* Too? Who else?

MRS. SOLNESS, *not replying.* Yes, yes; old Brovik—he'll die too now, Halvard. You'll see.

SOLNESS. Aline dear, don't you think you should go out and get a little fresh air?

MRS. SOLNESS. Yes, I should, shouldn't I?

Continues attending to the flowers.

SOLNESS, *bent over the drawings.* Is she still asleep?

MRS. SOLNESS *looks at him.* Is it Miss Wangel you're sitting there thinking about?

SOLNESS, *indifferently.* Just happened to think of her.

MRS. SOLNESS. Miss Wangel's been up a long time.

SOLNESS. Oh, has she?

MRS. SOLNESS. When I looked in she was seeing to her clothes. *She goes to the mirror and begins slowly to put on her hat.*

SOLNESS, *after a short pause.* Well, we've found a use for one of the nurseries after all, haven't we, Aline?

MRS. SOLNESS. Yes, we have.

SOLNESS. I think that's better than that they should all stand empty.

MRS. SOLNESS. Yes, that emptiness is horrible. You're right there.

SOLNESS *closes the portfolio, gets up, and goes over to her.* From now on things will be better, Aline. You'll see. Much more satisfactory. Life will be easier to bear. Especially for you.

MRS. SOLNESS *looks at him.* From now on?

SOLNESS. Yes, Aline, believe me——

MRS. SOLNESS. You mean—because she's come?

SOLNESS *controls himself.* I mean, of course, once we've moved into the new house.

MRS. SOLNESS *takes her overcoat.* Do you really think so, Halvard? Things will be better?

SOLNESS. I'm sure they will. You believe that too, don't you?

MRS. SOLNESS. I don't believe anything where that new house is concerned.

SOLNESS, *vexed.* I'm sorry to hear that, my dear. It was mainly for your sake I built it.

Tries to help her on with her coat.

MRS. SOLNESS *moves away.* You do much too much for me.

SOLNESS, *almost violently.* No, no, you mustn't talk like that, Aline. I can't bear to hear you say such things.

MRS. SOLNESS. Very well, Halvard, I won't say them.

SOLNESS. I'm right, though. You'll be happy in that new house —you'll see.

MRS. SOLNESS. God! *I*—happy——?

SOLNESS. Yes! Yes! I promise you! Don't you see, there'll be so much there that'll remind you of your own home——

MRS. SOLNESS. Father's and Mother's home. And it was burnt. All burnt.

SOLNESS, *subdued.* Yes, my poor Aline. That was a horrible blow for you.

MRS. SOLNESS. You can build as much as you like, Halvard— you'll never be able to build a real home for me again.

SOLNESS *turns and walks away across the room.* Well, in that case, for God's sake let's not talk about it any more.

MRS. SOLNESS. Well, we don't usually talk about it, anyway. You always avoid the subject——

SOLNESS *stops abruptly and looks at her.* I do? And why should I avoid the subject?

MRS. SOLNESS. Oh, I understand you so well, Halvard. You want to spare me. And stop me feeling guilty. As far as you can.

SOLNESS *stares amazed.* Stop *you* feeling guilty? Are you—are you talking about yourself, Aline?

MRS. SOLNESS. Yes, who else would I be talking about?

SOLNESS, *involuntarily, to himself.* That too!

MRS. SOLNESS. It's not so much what happened to the old house. I think I could resign myself to that. After all, that was an accident——

SOLNESS. Yes, you're right. Accidents will happen, and it's no use blaming oneself for them.

MRS. SOLNESS. But the dreadful thing that happened after the fire! That's what I can't forget. I can't, I can't, I can't!

SOLNESS, *violently.* Don't think about it, Aline.

MRS. SOLNESS. I have to think about it. And I must talk about it some time. I don't think I can endure it any longer. And I never can forgive myself——

SOLNESS. Forgive *yourself*——?

MRS. SOLNESS. Yes, because I had a duty to all of you. To you, and the children. I should have hardened myself, I shouldn't have let fear weaken me. Or grief for my burnt home. Oh, if only I'd had the strength, Halvard.

SOLNESS, *quiet, shaken, comes towards her.* Aline, you must promise me you'll never let these thoughts enter your head again. Promise me that, my dear.

MRS. SOLNESS. God—promise, promise! It's easy to promise anything—

SOLNESS *walks across the room.* Oh, this is hopeless, hopeless! Not a ray of light ever enters this home. Not a glimmer.

MRS. SOLNESS. This is no home, Halvard.

SOLNESS. No, you're so right. And, God knows, you may be

right, too, when you say it won't be any better in the new
house.

MRS. SOLNESS. Never. It'll be just as empty and just as desolate
there as it is here.

SOLNESS, *violently.* Why in God's name have we built it, then?
Can you tell me that?

MRS. SOLNESS. No, that you must answer yourself.

SOLNESS *looks at her suspiciously.* What do you mean by that,
Aline?

MRS. SOLNESS. What do I mean?

SOLNESS. Yes, damn it! You said it so strangely. As though
you meant something else.

MRS. SOLNESS. No, I assure you——

SOLNESS *goes closer.* Oh, thank you very much—I know what
I know. I've got eyes and ears, Aline. You can be sure of
that.

MRS. SOLNESS. What do you mean? What do you mean?

SOLNESS *stands in front of her.* You find some cunning, hidden
meaning in every harmless little thing I say, don't you, eh?

MRS. SOLNESS. I, Halvard? Do *I* do that?

SOLNESS *laughs.* Oh, it's very understandable, Aline. When
you've a sick man on your hands, well——

MRS. SOLNESS, *alarmed.* Sick? Are you sick, Halvard?

SOLNESS. An idiot, then! A lunatic! Call me what you like.

MRS. SOLNESS *gropes for the back of the chair and sits down.*
Halvard—for God's sake——

SOLNESS. But you're wrong, both of you. You and your doctor. There's nothing the matter with me.

He walks up and down the room. MRS. SOLNESS *watches
him anxiously. At length he comes over to her.*

SOLNESS, *calmly.* There's nothing the matter with me at all.

MRS. SOLNESS. No, of course not. But—what's worrying you,
then?

SOLNESS. It's this dreadful burden of debt that's crushing me——

MRS. SOLNESS. Debt? But you're not in debt to anyone, Halvard.

SOLNESS, *quietly.* I owe a boundless debt to you. To you, Aline.

MRS. SOLNESS *rises slowly.* What is behind all this?

SOLNESS. There's nothing *behind* it. I've never done you any harm. Not wittingly, anyway. And yet—it feels as though a huge stone of guilt lay on me, weighing me down, crushing me.

MRS. SOLNESS. Guilt? Towards me, you mean?

SOLNESS. Towards you, most of all.

MRS. SOLNESS. Then you really are—sick, Halvard.

SOLNESS. I suppose I must be. Sick—or something.

Glances towards the door on the right, as it is opened.

Ah! Now it grows lighter.

HILDE WANGEL *enters. She has made one or two changes in her dress, and has let down her skirt so that it reaches to her ankles.*

HILDE. Good morning, master builder.

SOLNESS *nods.* Slept well?

HILDE. Marvellously! Just as though I was in a cradle. Oh, I lay there and stretched myself like a—like a princess.

SOLNESS, *with a little smile.* Really comfortable?

HILDE. I should say so!

SOLNESS. And you dreamed too, I suppose?

HILDE. Yes. Ugh—beastly!

SOLNESS. Oh?

HILDE. Yes, I dreamed I'd fallen over a frightfully high, steep cliff. Do you ever have that dream?

SOLNESS. Er—yes—now and then——

HILDE. It's so exciting—as you fall and fall——

SOLNESS. It makes me go cold as ice.

HILDE. Do you hug your knees up under you as you fall?

SOLNESS. Yes, as high as I can.

HILDE. So do I.

MRS. SOLNESS *takes her parasol.* Well, I'd better be going into town now, Halvard.

To HILDE.

I'll see if I can bring back one or two things you might need.

HILDE *tries to embrace her.* Oh, darling, beautiful Mrs. Solness! You're really too sweet! Frightfully sweet——

MRS. SOLNESS, *freeing herself.* Not at all. It's my simple duty. And I'm only too glad to do it.

HILDE *pouts, piqued.* Actually, I think I'm all right to go into town as I am, now that I've made myself smart. Or perhaps I'm not?

MRS. SOLNESS. To speak frankly, I think one or two people might glance at you.

HILDE. Pooh! Is that all? That'd be rather a lark.

SOLNESS, *concealing his mood.* Yes, but people might think you were mad too, you see.

HILDE. Mad? Are there so many mad people in this town?

SOLNESS *points at his forehead.* Here you see one, anyway.

HILDE. *You*—master builder!

MRS. SOLNESS. Oh, but my dear Halvard, really!

SOLNESS. Haven't you noticed yet?

HILDE. No, I certainly haven't.

Thinks, and gives a little laugh.

Yes, perhaps, in just one little thing, now I think of it.

SOLNESS. You hear that, Aline?

MRS. SOLNESS. In what *thing*, Miss Wangel?

HILDE. No, I'm not telling.

SOLNESS. Yes, tell us.

HILDE. No, thanks—I'm not *that* mad.

MRS. SOLNESS. When you and Miss Wangel are alone, she'll tell you, Halvard.

SOLNESS. Oh, do you think so?

MRS. SOLNESS. Why, yes. You and she have been such good friends; ever since she was a child, you say.

She goes out through the door on the left.

HILDE, *after a moment*. Do you think your wife doesn't like me?

SOLNESS. Why, did you notice anything?

HILDE. Didn't you?

SOLNESS, *avoiding the question*. Aline's become very shy of people these last years.

HILDE. That too?

SOLNESS. But if only you could get to know her properly—she's very good and kind—a really good woman——

HILDE, *impatiently*. If she is, why did she have to talk like that about duty?

SOLNESS. About duty?

HILDE. Yes, she said she'd go out and buy something for me because it was her duty. Oh, I can't stand that nasty, beastly word.

SOLNESS. Why not?

HILDE. It sounds so cold and sharp, like a knife. Duty, duty, duty! Don't you feel that, too? That it—somehow—pierces you?

SOLNESS. Hm—I haven't given it much thought.

HILDE. Oh, yes! And if she's as good and kind as you pretend, why should she say a thing like that?

SOLNESS. Well, good Lord, what should she have said?

HILDE. She could have said she wanted to do it because she liked me so much. Or something like that, she could have said. Something really warm and kind, don't you think?

SOLNESS *looks at her*. So that's what you want?

HILDE. Yes.

Walks round the room, stops in front of the bookcase, and looks at the books.

You've an awful lot of books.

SOLNESS. Oh, I've collected a few.

HILDE. Do you read them all?

SOLNESS. I used to try. Do you read?

HILDE. No! Not any more. It all seems so meaningless.

SOLNESS. That's exactly how I feel.

HILDE wanders round for a few moments, stops by the small table, opens the portfolio, and glances through it.

HILDE. Have you done all these drawings?

SOLNESS. No, a young man I have here to help me.

HILDE. A pupil of yours?

SOLNESS. Oh, yes, I dare say he's learned something from me, too.

HILDE *sits.* He must be awfully clever, then?

Looks at a drawing for a moment.

Isn't he?

SOLNESS. Oh, not so bad. For my purposes——

HILDE. Oh, *yes.* He must be frightfully clever.

SOLNESS. You can tell that from his drawings, can you?

HILDE. What, this stuff? Oh, no. But if he's been studying with *you*——

SOLNESS. Oh, that? There are plenty of people round here who've studied under me. And nothing's become of them.

HILDE *looks at him and shakes her head.* Upon my soul, I don't understand how you can be so stupid.

SOLNESS. Stupid? Do you think I'm so very stupid, then?

HILDE. Yes, indeed I do. Letting these young men come here and pick your brains——

SOLNESS *starts.* Well? And why not?

HILDE *gets up, half in earnest, half laughing.* Oh, no, master builder, that's no good! No-one but you should be allowed to build. Only you. Do it all yourself. Now you know.

SOLNESS, *unwillingly.* Hilde——

HILDE. Yes?

SOLNESS. What on earth made you say that?

HILDE. Why—*that's* not such a wicked idea, is it?

SOLNESS. No, I didn't mean that. But—I'll tell you something.

HILDE. Well, what?

SOLNESS. I walk up and down in this house—incessantly—in

silence—and loneliness—turning that very idea over in my mind.

HILDE. Yes, well, that's very reasonable.

SOLNESS *glances searchingly at her.* I dare say you've noticed this?

HILDE. No, I haven't *noticed* anything.

SOLNESS. But just now—when you said you thought I was— wrong in the head—on one point of the compass. Did you mean——?

HILDE. Oh, I was thinking of something quite different then.

SOLNESS. What were you thinking of?

HILDE. Never you mind, master builder.

SOLNESS *walks across the room.* As you please.

Stops by the bay.

Come here, and I'll show you something.

HILDE *goes closer.* What is it?

SOLNESS *points.* Just beyond that big stone-pit——

HILDE. That new house?

SOLNESS. The one that's being built, yes. Almost finished now.

HILDE. It's got a very high tower, hasn't it?

SOLNESS. The scaffolding's still round it.

HILDE. Is that your new house?

SOLNESS. Yes.

HILDE. The house you're going to move into soon?

SOLNESS. Yes.

HILDE *looks at him.* Are there nurseries in that house, too?

SOLNESS. Three, the same as here.

HILDE. And no children?

SOLNESS. There won't be any, either.

HILDE, *with a half smile.* Well, wasn't I right?

SOLNESS. What do you mean?

HILDE. You are a little—mad—after all.

SOLNESS. Was *that* what you were thinking?

HILDE. Yes—all those empty nurseries, where I was sleeping.

SOLNESS, *quietly*. We have had children—Aline and I.

HILDE *looks at him tensely*. Have you?

SOLNESS. Two little boys. Both the same age.

HILDE. Twins?

SOLNESS. Yes, twins. It's nearly twelve years ago, now.

HILDE, *gently*. You mean they're both——? You haven't got these twins any longer?

SOLNESS, *quiet, moved*. We only had them three weeks. Hardly that.

Bursts out.

Oh, Hilde, I can't tell you how glad I am that you've come! Now at last I've found someone I can talk to.

HILDE. Can't you talk to—to her, too?

SOLNESS. Not about this. Not the way I want to—and need to. *Sadly.*

Nor about much else, either.

HILDE. Was that all you meant when you said you needed me?

SOLNESS. Must have been—I suppose so. Yesterday, at least. Today I'm no longer so sure.

Breaks off. Takes her by the hand and leads her to the sofa.

There. You can see the garden from there.

She sits on the corner of the sofa. He brings a chair nearer to her.

Would you like to hear about it?

HILDE. Yes, I love sitting and listening to you.

SOLNESS *sits*. Well, I'll tell you all about it.

HILDE. Now I can see you *and* the garden, master builder. Now then, tell me. Come on!

SOLNESS *points through the bay window*. Up there—where you see that new house——

HILDE. Yes?

SOLNESS. That's where Aline and I lived during the first years of our marriage. In those days there used to be an old house up there which had belonged to her mother. She left it to us. And all the grounds with it.

HILDE. Was there a spire on that house, too?

SOLNESS. No, nothing of the kind. To look at from the outside, it was a great, dark, ugly crate. But indoors it was nice and cosy enough.

HILDE. Did you pull the old thing down?

SOLNESS. No. It was burned down.

HILDE. The whole thing?

SOLNESS. Yes.

HILDE. Was that a terrible blow to you?

SOLNESS. It depends which way you look at it. It was that fire that made me a master builder.

HILDE. Oh? But——?

SOLNESS. Our two little boys had just been born——

HILDE. The poor little twins——

SOLNESS. They were so healthy and strong when they were born. And you could see them growing from day to day——

HILDE. Babies grow frightfully quickly the first few days.

SOLNESS. It was the prettiest sight you could wish to see, Aline lying there with the two of them. But then there came the night of the fire——

HILDE. What happened? Tell me! Was anyone burned alive?

SOLNESS. No, not that. Everyone got safely out of the house——

HILDE. Well, then, what——?

SOLNESS. It was a terrible shock for Aline. The alarm, and being rushed out of the house, into the ice-cold night—they had to be carried out, just as they were—she and the little boys.

HILDE. And they couldn't stand the cold?

SOLNESS. Oh, they stood up to that all right. But Aline caught a fever. And it infected her milk. She had to feed them herself. It was her duty, she said. And both our little boys—both of them——

HILDE. They didn't get over *that?*

SOLNESS. No, they didn't get over that. It—took them from us.

HILDE. That must have been a great loss for you.

SOLNESS. It was great enough for me. But ten times greater for her.

Clenches his hands in quiet fury.

How can such a thing be allowed to happen in this world?
Curtly.

From that day on, I lost interest in building churches.

HILDE. Then you didn't enjoy building the steeple on our church?

SOLNESS. I didn't. How relieved and glad I was when it was finished.

HILDE. I know that.

SOLNESS. And now I shall never build anything like that again. Neither churches, nor steeples.

HILDE *nods slowly.* Just houses, for people to live in.

SOLNESS. Homes, Hilde. Homes for men and women and children.

HILDE. But homes with high towers and spires on top.

SOLNESS. Yes, if possible.

Speaks more lightly.

Well, you see—as I said—that fire started me on my way. As a master builder.

HILDE. Why don't you call yourself an architect, like all the others?

SOLNESS. I've never really studied it properly. Most of what I know I've found out for myself.

HILDE. But you got to the top, master builder.

SOLNESS. Yes; fanned by those flames. I cut up nearly all the grounds into building plots. And *there* I was able to build, just the way I wanted. And from then on things went well for me.

HILDE *looks searchingly at him.* You must be a very happy man, then. With all the success you've had.

SOLNESS. Happy? You say that, too? Like all the others.

HILDE. Yes, I think you should be. If you could only stop thinking about those two little boys——

SOLNESS, *slowly.* Those two little boys—are not so easy to forget, Hilde.

HILDE, *a little uncertain.* So they still stand in your way? After so many years?

SOLNESS *stares at her without replying.* A happy man, you said——

HILDE. Yes, well, aren't you—apart from this?

SOLNESS, *still staring at her.* When I told you about the fire——

HILDE. Go on.

SOLNESS. Didn't anything particular strike you?

HILDE. No. I can't think of anything.

SOLNESS. If it hadn't been for that fire, I wouldn't have been able to build homes. Bright, peaceful, comfortable homes, where mothers and fathers could live with their children, secure and happy in the knowledge that it is good to be alive. And, above all, to belong to each other—in great things and in small.

HILDE. Yes, but doesn't it bring you great happiness to know that you can build such wonderful homes for them?

SOLNESS. But the price, Hilde. The terrible price I had to pay.

HILDE. Is there no way to put all that behind you?

SOLNESS. No. Because—to be able to build homes for other people, I had to renounce for ever all hope of having a home of my own. I mean a home with children. And for their father and mother.

HILDE. For ever, you say? Was that absolutely necessary?

SOLNESS *nods slowly.* That was the price I had to pay for this "happiness" people talk so much about.

Takes a deep breath.

That happiness—hm—that happiness wasn't to be had at a lesser price, Hilde.

HILDE. But perhaps things may still work out?

SOLNESS. No, they never can. Never. That is another consequence of the fire. And of Aline's illness which resulted from it.

HILDE *looks at him with an enigmatic expression.* And yet you are building all these nurseries?

SOLNESS. Haven't you noticed, Hilde, that the impossible beckons and calls to us?

HILDE *thinks.* The impossible?

Excitedly.

Why, yes! Is it like that with you as well?

SOLNESS. It is.

HILDE. Then you have something of the troll in you, too?

SOLNESS. Why troll?

HILDE. Well, what would you call it?

SOLNESS *gets up.* No, no, you may be right.

Violently.

But please God I may never become a troll like the one who mocks me in everything I do! Everything!

HILDE. What do you mean?

SOLNESS. Mark my words, Hilde. Everything that I have created—beautiful, secure, and friendly—yes, and magnificent, too!—I must sit here and expiate! Pay for it. Not with money. But with human happiness . . . And not only with my happiness, but with the happiness of others, too. You see, Hilde! That's the price that my success as an artist has cost me—and others. And every day of my life I have to sit here and see that price being paid for me—day after day after day!

HILDE *gets up and looks steadily at him.* You're thinking of *her*—aren't you?

SOLNESS. Yes. Aline had her calling in life. Just as I had mine. But she had to be destroyed and annihilated so that I could follow my calling and gain a—a kind of triumph. Yes —you see, Aline had a—a talent for building, too.

HILDE. She? For building?

SOLNESS *shakes his head.* Not houses and towers and steeples. Not the kind of things I bother with——

HILDE. Well, what, then?

SOLNESS, *softly, moved.* Children, Hilde. The souls of children.

So that they might grow into something noble, harmonious, and beautiful. So that they might become worthy human beings. That was where her talent lay. And it lies there, unused—and unusable; waste and barren, like the charred ruins left after a fire.

HILDE. Yes, but even if this were true——

SOLNESS. It is! I know it.

HILDE. Well, anyway, it's not your fault. You're not guilty.

SOLNESS. Aren't I? That's the terrible doubt that gnaws me night and day.

HILDE. What on earth—?

SOLNESS. Suppose it is true. Suppose I am guilty? In a kind of way.

HILDE. You? You mean—the fire?

SOLNESS. Everything. Everything. And on the other hand—I may be quite innocent.

HILDE. Oh, master builder! If you can talk like that, you must be—well—ill, anyway.

SOLNESS. Hm—incurably, I am afraid. Where this is concerned.

RAGNAR BROVIK *cautiously opens the small door in the corner on the left.* HILDE *walks across the room.*

RAGNAR, *as he sees* HILDE. Oh—I beg your pardon, Mr. Solness——

Is about to go.

SOLNESS. No, no, come in. Let's get this matter settled.

RAGNAR. Oh, yes—if we could!

SOLNESS. Your father's no better, I hear.

RAGNAR. He's sinking fast. So—please—I beg you—write a few kind words about one of the drawings. Something he can read before he——

SOLNESS, *violently.* You mustn't ask me any more questions about these drawings of yours.

RAGNAR. Have you looked at them?

SOLNESS. Yes—I have.

RAGNAR. And—they're no good? And I suppose I'm no good either?

SOLNESS. You stay here with me, Ragnar. You shall have whatever you want. Then you can marry Kaja, and all your cares will be over. You might even be happy. Only—don't think of building by yourself.

RAGNAR. Very well. I'd better go home and tell Father that. I promised him I would. Shall I tell Father this—before he dies?

SOLNESS, *distressed*. Oh, tell him—tell him what you like. Better not tell him anything.

Violently.

I can't help it, Ragnar! I have no choice.

RAGNAR. In that case, may I have the drawings?

SOLNESS. Yes, take them—take them away. They're on the table.

RAGNAR *goes across*. Thank you.

HILDE *puts her hand on the portfolio*. No, no. Leave them.

SOLNESS. Why?

HILDE. I'd like to look at them, too.

SOLNESS. But you've already——

To RAGNAR.

All right then. Leave them there.

RAGNAR. By all means.

SOLNESS. And now go home to your father.

RAGNAR. I suppose I must.

SOLNESS, *as though desperate*. Ragnar—you mustn't ask of me something I cannot do. Do you hear, Ragnar? You mustn't do that!

RAGNAR. No, no. I'm sorry.

Bows, and goes out through the corner door. HILDE *goes and sits on a chair by the mirror.*

HILDE *looks angrily at* SOLNESS. That was beastly of you.

SOLNESS. You think so, too?

HILDE. Yes, really beastly. Hard and vicious and cruel.

SOLNESS. Oh, you don't understand.

HILDE. All the same—no, you shouldn't be like that. Not you.

SOLNESS. You said yourself just now that I was the only person who should be allowed to build.

HILDE. I can say that. Not you.

SOLNESS. If anyone can, I can. I paid dearly enough for my position.

HILDE. Oh, yes. Domestic bliss, and all that.

SOLNESS. Peace of mind.

HILDE *gets up.* Peace of mind! Yes, of course! Poor master builder! You fancy that——

SOLNESS *chuckles.* You sit down again, Hilde, and I'll tell you a funny story.

HILDE *sits.* Well?

SOLNESS. It sounds so ludicrously trivial. You see, it all turns on a crack in a chimney.

HILDE. That all?

SOLNESS. Yes, to begin with.

He moves a chair closer to HILDE, *and sits.*

HILDE, *impatient, slaps her knee.* So there was a crack in the chimney?

SOLNESS. I'd noticed that crack in the pipe for a long time, long before the fire. Each time I went up to the loft, I looked to see if it was still there.

HILDE. And it was?

SOLNESS. Yes. No-one else knew about it.

HILDE. And you didn't say anything?

SOLNESS. No, I didn't.

HILDE. And you didn't think of getting it mended?

SOLNESS. Oh, I thought about it, but I didn't do anything. Each time I decided to get down to it, it was just as though a hand reached out and held me back. Not today, I thought. Tomorrow. So nothing ever came of it.

HILDE. But why did you always put it off?

SOLNESS. Because a thought had occurred to me.

Slow, quiet.

Through this little black crack in this chimney pipe, I might climb my way to the top. Become a master builder.

HILDE, *to herself.* That must have been exciting.

SOLNESS. It was irresistible—almost. Utterly irresistible! At the time, it all seemed so unimportant and trivial. I wanted it to happen some time in winter. Shortly before dinner. I would be out, driving Aline in the sleigh. The servant would have built up great fires in all the rooms——

HILDE. It'd be frightfully cold that day, wouldn't it?

SOLNESS. Pretty sharp, yes. And they'd want it to be good and warm for Aline when she came back.

HILDE. Yes, she suffers from the cold, doesn't she?

SOLNESS. She does. And then, it'd be on the way home that we'd see the smoke.

HILDE. Just the smoke?

SOLNESS. First of all the smoke. But then, when we reached the drive, the old crate was just a surging mass of flames! That's the way I wanted it to happen.

HILDE. Oh, why couldn't it have happened like that?
Pause.
Ah, but wait a moment, master builder. Are you quite sure that the fire was caused by this little crack in the chimney?

SOLNESS. No, on the contrary. I'm quite sure the crack in the chimney had nothing whatever to do with the fire.

HILDE. What!

SOLNESS. It's been established that the fire broke out in the linen room, on the other side of the house.

HILDE. Then why on earth are you sitting here drivelling about this cracked chimney?

SOLNESS. May I go on talking to you for a little, Hilde?

HILDE. Yes, but only if you talk sensibly——

SOLNESS. I'll do my best.
Moves his chair closer.

HILDE. Well! Out with it, master builder!

SOLNESS, *confidentially.* Don't you think, Hilde, that there are people singled out by fate who have been endowed with grace and power to wish for something, desire it so passionately, *will* it so inexorably that, ultimately, they must be granted it? Don't you believe that?

HILDE, *with an enigmatic expression in her eyes.* If that is so, the time will come when we shall see if I am one of them.

SOLNESS. No man can achieve such things alone. Oh, no—there are helpers and servers—who must be at our side if we are to succeed. But they never come of their accord. One must call on them with all one's strength. Silently, you understand.

HILDE. Who are these helpers and servers?

SOLNESS. Oh, let's talk about that some other time. For the moment let's concentrate on the fire.

HILDE. Don't you think there would have been a fire even if you hadn't wished for it?

SOLNESS. If that house had been owned by old Knut Brovik, it would never have burned down at such an opportune moment. I'm sure of that. Because he doesn't understand how to call on the helpers, or to summon those who serve him.

Gets up, restlessly.

So you see, Hilde, it *is* I who am guilty, and both those little boys had to pay with their lives. And is it not also true that it is my fault that Aline has not become what she should and could have become? And what she so longed to become.

HILDE. Yes, but if it's these helpers and servers who——?

SOLNESS. Who called to the helpers and to the servers? I did! And they came and bowed to my will.

In increasing turmoil.

This is what people call being lucky. But I'll tell you how it feels to be lucky! It feels as though the skin had been flayed from my breast. And the helpers and servers go round taking the skin from other people's bodies to cover the wound! But it can't be healed. Never, never! Oh, if you only knew how it burns sometimes!

HILDE. You are ill, master builder. Very ill, I think.

SOLNESS. Say mad. That's what you mean.

HILDE. No, I don't think there's anything wrong with your head.

SOLNESS. What, then? Out with it!

HILDE. I'm wondering if you weren't born with an under-developed conscience.

SOLNESS. Under-developed conscience? What the devil do you mean?

HILDE. I mean that your conscience is very frail. Over-sensitive; won't get to grips with things. Can't carry a heavy burden.

SOLNESS *growls*. Hm! How ought a conscience to be, if I may ask?

HILDE. In your case I wish it were a little more—well—robust.

SOLNESS. Indeed? Robust? Well! And have you a robust conscience?

HILDE. Yes, I think so. I haven't noticed anything to the contrary.

SOLNESS. I don't suppose you've had much opportunity to test it, have you?

HILDE, *with a tremble round her mouth*. Oh, it wasn't all that easy to leave Father. I'm frightfully fond of him.

SOLNESS. Oh, just for a month or two——

HILDE. I don't think I shall ever go back.

SOLNESS. What, never? Why did you leave him, then?

HILDE, *half serious, half teasing*. Have you forgotten again? The ten years are up!

SOLNESS. Nonsense. Was there anything wrong at home? Mm?

HILDE, *in earnest*. This thing inside me drove me to come here. Tempted and drove me.

SOLNESS, *eagerly*. That's it! That's it, Hilde! There's troll in you, too; the same as in me. And it's the troll, you see, that calls to the powers outside! And we have to submit whether we like it or not.

HILDE. I begin to think you're right, master builder.

SOLNESS *paces the floor again.* Oh, there are so many invisible demons in the world, Hilde.

Stops.

Good demons and evil demons. Fair demons and dark. If only one always knew whether it was the fair that had hold of one or the dark!

Starts walking again.

Ha, ha! It would all be so simple.

HILDE *watches him as he walks.* Or if only one had a really brash and hearty conscience! If one *dared* to do what one wanted.

SOLNESS *stops by the console table.* Oh, I think most people are as cowardly as I, in that respect.

HILDE. That may well be.

SOLNESS *leans against the table.* In the sagas—have you read any of those old sagas?

HILDE. Oh, yes! In the days when I used to read——

SOLNESS. Those sagas tell about vikings, who sailed to foreign lands and plundered and burned and killed——

HILDE. And carried away women——

SOLNESS. And kept them——

HILDE. Took them home with them in their ships——

SOLNESS. And used them like—like the worst kind of trolls.

HILDE, *to herself, with her eyes half closed.* I think that must be so exciting!

SOLNESS, *with a short, gruff laugh.* To take a woman, you mean?

HILDE. To be taken.

SOLNESS *looks at her for a moment.* I see.

HILDE, *as though changing the subject.* But what were you going to say about these vikings, master builder?

SOLNESS. Oh, yes—well, those fellows, their consciences were robust enough. When they came home they ate and drank and were as merry as children. And what about the women! Quite often they didn't want to leave these men! Can you understand that, Hilde?

HILDE. I can understand the women frightfully well.

SOLNESS. Ah! Perhaps you would do the same yourself?

HILDE. Why not?

SOLNESS. Live—willingly—with a brute like that?

HILDE. If he was a brute I'd come to grow really fond of—

SOLNESS. *Could* you grow fond of a man like that?

HILDE. Oh, God, one can't help whom one grows fond of, can one?

SOLNESS *looks at her thoughtfully.* No, no—I suppose it's the troll in us that decides that.

HILDE, *with a little laugh.* And all these blessed demons you know so much about. The fair and the dark.

SOLNESS, *warmly and quietly.* I hope the demons choose kindly for you, Hilde.

HILDE. They have chosen for me. Once and for all.

SOLNESS *looks deep into her eyes.* Hilde—you are like a wild bird of the forest.

HILDE. Far from it. I'm not shy.

SOLNESS. No, no. There's more of the falcon in you.

HILDE. Yes—perhaps.

Violently.

And why not a falcon? Why shouldn't I go hunting, too? Get the prey I want? If only I can get my claws into it! Bring it to the ground!

SOLNESS. Hilde—do you know what you are?

HILDE. Yes, I'm a strange kind of bird.

SOLNESS. No. You are like a new dawn. When I look at you, it is as though I were watching the sunrise.

HILDE. Tell me, master builder—are you sure you've never called to me? Silently?

SOLNESS, *quietly.* I think I must have done.

HILDE. What do you want from me?

SOLNESS. Your youth, Hilde.

HILDE *smiles.* Youth, which you are so frightened of?

SOLNESS *nods slowly.* And which, in my heart, I long for.

HILDE *gets up, goes over to the small table, and fetches* RAGNAR BROVIK'S *portfolio.*

HILDE *holds out the portfolio towards him.* What about these drawings, now?

SOLNESS, *curtly.* Put those things away. I've seen enough of them.

HILDE. Quite, but you're going to approve them.

SOLNESS. Approve them? I'm damned if I will.

HILDE. Can't you do this little thing for him? But the poor old man is dying! And then perhaps his son might get the chance to build the house, too.

SOLNESS. Yes, that's just it. He can. He's made sure of that, that young gentleman.

HILDE. Well, for goodness' sake, if he has, can't you bring yourself to lie a tiny bit?

SOLNESS. Lie?

Furiously.

Hilde, take those damned drawings away from me!

HILDE *draws the portfolio a little towards her.* Now, now, now, don't snap at me. You talk about trolls. I think you behave like one yourself.

Looks round.

Where do you keep your pen and ink?

SOLNESS. I haven't any in here.

HILDE *goes towards the door.* Well, that girl'll have some—

SOLNESS. Stay where you are, Hilde! I must tell a lie, you said. Oh, I wouldn't mind doing it for his old father. A man I once ruined.

HILDE. You ruined him too?

SOLNESS. I needed room. But this young Ragnar—he mustn't on any account be allowed to come to the front.

HILDE. He won't, either, will he, poor boy? If he's no good—

SOLNESS *comes closer, looks at her and whispers.* If Ragnar Brovik gets started, he will break me to the ground. Just as I broke his father.

HILDE. Break *you?* He is some good, then?

SOLNESS. Yes, he's good, make no mistake. He is the youth who is waiting, standing ready to bang upon my door. And make an end of master builder Solness.

HILDE. And yet you wanted to shut him out? For shame, master builder!

SOLNESS. This struggle has cost me enough. Besides, I'm afraid the helpers and the servers won't obey me any longer.

HILDE. Then you'll have to paddle your own canoe. There's nothing for it.

SOLNESS. Hopeless, Hilde. The tide will turn. Sooner or later. Retribution will come.

HILDE, *frightened, puts her hands over her ears.* Don't talk like that! Do you want to take away from me what I value more than my life?

SOLNESS. And what's that?

HILDE. To see you great. See you with a wreath in your hand. High, high up on a church tower.

Calm again.

Well, at least you must have a pencil. Give it to me.

SOLNESS *takes out his notebook.* Yes, I've got one here.

HILDE *puts the portfolio on the table by the sofa.* Right. And now we'll sit down here, master builder.

SOLNESS *sits at the table.*

HILDE, *behind him, leaning over the back of his chair.* And then we'll write on the drawings. Really, really nicely and kindly, we'll write. For this beastly Ragnvald or whatever his name is.

SOLNESS *writes a few lines, turns his head, and looks up at her.* Tell me something, Hilde.

HILDE. Yes?

SOLNESS. If you've really been waiting for me for ten years——

HILDE. Well?

SOLNESS. Why didn't you write to me?

HILDE, *quickly.* No, no, no! That was just what I didn't want.

SOLNESS. Why not?

HILDE. I was afraid that then it might all go wrong. But we were going to write on the drawings, master builder.

SOLNESS. So we were.

HILDE *leans over him and watches while he writes.* How good and kind. Oh, how I hate—how I hate this Ragnvald——

SOLNESS, *as he writes.* Have you never been—really fond of anyone, Hilde?

HILDE, *in a hard voice.* What did you say?

SOLNESS. I asked if you had ever been really fond of anyone.

HILDE. Anyone else, you mean?

SOLNESS *looks up at her.* Yes, of course—anyone else. Haven't you? In all these years? Ever?

HILDE. Oh, yes, once in a while. When I was really mad with you for not coming.

SOLNESS. Then you—cared about others, too?

HILDE. A little. For a week or two. Oh, God, master builder, you know how it is?

SOLNESS. Hilde—why have you come?

HILDE. Don't waste time. That poor old man may be dying while you talk.

SOLNESS. Answer me, Hilde. What is it you want from me?

HILDE. I want my kingdom.

SOLNESS. Hm——

He glances quickly towards the door on the left and continues writing on the drawings. MRS. SOLNESS *enters, carrying some parcels.*

MRS. SOLNESS. I've bought you a few things, Miss Wangel. There are some big parcels being sent on later.

HILDE. Oh, how very sweet of you!

MRS. SOLNESS. It's my simple duty. That's all.

SOLNESS, *reading through what he has written.* Aline!

MRS. SOLNESS. Yes?

SOLNESS. Did you see if she—if the bookkeeper was out there?

MRS. SOLNESS. Yes, of course she was there.

SOLNESS, *replacing the drawings in the portfolio.* Hm——

MRS. SOLNESS. She was standing at the desk, as she always does—when I'm in the room.

SOLNESS *gets up.* I'll give this to her, then, and tell her that——

HILDE, *taking the portfolio from him.* Oh, no, let me, please!
Goes to the door, then turns.
What's her name?

SOLNESS. Her name is Miss Fosli.

HILDE. Ugh, that sounds so formal. What's her first name, I mean?

SOLNESS. Kaja, I think.

HILDE *opens the door and calls.* Kaja! Come in here. Hurry! The master builder wants to speak with you.

KAJA *comes inside the door.*

KAJA *looks at him, frightened.* Here I am——?

HILDE *holds out the portfolio to her.* Look, Kaja! You can take this, now. The master builder's written on them.

KAJA. Oh—at last!

SOLNESS. Give them to the old man as soon as you can.

KAJA. I'll take them home at once.

SOLNESS. Yes, do that. And then Ragnar can begin to build.

KAJA. Oh, may he come and thank you for everything——?

SOLNESS. I want no thanks. Tell him so from me.

KAJA. Yes, I'll——

SOLNESS. And tell him at the same time that from now on I've no use for him. Nor for you.

KAJA, *quietly trembling.* Nor for me?

SOLNESS. You'll have other things to think about now. And someone else to look after. And that's as it should be. All right, go home now with your drawings, Miss Fosli. Quickly! Do you hear?

KAJA. Yes, Mr. Solness.
Goes out.

MRS. SOLNESS. Oh, what sly eyes she has!

SOLNESS. That poor little creature.

MRS. SOLNESS. Oh, I'm not blind, Halvard. Are you really dismissing them?

SOLNESS. Yes.

MRS. SOLNESS. Her too?

SOLNESS. Well, wasn't that what you wanted?

MRS. SOLNESS. But how can you manage without her? Oh, I see; you've someone else up your sleeve, haven't you, Halvard?

HILDE, *gaily.* Well, I'm no good for standing at desks, anyway.

SOLNESS. I shall manage somehow, Aline. You just make arrangements for moving into our new home, as soon as possible. This evening we shall hoist the wreath——

Turns to HILDE.

—to the top of the spire. What do you say to that, Miss Hilde?

HILDE *looks at him excitedly.* It'll be so marvelous to see you standing high up there again!

SOLNESS. Me!

MRS. SOLNESS. Oh, God, Miss Wangel, you mustn't think of it. My husband gets dizzy. He has no head for heights.

HILDE. Dizzy? I don't believe it.

MRS. SOLNESS. Oh, yes, he's always been like that.

HILDE. But I've seen him myself, high up on the top of a church steeple.

MRS. SOLNESS. Yes, I've heard people talk about that. But it's impossible.

SOLNESS, *violently.* Impossible, yes! But nevertheless I stood up there!

MRS. SOLNESS. How can you say that, Halvard? You hardly even dare to go out on to the balcony on the second floor. You've always been like that.

SOLNESS. You may think otherwise this evening.

MRS. SOLNESS, *frightened.* No, no, no! God will help me to prevent that. I'll write a message to the doctor at once. He'll talk you out of it.

SOLNESS. But, Aline——

MRS. SOLNESS. Yes, you're ill, Halvard! That's what it is, you're ill! Oh, God, oh, God——!

She hurries out to the right.

HILDE *looks at him, tensely.* Is it true?

SOLNESS. That I have no head for heights?

HILDE. That *my* master builder dare not—cannot rise as high as he can build?

SOLNESS. That is how you see it?

HILDE. Yes.

SOLNESS. I begin to think there is no part of me that is safe from you.

HILDE *looks towards the bay window.* Up there! Right up there!

SOLNESS *goes closer.* You could live up there, Hilde. In the highest room in the tower. You could live there like a princess.

HILDE, *enigmatically, half serious, half jesting.* Yes, that's what you promised me.

SOLNESS. *Did* I?

HILDE. For shame, master builder! You said you'd make me a princess, and that you would give me a kingdom. And then you took me and—— Well?

SOLNESS, *gently.* Are you quite sure it wasn't a dream? Something you just imagined?

HILDE, *sharply.* You think you didn't do it?

SOLNESS. I hardly know myself——

More quietly.

But I know one thing—that I——

HILDE. That you——? Say it!

SOLNESS. That I should have done it.

HILDE. *You*—dizzy!

SOLNESS. Tonight we shall hang up our wreath—Princess Hilde.

HILDE, *with a touch of bitterness.* Over your new home.

SOLNESS. Over the new house. It will never be a home for me.

He goes out through the garden door.

HILDE, *with half closed eyes, whispers to herself. Only two words can be heard.* . . . frightfully exciting!

ACT THREE

A large, broad verandah belonging to SOLNESS's *house. Part of the house, with a door leading to the verandah, can be seen on the left. In front, to the right, a railing. Backstage, at one end of the verandah, a flight of steps leads down to the garden below. Large old trees stretch their branches over the verandah towards the house. On the extreme right, through the trees, can be glimpsed the lower part of the new villa, with scaffolding round the base of the tower. Backstage, the garden is bounded by an old fence. Beyond the fence is a street, with low, tumbledown cottages. Evening sky, with clouds irradiated by the sun.*

On the verandah, against the wall of the house, stands a garden seat, and in front of the seat is a long table. On the other side of the table, an armchair and some stools. All the furniture is of wicker.

MRS. SOLNESS, *wrapped in a large, white, crepe shawl, is resting in the armchair, gazing over towards the right. After a few moments,* HILDE WANGEL *comes up the steps from the garden. She is dressed as before, and is wearing her hat. On her breast is pinned a little bouquet of common flowers.*

MRS. SOLNESS *turns her head slightly.* Have you been in the garden, Miss Wangel?

HILDE. Yes, I've been having a look round.

MRS. SOLNESS. You've found some flowers, too, I see.

HILDE. Oh, yes! There are heaps of them. Among the bushes.

MRS. SOLNESS. No, are there really? Still? I hardly ever go down there.

HILDE *comes closer.* What? I should have thought you'd skip down every day.

MRS. SOLNESS *smiles wanly.* I don't *skip* anywhere, I'm afraid. Not any longer.

HILDE. But don't you go down now and then to say hello to all the beautiful things there?

MRS. SOLNESS. It's all become so foreign to me. I'm almost afraid to look at it again.

HILDE. Your own garden?

MRS. SOLNESS. I don't feel it's mine any longer.

HILDE. Oh, what rubbish!

MRS. SOLNESS. No, no, it isn't. It's not like it was in Mother's and Father's time. They've taken such a dreadful lot of it away, Miss Wangel. Can you imagine—they've broken it up, and built houses in it, for strangers. People I don't know. They can look at me from their windows.

HILDE, *with a sunny expression.* Mrs. Solness?

MRS. SOLNESS. Yes?

HILDE. May I sit here with you for a little?

MRS. SOLNESS. Yes, please do, if you'd really like to.

HILDE *moves a stool close to the armchair and sits on it.*

HILDE. Ah, one can sit and sun oneself here. Like a cat.

MRS. SOLNESS *puts her hand gently on* HILDE's *neck.* It's very sweet of you to want to sit with me. I thought you were going inside to my husband.

HILDE. What would I want with him?

MRS. SOLNESS. I thought you'd want to help him.

HILDE. No, thank you. Anyway, he's not in. He's over there among the workmen. But he looked so fierce I didn't dare to talk to him.

MRS. SOLNESS. Oh, he's very soft and gentle really.

HILDE. *He?*

MRS. SOLNESS. You don't know him well enough yet, Miss Wangel.

HILDE *looks affectionately at her.* Are you happy to be moving over to the new house?

MRS. SOLNESS. I should be happy. That's what Halvard wants.

HILDE. Oh, I didn't mean just because of that.

MRS. SOLNESS. Yes, Miss Wangel, yes. That's my duty, don't you see, to do what he wants. But it's often so difficult to force oneself to be obedient.

HILDE. Yes, that must be difficult.

MRS. SOLNESS. Yes, indeed. When one's as weak a person as I am——

HILDE. When one has suffered as much as you have——

MRS. SOLNESS. How do you know that?

HILDE. Your husband told me.

MRS. SOLNESS. He so seldom speaks to me about these things. Yes, I've had more than my share of suffering in my lifetime, Miss Wangel.

HILDE *looks at her sympathetically, and nods slowly.* Poor Mrs. Solness. First there was the fire——

MRS. SOLNESS *sighs.* Yes. Everything I had was burned.

HILDE. And then there was worse to follow.

MRS. SOLNESS. Worse?

HILDE. The worst thing of all.

MRS. SOLNESS. What do you mean?

HILDE, *quietly.* You lost both your little boys.

MRS. SOLNESS. Oh, them, yes. Well, that was different. That was an act of God. One must resign oneself to such things. And be thankful.

HILDE. Are you?

MRS. SOLNESS. Not always, I'm afraid. I know so well that it's my duty. But I can't.

HILDE. No, well, I think that's very understandable.

MRS. SOLNESS. Time and again I have to remind myself that I've been justly punished——

HILDE. Why?

MRS. SOLNESS. Because I wasn't resolute enough in the face of adversity.

HILDE. But I don't see that——

MRS. SOLNESS. No, no, Miss Wangel—don't talk to me any more about the two little boys. We should be happy for them. They're so much, much better off where they are. No, it's the little losses which leave the deepest wound. Things which other people would regard as unimportant.

HILDE *puts her arms on* MRS. SOLNESS's *knee and looks up at her warmly.* Dear Mrs. Solness, tell me—what kind of things?

MRS. SOLNESS. Just little things. All the old portraits on the walls were burned. And all the old silk dresses that had been in our family for generations. And all Mama's and Grandmama's lace, that was burned too. And think of the jewels!
Sadly.
And all the dolls.

HILDE. The dolls?

MRS. SOLNESS, *tearfully.* I had nine beautiful dolls.

HILDE. And they were burned too?

MRS. SOLNESS. All of them. Oh, it was so hard for me—so hard.

HILDE. Had you kept all those dolls, then? Ever since you'd been a child?

MRS. SOLNESS. I didn't just keep them. They lived with me.

HILDE. After you'd grown up?

MRS. SOLNESS. Yes, long after.

HILDE. After you were married?

MRS. SOLNESS. Oh, yes. As long as he didn't see them—— But then they were burned, poor dears. No-one thought of saving them. Oh, it makes me so sad to think about it! Now you mustn't laugh at me, Miss Wangel.

HILDE. I'm not laughing.

MRS. SOLNESS. They were alive, too, in a way, you see. I carried them under my heart. Like little unborn children.

DR. HERDAL, *hat in hand, comes out through the door and catches sight of* MRS. SOLNESS *and* HILDE.

HERDAL. Giving yourself a cold, I see, Mrs. Solness!

MRS. SOLNESS. I think it's so nice and warm out here today.

HERDAL. Yes, yes. But is something the matter? I got a note——

MRS. SOLNESS *gets up.* Yes, there's something I have to talk to you about.

HERDAL. By all means. Perhaps we'd better go inside.

To HILDE.

Still wearing your climbing outfit, young lady?

HILDE, *gaily, as she gets up.* Rather! Dressed to kill! No climbing for me today, though. You and I will stay down here and watch like good little children.

HERDAL. Watch what?

MRS. SOLNESS, *quietly, frightened, to* HILDE. Ssh, please, for heaven's sake! He's coming! Try to dissuade him from this idea! And—do let us be friends, Miss Wangel. Can't we?

HILDE *throws her arms impetuously round* MRS. SOLNESS's *neck.* Oh, if only we could!

MRS. SOLNESS *frees herself gently.* Now, now, now. Here he comes, Doctor. Let me talk to you for a moment.

HERDAL. Is it about him?

MRS. SOLNESS. Yes, it's about him. Come inside.

She and HERDAL *go into the house. The next moment,* SOLNESS *comes up the steps from the garden. A serious expression comes over* HILDE's *face.*

SOLNESS *glances at the door as it is carefully shut from inside.*

Have you noticed, Hilde? As soon as I come, she goes.

HILDE. I've noticed that when you come that makes her go.

SOLNESS. Possibly. But I can't help that.

Looks closely at her.

Are you cold, Hilde? You look as if you were.

HILDE. I've just come up out of a tomb.

SOLNESS. What does that mean?

HILDE. The frost's got into me, master builder.

SOLNESS, *slowly.* I think I understand——

HILDE. Why have you come up here?

SOLNESS. I saw you.

HILDE. You must have seen her, too?

SOLNESS. I knew she'd go as soon as I came.

HILDE. Does it hurt you that she always avoids you?

SOLNESS. In a way it's a kind of relief.

HILDE. That you don't always have to be looking at her?

SOLNESS. Yes.

HILDE. That you don't have to be reminded the whole time of how much she grieves for her little boys?

SOLNESS. Yes. That above all.

HILDE *wanders along the verandah with her hands behind her back, stops by the railing, and gazes out across the garden.*

SOLNESS. How long did you talk to her?

HILDE *does not move or reply.*

SOLNESS. How long, I asked?

HILDE *remains silent.*

SOLNESS. What did she talk about, then?

HILDE *still does not speak.*

SOLNESS. Poor Aline! About the children, I suppose.

HILDE *shivers nervously, then nods twice rapidly.*

SOLNESS. She can't get over it. She will never get over it. *Goes closer.*

Now you're standing there like a statue again. You stood like that last night.

HILDE *turns and looks at him, large-eyed, serious.* I want to go.

SOLNESS, *sharply.* Go?

HILDE. Yes.

SOLNESS. No. I won't allow it.

HILDE. What can I do here now?

SOLNESS. Just—stay here, Hilde.

HILDE *looks at him scornfully.* Thank you very much. But it wouldn't end there.

SOLNESS, *without thinking.* So much the better!

HILDE, *violently*. I can't hurt someone I *know*. I can't take what belongs to her.

SOLNESS. Who says you will?

HILDE *continues*. From a stranger, yes. That's different. Someone I've never set eyes on. But someone I've got close to——! No! No! Ugh!

SOLNESS. But I haven't suggested that you should.

HILDE. Oh, master builder, you know very well how it would end. That's why I'm leaving.

SOLNESS. And what's to become of me when you've gone? What shall I have to live for? Afterwards?

HILDE, *with the enigmatic expression in her eyes*. It's easy for you. You have your duty towards her. You must live for that duty.

SOLNESS. Too late. These powers—these——

HILDE. Demons——

SOLNESS. Yes, demons! And the troll in me! They've sucked her blood.

Laughs desperately.

It was done for my happiness.

Heavily.

And for my sake she died. And I am chained to the corpse.

In anguish.

I—I, who cannot live without joy!

HILDE *walks round the table and sits down on the seat with her elbows on the table, leaning her head on her hands.*

HILDE *sits for a moment, looking at him*. What are you going to build next?

SOLNESS *shakes his head*. I don't think I shall build much more.

HILDE. No more happy homes for Mummy and Daddy? And all the little children?

SOLNESS. God knows whether people will want that kind of thing any more.

HILDE. Poor master builder! And you've spent ten years thinking of nothing else? You've given your life to it.

SOLNESS. I have, haven't I, Hilde?

HILDE *bursts out.* Oh, I think it's all so wrong, so wrong!

SOLNESS. What?

HILDE. That one should be afraid to seize happiness! To seize hold of life! Just because someone stands in the way. Someone one knows.

SOLNESS. Someone one has no right to pass by.

HILDE. Haven't we that right? I wonder. But even so—— Oh, if one could only sleep and forget it all!

She lays her arms flat on the table, rests her left cheek on her hands, and closes her eyes.

SOLNESS *turns the armchair round and sits down by the table.* Did you have a happy home with your father, Hilde?

HILDE, *without moving, replies as though half asleep.* I only had a cage.

SOLNESS. And you don't want to go back into it?

HILDE, *as before.* Wild birds don't fly into cages.

SOLNESS. They want to chase the free air——

HILDE, *still in the same tone.* Eagles love the chase.

SOLNESS, *resting his eyes on her.* If only one were a viking. They had hunting in their blood.

HILDE *opens her eyes, but does not move, and says in her normal voice.* What else did they have? Tell me!

SOLNESS. A robust conscience.

HILDE *sits up, alive. Her eyes are again excited and aflame.*

HILDE *nods at him.* I know what you're going to build next!

SOLNESS. Then you know more than I do, Hilde.

HILDE. Yes. Master builders are very stupid people.

SOLNESS. What is it to be, then?

HILDE *nods again.* The castle.

SOLNESS. What castle?

HILDE. *My* castle, of course.

SOLNESS. You want a castle, now?

HILDE. You owe me a kingdom, don't you?

SOLNESS. So you tell me.

HILDE. Well, then! You owe me this kingdom. And a kingdom's got to have a castle, hasn't it?

SOLNESS, *more and more exhilarated.* Yes, they usually do.

HILDE. Good. Build it for me, then! At once!

SOLNESS *laughs.* Within the hour?

HILDE. Yes! The ten years are up now! And I don't intend to wait any longer! I want my castle, master builder!

SOLNESS. It's no joke to have you as a creditor, Hilde.

HILDE. You should have thought of that before. Now it's too late. Now then——

Thumps on the table.

—Where's my castle? It's *my* castle! I want it now!

SOLNESS, *more earnestly, leans closer to her, with his arms on the table.* What does it look like, this castle of yours, Hilde?

HILDE, *slowly.* My castle must stand high up. High above everything! Open and free on every side. So that I can see for miles around.

SOLNESS. It's got a tower, I suppose?

HILDE. A frightfully high tower. And right up on the top of the tower there'll be a balcony. And that's where I shall stand——

SOLNESS *involuntarily clutches his head.* How can you want to stand so high? Doesn't it make you giddy——?

HILDE. I want to stand up there and look down at the others— the ones who build churches! And homes for mothers and fathers and children. And you can come up there and look down too.

SOLNESS, *humbly.* Has the master builder leave to climb up to the princess?

HILDE. If the master builder wishes.

SOLNESS *whispers.* Then—I think the master builder will come.

HILDE *nods.* The master builder—he will come.

SOLNESS. But he will never build again. Poor master builder!

HILDE, *alive.* Oh, yes he will! We'll do it together! And we'll build the most beautiful thing—the most beautiful thing in all the world!

SOLNESS. Hilde—tell me! What is that?

HILDE *looks at him with a smile, gives a little shake of her head, pouts, and says, as though to a child.* Master builders —they are vewy—vewy stupid people.

SOLNESS. Yes, I know they're stupid. But tell me—what is the most beautiful thing in the world? The thing we two are going to build together.

HILDE *is silent for a moment, then says, with the enigmatic expression in her eyes.* A castle in the air.

SOLNESS. A castle in the air?

HILDE *nods.* A castle in the air, yes. Do you know what a castle in the air is?

SOLNESS. It's the most beautiful thing in the world, you say.

HILDE *jumps up angrily and makes a contemptuous gesture with her hand.* Yes, of course! Castles in the air are so safe to hide in. And easy to build.

Looks at him scornfully.

Especially for master builders with a—a giddy conscience.

SOLNESS *gets up.* From now on we two shall build together, Hilde.

HILDE, *with a doubting smile.* A real castle in the air?

SOLNESS. Yes. Built on a true foundation.

RAGNAR BROVIK *comes out of the house. He is carrying a big, green wreath with flowers and silk ribbons.*

HILDE *exclaims joyfully.* The wreath! Oh, it's going to be absolutely marvelous!

SOLNESS, *amazed.* Have you brought the wreath, Ragnar?

RAGNAR. I promised the foreman I would.

SOLNESS, *relieved.* Your father's better, then?

RAGNAR. No.

SOLNESS. Didn't it cheer him up, what I wrote?

RAGNAR. It came too late.

SOLNESS. Too late?

RAGNAR. By the time she came with it, he'd lost consciousness. He'd had a stroke.

SOLNESS. Get back home to him, then! Look after your father!

RAGNAR. He doesn't need me any more.

SOLNESS. But surely you ought to be with him?

RAGNAR. She's sitting with him.

SOLNESS, *a little uncertainly.* Kaja?

RAGNAR *looks darkly at him.* Yes. Kaja.

SOLNESS. Go home, Ragnar. Go home to them. Give me the wreath.

RAGNAR *represses a scornful smile.* Surely *you're* not going to——?

SOLNESS. I'll take it down there myself.

Takes the wreath from him.

Go home, now. We won't need you today.

RAGNAR. I know you won't. But today, I'm staying.

SOLNESS. Oh, stay—stay, by all means.

HILDE, *at the railing.* Master builder—I shall stand here and watch you.

SOLNESS. Watch me?

HILDE. It'll be frightfully exciting.

SOLNESS, *subdued.* We'll—talk about that later, Hilde.

He descends the steps with the wreath and goes out through the garden.

HILDE *watches him go, then turns to* RAGNAR. You might at least have thanked him.

RAGNAR. Thanked him? Should I have thanked *him?*

HILDE. Yes, you should.

RAGNAR. I ought to thank you, if anyone.

HILDE. How can you say such a thing?

RAGNAR. But you watch out! You don't know him yet.

HILDE, *angrily.* I know him better than anyone.

RAGNAR *laughs bitterly.* Thank *him,* who's kept me back year after year? Who made my father lose his belief in me. Made me lose belief in myself. And all just so that he could——

HILDE, *as though sensing his meaning.* So that he could—what? Tell me!

RAGNAR. So that he could keep *her*.

HILDE, *with a movement towards him*. The girl at the desk?

RAGNAR. Yes.

HILDE *clenches her fists*. It's not true! You're lying!

RAGNAR. I didn't want to believe it either, until today. When she told me.

HILDE. What did she tell you? I want to know! Now! Now!

RAGNAR. She said he'd taken possession of her mind. That he'd directed all her thoughts towards himself. She says she'll never be able to free herself from him. That she'll stay wherever he is——

HILDE. She won't!

RAGNAR. Who's going to stop her? Are you?

HILDE, *quickly*. I won't be the only one.

RAGNAR. Oh, yes. I see. Now she'd only be a nuisance to him.

HILDE. You don't understand anything, if you talk like that. No, I'll tell you why he kept her on.

RAGNAR. Why?

HILDE. To keep you.

RAGNAR. Did he tell you that?

HILDE. No, but it's true! It *must* be.

Wildly.

It is, it is, I want it to be!

RAGNAR. And the moment *you* came, he let her go.

HILDE. It was *you* he let go! What do you think he cares about girls like her?

RAGNAR, *thoughtfully*. You mean he's been afraid of me all these years?

HILDE. Afraid of you? You fancy yourself!

RAGNAR. Oh, he must have realized a long time ago that I've got something in me. Besides—afraid—that's just what he is, don't you see?

HILDE. Try to make me believe that!

RAGNAR. In some ways he's afraid. The great master builder! Oh, he's not afraid to destroy people's happiness, the way he has Father's and mine. But ask him to climb up a few feet of scaffolding, and he'll go down on his knees and pray to God to be delivered.

HILDE. Oh, if only you'd seen him high up there! As giddily high as I once saw him!

RAGNAR. Have you seen that?

HILDE. Yes, I've seen it! Oh, so proud and free he stood up there as he tied the wreath to the church weathercock!

RAGNAR. I know he dared to do it once in his life. Just once. We've often talked about it. But no power on earth will persuade him to do it again.

HILDE. He'll do it again today!

RAGNAR. Don't you believe it.

HILDE. You'll see!

RAGNAR. I won't, and neither will you.

HILDE, *violently, uncontrollably.* I will! I will—I *must* see it!

RAGNAR. But he won't do it. He just daren't. He's got this yellow streak—the great master builder!

MRS. SOLNESS *comes out of the house on to the verandah.*

MRS. SOLNESS, *looking round.* Isn't he here? Where's he gone?

RAGNAR. The master builder is over there with the workmen.

HILDE. He took the wreath.

MRS. SOLNESS, *in terror.* Took the wreath? Oh, my God, my God! Brovik—you must go down to him. Get him to come back here!

RAGNAR. Shall I say you want to speak to him?

MRS. SOLNESS. Oh, yes, my dear boy, please do. No, no—don't tell him I want him. Tell him there's someone here. That he must come at once.

RAGNAR. Very well. I'll tell him that, Mrs. Solness.

He goes down the steps and out through the garden.

MRS. SOLNESS. Oh, Miss Wangel, you can't imagine how frightened I am for him.

HILDE. But what is there to be so frightened about?

MRS. SOLNESS. Suppose he's serious! Suppose he takes it into his head to climb up the scaffolding!

HILDE, *tensely*. Do you think he will?

MRS. SOLNESS. Oh, one can never be sure what he might do. He's quite capable of doing anything.

HILDE. Oh, so you, too, think he's a bit—er——?

MRS. SOLNESS. I no longer know what to think. The doctor's been telling me so many strange things. And when I think of some of the things I've heard *him* say——

DR. HERDAL *looks out through the door*.

HERDAL. Not here yet?

MRS. SOLNESS. He'll be back soon. I've sent him a message.

HERDAL, *closer*. You'd better go inside, Mrs. Solness.

MRS. SOLNESS. No, no. I want to stay out here and wait for Halvard.

HERDAL. Yes, but some ladies have come to see you——

MRS. SOLNESS. Oh, my God—no, not now!

HERDAL. They say they simply must watch the ceremony.

MRS. SOLNESS. Oh, well, I'll have to go in to them. It's my duty.

HILDE. Can't you ask them to go away?

MRS. SOLNESS. No, no, that's impossible. Since they've come, it's my duty to receive them. You stay out here, though, and talk to him when he gets back.

HERDAL. Yes, talk to him and keep him here as long as possible.

MRS. SOLNESS. Yes, do that, please, dear Miss Wangel. Keep him as long as you can.

HILDE. Hadn't you better do it yourself?

MRS. SOLNESS. Oh, dear, yes—it's *my* duty, really. But one has so many duties——

HERDAL, *looking towards the garden*. Here he is.

MRS. SOLNESS. Oh, dear, just as I have to go inside.

HERDAL, *to* HILDE. Don't tell him I'm here.

HILDE. Oh, no. I'll find other things to talk about with the master builder.

MRS. SOLNESS. And keep him here. I think you can do that better than anyone.

MRS. SOLNESS *and* DR. HERDAL *go into the house.* HILDE *remains standing on the verandah.* SOLNESS *comes up the steps from the garden.*

SOLNESS. I'm told there's someone here who wants to speak to me.

HILDE. Yes, master builder. I want to speak to you.

SOLNESS. Oh it's you, Hilde. I was afraid it might be Aline and the doctor.

HILDE. You scare very easily, don't you?

SOLNESS. You think so, do you?

HILDE. Yes. People say you're scared of clambering round on the scaffolding.

SOLNESS. That's different.

HILDE. Then you are afraid of it?

SOLNESS. Yes, I am.

HILDE. Afraid you might fall down and kill yourself?

SOLNESS. No, not that.

HILDE. What, then?

SOLNESS. I am afraid of retribution, Hilde.

HILDE. Of retribution?

Shakes her head.

I don't understand.

SOLNESS. Sit down and I'll tell you something.

HILDE. Yes, tell me. Out with it!

She sits down on a stool by the railing and looks at him expectantly.

SOLNESS *throws his hat on the table.* As you know, I began by building churches.

HILDE *nods.* Yes, I know that.

SOLNESS. When I was a boy, you see, my parents were pious, country people. So I thought building churches was the finest work that a man could choose to do.

HILDE. Yes, yes.

SOLNESS. And I think I may say that I built these humble little churches with such honesty and tenderness and devotion that—that——

HILDE. That——? Well?

SOLNESS. Yes—that I think He ought to have been pleased with me.

HILDE. He? Which he?

SOLNESS. He—Whom the churches were meant for, of course. He Whose honour and glory they were meant to proclaim.

HILDE. I see! But are you so sure that—that He wasn't—well— pleased with you?

SOLNESS, *scornfully. He* pleased with me? How can you talk so foolishly, Hilde? He, who let the troll in me cut loose? He who bade them wait on me day and night, these— these——

HILDE. Demons?

SOLNESS. Yes. And the others. Oh, no, I was made to realize He wasn't pleased with me.

Secretively.

That's why He let the old house be burned down, you see.

HILDE. Was that why?

SOLNESS. Yes, don't you understand? He wanted to give me the chance to be a real master in my own field, and build greater churches to His glory. At first I didn't realize what He wanted. But then, suddenly, it all became clear to me.

HILDE. When was that?

SOLNESS. When I built the church tower up at Lysanger.

HILDE. I thought so.

SOLNESS. You see, Hilde, up there, where I was a stranger, I spent so much time by myself, brooding and puzzling. Then I saw so clearly why He had taken my little children from me. It was so that I should have nothing to bind me. No love or happiness or anything, you see. I was to be a master builder—nothing else. And all my life was to be spent building for Him.

Laughs.

But that wasn't the way it worked out.

HILDE. What did you do?

SOLNESS. First, I examined and tried myself——

HILDE. And then——?

SOLNESS. Then, like Him, I did the impossible.

HILDE. The impossible!

SOLNESS. I could never bear to climb up high before. But that day, I did it.

HILDE *jumps up*. Yes, yes, you did!

SOLNESS. And as I stood high up there, right at the top, and placed the wreath over the weathercock, I said to Him: "Listen to me, mighty One! Henceforth I, too, want to be a free master builder. Free in my field, as You are in Yours. I never want to build churches for You again. Only homes, for people to live in.

HILDE, *her eyes wide and glittering*. That was the song I heard in the air.

SOLNESS. But He took His revenge later.

HILDE. What do you mean by that?

SOLNESS *looks at her dejectedly*. Building homes for people isn't worth twopence, Hilde.

HILDE. How can you say that now?

SOLNESS. Because I realize now that people have no use for the homes they live in. They can't be happy in them. And a home wouldn't have been any use to me, even if I'd had one.

Laughs quietly and savagely.

So when all the accounts are closed, I have built nothing really. And sacrificed nothing. It all adds up to nothing. Nothing. Nothing.

HILDE. And are you never going to build again?

SOLNESS. Yes, now I shall begin!

HILDE. What will you build? What? Tell me. Quickly!

SOLNESS. Now I shall build the only place where I believe that happiness can exist.

HILDE *looks at him*. Master builder—you mean our castles in the air.

SOLNESS. Yes. Castles in the air.

HILDE. I'm afraid you'll get giddy before we've climbed half-way.

SOLNESS. Not when I can go hand in hand with you, Hilde.

HILDE. Just with me? Won't there be others?

SOLNESS. What others? What do you mean?

HILDE. Oh—that Kaja at the desk. Poor thing, aren't you going to take her along too?

SOLNESS. Oh. So that's what Aline and you were sitting here talking about?

HILDE. Is it true, or isn't it?

SOLNESS, *angrily*. I won't answer that. You must believe in me unquestioningly.

HILDE. I have believed in you for ten years. Unquestioningly.

SOLNESS. You must go on believing in me.

HILDE. Then let me see you stand up there, high and free!

SOLNESS, *heavily*. Oh, Hilde! One can't do things like that every day.

HILDE, *passionately*. But I want you to! I want you to!
Pleadingly.
Just once more, master builder! Do the impossible again!

SOLNESS *looks deeply into her eyes*. If I try, Hilde, I shall stand up there and speak to Him the way I spoke to Him before.

HILDE, *in mounting excitement*. What will you tell Him?

SOLNESS. I shall say to Him: "Hear me, mighty Master! Judge me as you will. But from now on I shall build only one thing—the most beautiful thing in the world——"

HILDE. Yes, yes, yes!

SOLNESS. "I shall build it together with a princess, whom I love——"

HILDE. Yes, tell Him that! Tell Him that!

SOLNESS. I will. And then I shall say to Him: "Now I go down, to take her in my arms, and kiss her——"

HILDE. Many times! Tell Him that!

SOLNESS. "Many, many times," I shall tell Him.

HILDE. And then——?

SOLNESS. Then I shall wave my hat—and come down to the ground—and do as I told Him.

HILDE *flings her arms wide.* Now I see you again as you were when I heard that song in the air!

SOLNESS *looks at her with bowed head.* How have you come to be what you are, Hilde?

HILDE. How did you make me what I am?

SOLNESS, *curtly, decisively.* The princess shall have her castle.

HILDE, *jubilant, claps her hands.* Oh, master builder! My beautiful, beautiful castle! Our castle in the air!

SOLNESS. Built on a true foundation.

In the street, a crowd of people has gathered; they can be indistinctly glimpsed through the trees. A brass band can be distantly heard from behind the new house. MRS. SOLNESS, *with a fur collar round her neck,* DR. HERDAL, *carrying her white shawl on his arm, and several* LADIES *come out on to the verandah. At the same moment,* RAGNAR BROVIK *comes up from the garden.*

MRS. SOLNESS, *to* RAGNAR. Are we going to have music, too?

RAGNAR. Yes. It's the Builders' Association.

To SOLNESS.

The foreman asked me to tell you he's ready to go up with the wreath.

SOLNESS *takes his hat.* Good. I'll go down there myself.

MRS. SOLNESS, *anxiously.* What are you going to do down there, Halvard?

SOLNESS, *curtly.* I must be down below with the men.

MRS. SOLNESS. Yes—down below, of course. Down below.

SOLNESS. I always do it. It's my everyday custom.

He goes down the steps and out through the garden.

MRS. SOLNESS *shouts over the railing after him.* Do tell the man to be careful when he climbs up! Promise me that, Halvard!

HERDAL, *to* MRS. SOLNESS. There, you see, I was right. He's put these mad ideas out of his head.

MRS. SOLNESS. Oh, what a relief! Two of our men have fallen.
And they were both killed instantaneously.

Turns to HILDE.

Thank you so much for holding on to him, Miss Wangel.
I'd never have been able to budge him.

HERDAL. Yes, yes, Miss Wangel, I'm sure you know how to
hold on to someone when you really want to.

MRS. SOLNESS *and* DR. HERDAL *go over to the* LADIES, *who
are standing by the steps and looking out across the garden.*

HILDE *remains standing by the railing downstage.* RAGNAR
goes across to her.

RAGNAR, *quietly, trying not to laugh.* Do you see all those
young men down in the street, Miss—er——?

HILDE. Yes.

RAGNAR. They're my fellow apprentices, come to watch the
master.

HILDE. What do they want to watch him for?

RAGNAR. They want to see him not dare to climb up his own
house.

HILDE. Is that what the little boys want?

RAGNAR. He's kept us down for so long. Now we want to see
him keeping himself down for a change.

HILDE. You won't. Not this time.

RAGNAR *smiles.* Oh? Where shall we see him, then?

HILDE. High, high up by the weathercock! That's where
you'll see him!

RAGNAR *laughs.* Him? Not likely!

HILDE. He intends to climb to the top. And you'll see him
there.

RAGNAR. Oh, he intends to, I'm sure. But he can't, he just
can't. He'd get giddy long before he'd climbed halfway.
He'd have to crawl down again on his hands and knees.

HERDAL, *pointing.* Look. There's the foreman climbing up.

MRS. SOLNESS. He's got the wreath, too. Oh, I do hope he
takes care.

RAGNAR *stares incredulously and shouts.* But that's not——!

HILDE *cries ecstatically*. It's the master builder himself!

MRS. SOLNESS *screams in terror*. Yes, it's Halvard! Oh, my God, my God! Halvard! Halvard!

HERDAL. Ssh! Don't shout to him!

MRS. SOLNESS, *almost out of her mind*. I must go to him! I must make him come down!

HERDAL, *restraining her*. Stand still, all of you! Don't make a sound!

HILDE, *standing motionless, follows* SOLNESS *with her eyes*. He's climbing and climbing! Higher, always higher! Look! Just look!

RAGNAR, *breathlessly*. He must turn back now! He must!

HILDE. He's climbing, climbing! Soon he'll be up!

MRS. SOLNESS. Oh, I shall die of fright. I can't bear to look.

HERDAL. Don't look up at him, then.

HILDE. There he is on top of the scaffolding! Right at the top!

HERDAL. Don't move, anyone! Do you hear?

HILDE, *quiet but jubilant*. At last! At last! Now I see him great and free again!

RAGNAR, *almost speechless*. But this is——

HILDE. That's how I've seen him all these ten years. How squarely he stands! Frightfully exciting, though! Look at him! Now he's hanging the wreath over the spire!

RAGNAR. But—I can't believe it! This is impossible!

HILDE. Yes! That's what he's doing now! The impossible!

With the enigmatic expression in her eyes.

Can you see anyone else up there with him?

RAGNAR. There's no-one else.

HILDE. Oh, yes! There's someone he's arguing with.

RAGNAR. You're mistaken.

HILDE. Perhaps you can't hear a song in the air, either?

RAGNAR. It must be the wind in the treetops.

HILDE. I hear a song. A mighty song!

Cries jubilantly.

Look, look! Now he's waving his hat! He's waving to us

down here! Oh, wave back to him! He's done it at last, he's done it!

She tears the white shawl from the doctor, waves it, and cries up.

Hurrah for Solness! Hurrah for the master builder!

HERDAL. Stop it! Stop it, for God's sake——!

The LADIES *on the verandah wave their handkerchiefs, and the shouting is taken up in the street. Suddenly there is a silence; then the crowd utters a shriek of terror. A human body and some planks and poles can be indistinctly glimpsed falling through the trees.*

MRS. SOLNESS *and the* LADIES, *simultaneously.* He's falling! He's falling!

MRS. SOLNESS *staggers and falls back unconscious. The* LADIES *pick her up amid noise and confusion. The people in the street break down the fence and storm into the garden.* DR. HERDAL *hurries down. Short pause.*

HILDE, *still staring upwards, as though turned to stone.*

My master builder!

RAGNAR *supports himself, trembling, against the railing.* He must have been smashed to pieces. Killed outright.

ONE OF THE LADIES, *while* MRS. SOLNESS *is carried into the house.* Run down to the doctor——

RAGNAR. I can't move a step——

ANOTHER LADY. Call down to someone, then.

RAGNAR *tries to shout.* How is he? Is he alive?

A VOICE, *from down in the garden.* The master builder is dead.

OTHER VOICES, *nearer.* His head was crushed. He fell into the stonepit.

HILDE *turns to* RAGNAR, *and says quietly.* Now I can't see him up there any longer.

RAGNAR. This is terrible. He hadn't the strength after all.

HILDE, *in quiet, crazed triumph.* But he got right to the top! And I heard harps in the air!

Waves her shawl upwards and cries wildly and ecstatically.

My—my master builder!

John Gabriel Borkman

INTRODUCTION

JOHN GABRIEL BORKMAN was Ibsen's last play but one; he wrote it in 1896, at the age of sixty-eight. Its theme, like that of the strange, abbreviated experiment which followed, *When We Dead Awaken,* is what Ibsen himself, in one of his most merciless phrases, called "the coldness of the heart." Edvard Munch described JOHN GABRIEL BORKMAN as "the most powerful winter landscape in Scandinavian art."

The plot of JOHN GABRIEL BORKMAN is based on a story which Ibsen had heard long ago in his student days in Christiania. In 1851 a high-ranking army officer was charged with embezzlement. At first he denied the charge, but then, like Old Ekdal before the beginning of *The Wild Duck,* he unsuccessfully tried to shoot himself. He was sentenced to four years' penal servitude and, when he was released, shortly before Ibsen returned to Christiania as theatrical director, he shut himself up in his house and spent the rest of his life brooding in solitude, unable even to speak to his wife. Later, in the 1880s, a great scandal occurred at Arendal; a bank director speculated and embezzled his clients' money and was sent to prison. Bankruptcy was a subject that held a painful interest for Ibsen, for when he had been seven this fate had befallen his father.

In the year in which the officer was charged, Ibsen, then aged twenty-three, had written a poem in no way connected with that incident, but which anticipated many of the sentiments that, nearly half a century later, he was to put into Borkman's mouth. It is called "The Miner," and it tells of the fascination the poet felt for the darkness of the subterranean pit, and of his conviction that the answer to the secrets of life lay there.

Groan and thunder, mountain wall,
Before my heavy hammer blow.
Downwards I must carve my way
Till I hear the iron ore ring.

Deep in the mountain's desolate night
The rich treasure beckons me.
Diamonds and precious stones
Among the red branches of the gold.

And in the darkness there is peace.
Peace and rest for eternity.
Heavy hammer, break me the way
To the heart-chamber of what lies hidden there . . .

When I first entered here
I thought in my innocence:
"The spirits of the dark will solve for me
Life's endless riddles."

No spirit has yet taught me that strange answer.
No ray has shone from the depths.

Was I wrong? Does this path
Not lead to the light?
But the light blinds my eyes
If I seek it in the mountains.

No, I must go down into the dark.
Eternal peace lies there.
Heavy hammer, break me the way
To the heart-chamber of what lies hidden there.

Hammer blow on hammer blow
Till the last day of life.
No ray of morning shines.
No sun of hope rises.

It is interesting that, when Ibsen recalled the trial which had so impressed him in his youth, he should at the same time have taken up the theme of the poem which he had written in the year the tragedy took place.

Another memory from fifty years before found its way into the play. As a young man Ibsen had a friend named Vilhelm Foss, an old copying clerk who had once published a collection of verses and still cherished the hope that he might some day achieve poetic fame. Ibsen had remembered Foss when planning *The Lady from the Sea* eight years previously, for we find a reference to him in the first rough notes for that play. In the event, Ibsen found no place for him in *The Lady from the Sea*, but he often retained a discarded character for use in a subsequent play, so that Vilhelm Foss finally achieved immortality as Vilhelm Foldal in JOHN GABRIEL BORKMAN.

A more recent and painful memory left its mark on the play. Shortly before Ibsen wrote BORKMAN, his only son, Sigurd, to whom he was deeply attached, had left home to get married. The household must have seemed empty without him, and one imagines this was in Ibsen's mind when he wrote the scene in which Erhart leaves his parents to elope with Mrs. Wilton. The theme of young people rebelling against the domination of their parents had, of course, long been a favourite with Ibsen; we find it, for example, in *The Wild Duck* (Gregers Werle) and in *Ghosts*.

The danger of a loveless marriage was another theme to which Ibsen constantly returned (*Love's Comedy, The Pillars of Society, A Doll's House, The Lady from the Sea, Hedda Gabler*); so was that of the man who sacrifices the happiness of his wife or the woman he loves for the sake of a cause or a personal ambition (*Brand, An Enemy of the People, The Master Builder, When We Dead Awaken*). Ibsen's own marriage, though not unhappy, seems to have been more or less loveless; and he was obsessed by the feeling that, in choosing the life of an author, he had sacrificed his own chances of happiness and, to some extent, those of his wife.

Formally, the last act of JOHN GABRIEL BORKMAN marks a return towards the kind of epic-poetic-symbolic drama which Ibsen had perfected to a high degree in *Brand* and *Peer*

Gynt thirty years before. After completing *Peer Gynt* in 1867, he had deliberately abandoned poetry as a dramatic medium; in a letter to Edmund Gosse, dated January 15, 1874, explaining why he had chosen to write *Emperor and Galilean* in prose, he said: "I wished to produce on the reader the impression that what he was reading was something that had actually happened . . . We are no longer living in the age of Shakespeare . . . What I desired to depict was human beings, and therefore I would not let them talk in 'the language of the gods.'" He had done his best to remain faithful to this resolve and, although there are moments in every play he wrote in which we sense the buried river beneath the surface, it is not, I think, until the final act of JOHN GABRIEL BORKMAN that we again find the recorder of realistic dialogue being edged aside by the symbolist and the poet. In *When We Dead Awaken* this process was carried a stage further.

Ibsen's early drafts show that he originally gave Borkman the single Christian name of Jens, and then altered it successively to Jens Jørgen, Jens Adolf, Jens Gabriel, John, and, finally, John Gabriel. He told his doctor, Edvard Bull, that he decided on this last combination because the English name John would suggest big business, while that of Gabriel, the archangel, would signify power and glory.

In this first draft of the play, the second act opens with Borkman playing the final bars of "a piece by Beethoven" on the violin, and Frida accompanying him on the piano. But Ibsen took away Borkman's violin, so as to allow him to pace up and down the room, and altered the music from Beethoven to Saint-Saëns' *Danse Macabre*, which was especially popular in Norway during the summer of 1896 and which the young pianist, Hildur Andersen, with whom Ibsen was on terms of close friendship, often played to him.

It is not the purpose of these introductions to interpret the plays; that is something that should be left to individual producers, and few things are more irritating than a translator who tries to saddle a play with a rigid interpretation. Ibsen's plays, like Shakespeare's, are capable of many interpretations; for example, before World War I, Borkman was commonly presented in Scandinavian productions as a Nietzsche-figure; in 1916 as a wartime speculator; in the Thirties he was likened to Ivar Kreuger, the match king, and in the Forties to Hitler. Ibsen did, however, express a strong view as to how the character of Mrs. Borkman should be played—one of the few occasions on which he committed himself on paper about any of his characters. In a letter to a correspondent of the newspaper *Kjøbenhavns Aftenblad,* complaining that Mrs. Borkman's character had been misinterpreted in performance, Ibsen wrote:

"The main point is that Mrs. Borkman loves her husband. She is not at heart a hard or evil woman; she was, to begin with, a loving wife, and has only become hard and evil because she has been deceived. Her husband has deceived her doubly—firstly, in love, and secondly, because she had believed in his genius. It is above all important that the actress should make this clear. If Mrs. Borkman did not love her husband, she would long ago have forgiven him. Despite having been doubly deceived, she still waits for the sick wolf whose tread she hears every day. As he waits for 'the world' to come to him, so she waits for him to come to her. This is made clear in the dialogue, and it is above all else important that the actress who plays Mrs. Borkman should bring out this side of her character."

In the absence of any hard-and-fast international copyright agreement, Ibsen earned little from foreign productions of his plays and relied much on royalties from their sale in book form in Scandinavia. Ever since *The Pillars of Society,* he had, with formidable regularity, completed a play every second autumn, so as to have it in the bookshops in time for the Christmas sales. (The only exception during this period was *An Enemy of the People,* which he wrote the year after *Ghosts.*) His routine was to relax for a year after finishing a play, and then to spend the winter considering plots and ideas, one of which he would work out during the summer. The summer was always his favourite season for writing, at any rate after he left Norway for Italy in 1864.

True to this routine, he had completed *The Master Builder* in October 1892, and *Little Eyolf* in October 1894. William

Archer cannot, therefore, have been surprised when, the following June, Ibsen wrote to him: "I hope I may get down to writing a new play next year. But I don't know for sure—there's so much else I have to attend to which takes up my time." However, his fears, if he really entertained them, proved unjustified, for six months later, on April 24, 1896, he wrote to Georg Brandes that he could not travel to England, as Brandes had suggested, firstly because he did not know enough English, and secondly because he was "busy preparing a new work, and I don't want to put off writing it for longer than necessary." On July 11 he began the actual writing of his first draft. On July 27 he wrote to his publisher: "My play progresses with surprising speed and ease. Thanks to the more than southerly heat this summer, I am able to work uninterruptedly." By August 26 he had completed his first draft, and the next day he began to revise it. This took seven and a half weeks. By October 18 the final version was ready to go to press, and on December 15 JOHN GABRIEL BORKMAN was published by Gyldendals in Copenhagen in a first printing of 15,000 copies—an enormous edition for the Scandinavia of those days. (Since *The Pillars of Society,* nineteen years before, 10,000 had been the normal first printing for Ibsen's plays.)

On the day before publication (December 14, 1896), JOHN GABRIEL BORKMAN was read in public in London (in Norwegian) to secure the English copyright. It was first performed on January 10, 1897, when the Finnish and Swedish theatres in Helsinki staged it simultaneously.[1] On January 16 it was produced at Frankfurt-am-Main. The German censor had demanded the excision of two passages, Ella's remark in Act II about "the sin for which there is no forgiveness," and Mrs. Wilton's in Act IV about the importance of Erhart's having another girl to fall back on if he should tire of her, or she of him. Despite the censor, the performance was a success. Three days later, the play received its Norwegian premi̇ère, under strange circumstances. The Swedish actor, August Lindberg, had secured the rights to perform JOHN

---

[1] Finland being a bilingual country, a Swedish theatre has long existed in Helsinki for the benefit of the Swedish-speaking minority.

GABRIEL BORKMAN in the Norwegian provinces, and managed to stage his première at the little town of Drammen, about thirty miles from Christiania, on January 19, six days before the Christiania Theatre were ready with theirs. To annoy the Christiania Theatre, with the management of which he was on bad terms, Lindberg ran special trains from the capital to Drammen, and so drew off a large proportion of the Christiania Theatre's public. Before the end of the month, the play had also been staged in Stockholm, Berlin (where Hermann Nissen played Borkman with a make-up suggesting both Bjørnson and Ibsen, and the play was coolly received), and Copenhagen.

In London that winter, Ellen Terry tried to interest Henry Irving in the role of Borkman. He was ill, and "she took advantage of his enforced immobility by reading to him the first two acts of JOHN GABRIEL BORKMAN; he read the third to her. 'What a play!' he commented, with an inflection that left no doubt as to his opinion of it."[2] We are not told which of them, if either, read the fourth act. In any event, Londoners had to wait until May 3 before they could see the play. On that afternoon, it was performed at the Strand Theatre by the association called the New Century Theatre. Borkman was played by W. H. Vernon, Mrs. Borkman by Geneviève Ward, Ella by Elizabeth Robins, Erhart by Martin Harvey, Mrs. Wilton by Mrs. Beerbohm Tree, Foldal by James Welch, and Frida by Dora Barton. It seems to have been a very bad performance; even Bernard Shaw, anxious to encourage people to go and see it, could find little to praise. After denouncing the poverty of the sets ("I beg the New Century Theatre, when the next Ibsen play is ready for mounting, to apply to me for assistance. If I have a ten-pound note, they shall have it; if not, I can at least lend them a couple of decent chairs") he continued:

"I regret to say that the shortcomings of the scenery were not mitigated by imaginative and ingenious stage management. Mr. Vernon's stage management is very actor-like; that is to say, it is directed, not to secure the maximum of illusion for the play, but the maximum of fairness in distributing good

[2] *Henry Irving,* by Laurence Irving (London, 1951).

places on the stage to the members of the cast . . . The tra-
ditional stage management of tragedy ignores realism . . . it
lends itself to people talking at each other rhetorically from
opposite sides of the stage, taking long sweeping walks up to
their 'points', striking attitudes in the focus of the public vision
with an artificiality which, instead of being concealed, is not
only disclosed but insisted on, and being affected in all their
joints by emotions which a fine comedian conveys by the
faintest possible inflexion of tone or eyebrow . . . Mr. Vernon's Borkman was not ill acted; only, as it was not Ibsen's
Borkman, but the very reverse and negation of him, the better
Mr. Vernon acted, the worse it was for the play . . . Mr.
Vernon was as earthly and sane as a man need be until he
went for his walk in the snow, and a Borkman who is that is
necessarily a trifle dull." Shaw thought Elizabeth Robins "too
young and too ferociously individualistic" for the part of Ella;
and of Geneviève Ward as Mrs. Borkman, he wrote: "The
truth is, her tragic style derived from Ristori, was not made
for Ibsen." James Welch, "though his scene in the second act
was a triumph, made a fundamental mistake in the third.
. . . He played the heartbroken old man pretending to laugh
—a descendant of the clown who jokes in the arena while
his child is dying at home—and so wrecked what would otherwise have been the best piece of character work of the
afternoon." Martin Harvey, as Erhart, "shewed, as we all
knew he would shew, considerable stage talent and more than
ordinary dramatic intelligence; but in the first act he was not
the embarrassed young gentleman of Ibsen, but rather the
'soaring human boy' imagined by Mr. Chadband." The best
performances, in Shaw's view, came from Mrs. Beerbohm
Tree as Mrs. Wilton and Dora Barton as Frida—"but then
these two parts are comparatively easy." Other critics were,
as can be imagined, even less favourable.

JOHN GABRIEL BORKMAN was first performed in America
on November 18, 1897, when it was produced by the Cri-
terion Independent Theatre in New York. Borkman was
played by E. J. Henley, Mrs. Borkman by Maude Banks, Ella
by Ann Warrington, Erhart by John Blair, Mrs. Wilton by
Carrie Keeler, Foldal by Albert Brunning, and Frida by Dorothy Usner. This appears to have been a better production

than the one in London; the *New York Dramatic Mirror* called Henley's performance "a memorable achievement." In the same month, Lugné-Poe, a great Ibsen enthusiast, staged the play at his Théâtre de l'Oeuvre in Paris. Prague, Vienna, and Bologna soon followed suit, and by 1909, JOHN GABRIEL BORKMAN had reached even Tokyo. Ella Rentheim was one of the many roles in which Eleonora Duse excelled; Max Reinhardt, as a young actor in Berlin, scored one of his greatest successes as Vilhelm Foldal; Cathleen Nesbitt played Frida Foldal in 1910 in London, and Mrs. Wilton in 1911; and John Gielgud made one of his first professional appearances on the stage as Erhart Borkman, at Oxford at the age of nineteen. Sir Laurence Olivier chose the role of John Gabriel Borkman for his television début in 1958, in a production for which this translation was specially commissioned.

M.M.

CHARACTERS

JOHN GABRIEL BORKMAN, sometime banker
MRS. GUNHILD BORKMAN, his wife
ERHART BORKMAN, their son, a student
MISS ELLA RENTHEIM, Mrs. Borkman's twin sister
MRS. FANNY WILTON
VILHELM FOLDAL, supernumerary clerk in a Government Office
FRIDA FOLDAL, his daughter
MRS. BORKMAN'S MAID

The action takes place during a winter evening in the Rentheim family mansion outside the Norwegian capital.

This translation was first performed on November 19, 1958, in an H. M. Tennent Globe Production for Associated Television, with the following cast:

JOHN GABRIEL BORKMAN	Laurence Olivier
MRS. BORKMAN	Irene Worth
ERHART BORKMAN	Anthony Valentine
ELLA RENTHEIM	Pamela Brown
MRS. WILTON	Maxine Audley
VILHELM FOLDAL	George Relph
FRIDA FOLDAL	Anne Castaldini
MAID	Carmel McSharry

Produced by Casper Wrede
Settings by Richard Negri

ACT ONE

MRS. BORKMAN'S *sitting room, furnished with old-fashioned and faded splendour. At the back, an open sliding door leads to a garden room, with windows and a glass door. Through these can be seen the garden, with snow driving in the evening dusk. In the side wall on the right is a door leading from the hall. Further downstage is a large, old-fashioned iron stove, in which a fire is burning. On the left, some way back, a smaller, single door. Downstage on the same side is a window, hidden by thick curtains. Between the window and the door is a sofa with a horsehair cover; in front of it stands a table with a cloth on it. On the table is a lighted lamp, with a shade. By the stove stands a high-backed armchair.*

MRS. GUNHILD BORKMAN *is seated on the sofa, crocheting. She is an elderly lady of coldly aristocratic appearance, with a stiff demeanour and immobile features. Her rich hair is heavily streaked with grey. Delicate, transparent hands. She is wearing a thick, dark, silk dress, which was once elegant but is now somewhat worn and tired-looking. A woollen shawl covers her shoulders. For a few moments she sits upright and motionless at her crocheting. Then the sound of bells is heard from a sleigh passing outside.* MRS. BORKMAN *listens.*

MRS. BORKMAN. Erhart! At last!

She gets up and peers out through the curtains. Looks disappointed, sits down again on the sofa, and resumes her work. A few moments later, the MAID *comes in through the door with a visiting card on a small tray.*

MRS. BORKMAN, *quickly.* Was that Mr. Erhart?

MAID. No, madam. But there's a lady out in the——

MRS. BORKMAN *puts down her work.* Oh, Mrs. Wilton——

MAID. No, it's a strange lady.

MRS. BORKMAN *reaches out her hand for the card.* Let me see. *Reads it, rises quickly to her feet and looks coldly at the* MAID.

Are you sure it's me she wants to speak to?

MAID. Yes, I understood she meant you, madam.

MRS. BORKMAN. Did she ask to speak with Mrs. Borkman?

MAID. Oh yes, madam.

MRS. BORKMAN. Very well. Tell her I am at home.

The MAID *opens the door for the visitor, and goes out.* MISS ELLA RENTHEIM *enters the room. In appearance she resembles her sister, but her face bears evidence of suffering rather than of hardness. It still retains traces of her early beauty, strong and full of character. Her abundant and once black hair is combed up in natural waves from her forehead, and is completely white. She is dressed in black velvet, with hat and fur-lined coat of the same material. For a moment the two sisters stand in silence looking searchingly at each other. Each seems to be waiting for the other to speak first.*

ELLA, *remaining near the door.* I know you're surprised to see me, Gunhild.

MRS. BORKMAN *stands rigidly upright between the sofa and table, pressing her fingers against the cloth.* You've made a mistake. The bailiff lives in the side wing, you know.

ELLA. It's not the bailiff I've come to see today.

MRS. BORKMAN. You want to speak to me?

ELLA. Yes. I must have a few words with you.

MRS. BORKMAN *moves towards her.* Hm. Well, sit down, then.

ELLA. Thank you, I'll stand.

MRS. BORKMAN. As you please. Unfasten your coat, anyway.

ELLA, *unbuttoning her coat*. Yes, it's very hot in here.

MRS. BORKMAN. I am always cold.

ELLA *stands for a moment and looks at her, her arm resting on the back of the armchair.* Yes, Gunhild, it's nearly eight years now since we saw each other last.

MRS. BORKMAN, *coldly*. Since we spoke, at any rate.

ELLA. Since we spoke, yes. You must have seen me when I had to come out here on my annual visit to the bailiff.

MRS. BORKMAN. Once or twice, perhaps.

ELLA. I have caught a glimpse of you, too, once or twice. In that window.

MRS. BORKMAN. You must have sharp eyes to see through the curtains, Ella. But the last time we spoke was in here——

ELLA. Yes, I know.

MRS. BORKMAN. The week before they let him out.

ELLA. Oh, don't, Gunhild, don't!

MRS. BORKMAN. It was the week before John—before Borkman was released from prison.

ELLA, *coming towards her*. I haven't forgotten. But I can't bear to think about it.

MRS. BORKMAN. And yet one is never allowed to think about anything else—ever. I don't believe it—I can't—I cannot understand that anything so terrible could happen to a family. And to *our* family. Such a noble family as ours!

ELLA. Oh, Gunhild—it wasn't only our family that suffered. There were so many others.

MRS. BORKMAN. Oh yes—but I don't care so much about them. All they lost was money or pieces of paper—but we—I—and Erhart! Only a child at the time! The shame he brought on us, who were innocent—the disgrace, the terrible disgrace! And we were utterly ruined!

ELLA, *carefully*. Tell me, Gunhild. How does he take it?

MRS. BORKMAN. Erhart, you mean?

ELLA. No. He. How does he take it?

MRS. BORKMAN. Do you think I ask him?

ELLA. Ask? Surely you don't need to *ask* him——?

MRS. BORKMAN. Do you think I talk to him? Or see him?

ELLA. Don't you even see him?

MRS. BORKMAN. A man who spent five years in prison? Oh, the disgrace! And remember what the name of John Gabriel Borkman meant once! No, no, no—I shall never see him again, never!

ELLA. You are hard, Gunhild.

MRS. BORKMAN. Towards him, yes.

ELLA. But he is your husband.

MRS. BORKMAN. Didn't he tell the court that I had started him on the path to ruin? That I spent too much money——

ELLA. Wasn't there some truth in that?

MRS. BORKMAN. But he wanted it that way! He wanted everything to be so absurdly luxurious——

ELLA. I know. But shouldn't you have restrained him?

MRS. BORKMAN. Was I to know it wasn't his own money he was giving me to squander? And wasn't he ten times as extravagant as I?

ELLA, *quietly.* Well, I suppose he had to keep up his position.

MRS. BORKMAN. Oh yes! He always said we had to "put on a show"! Oh, he put on a show all right! Drove a four-in-hand, as though he were a king. Made people bow and scrape to him, the way they would to a king.
Laughs.
And they called him by his Christian names—throughout the country—just as though he *was* the King. "John Gabriel." Oh, he was a great man in their eyes, was John Gabriel.

ELLA. He *was* a great man then, Gunhild.

MRS. BORKMAN. So it seemed. But he never said one word to me about his real position. He never hinted where he took his money from.

ELLA. I don't suppose any of the others suspected.

MRS. BORKMAN. Oh, the others! But it was his duty to tell

me the truth. And he never did. He simply lied—lied to me endlessly——

ELLA. No, Gunhild. He may have concealed the truth from you. But he didn't lie.

MRS. BORKMAN. Call it what you like. It comes to the same thing. But then it all crashed about our ears. The whole magnificent edifice.

ELLA, *to herself*. Yes, everything crashed—for him—and for others.

MRS. BORKMAN. But I tell you, Ella, I shall not give up. I shall find redress somehow. You can be sure of that.

ELLA. Redress? What do you mean?

MRS. BORKMAN. Redress for our name, our honour, our fortunes. For the wreck that's been made of my life. I've got a trick up my sleeve. You'll see. Someone who will redeem everything that *he* defiled!

ELLA. Gunhild!

MRS. BORKMAN. Someone who will right all the wrongs his father did to me.

ELLA. You mean Erhart?

MRS. BORKMAN. Yes, Erhart—my son. He will know how to restore our family, our house, our name. Everything that *can* be restored.

ELLA. How do you expect him to achieve this?

MRS. BORKMAN. It'll happen some way. I don't quite know how. But it must and shall happen sometime. Tell me, Ella—honestly—hasn't this been in your mind ever since Erhart was a child?

ELLA. No, I can't say it has.

MRS. BORKMAN. Then why did you take him and look after him?

ELLA. You weren't able to, Gunhild.

MRS. BORKMAN. Oh no. I wasn't able to. And his father—the law wouldn't let him. Oh, he was nicely tucked away from all responsibility.

ELLA. Oh—how can you?

MRS. BORKMAN. And you? How could *you* bring up the child

of a—— John Gabriel's child? Just as though he were your own son—take him away from me—and keep him with you, till he was nearly grown up? Why did you do it, Ella?

ELLA. I grew to love him so dearly.

MRS. BORKMAN. More than I—his mother?

ELLA. That I can't judge. And Erhart was rather a weak child.

MRS. BORKMAN. Erhart—weak?

ELLA. I thought so—at the time, anyway. And the air over there on the west coast is so much milder than it is here, as you know.

MRS. BORKMAN *smiles bitterly.* Hm. Is it? Oh yes, you've certainly done a great deal for Erhart. Well, you've been able to afford it. You were lucky, Ella. You managed to get back everything you'd invested.

ELLA. Not because of anything I did. I didn't know until years later that my investments in the bank had been saved.

MRS. BORKMAN. Well, I don't understand these things. I merely point out that you were lucky. But when you took it on yourself to bring up Erhart for me—what was your motive then?

ELLA. My motive——?

MRS. BORKMAN. Yes, you must have had some motive. What did you want to make of him? What did you want to turn him into?

ELLA. I wanted to give Erhart a chance to find happiness.

MRS. BORKMAN, *scornfully.* Psh. People in our position have more important things to do than bother about happiness.

ELLA. What do you mean?

MRS. BORKMAN. Erhart's first duty is to shine so bright that no one in this land will remember the shadow his father cast over me—and my son.

ELLA. Tell me, Gunhild—is that the aim to which Erhart has pledged his life?

MRS. BORKMAN. I sincerely hope so.

ELLA. Or isn't it rather an aim to which you have pledged him?

MRS. BORKMAN. I and Erhart always have the same aims.

ELLA. You are very sure of your son, aren't you, Gunhild?

MRS. BORKMAN. Yes, I thank God I am.

ELLA. Then you must be happy, in spite of everything.

MRS. BORKMAN. I am, as far as that goes. But then, every moment, Ella, those memories blow into my heart like a bitter wind.

ELLA. Gunhild, I might as well come to the point. There's something I have to talk to you about.

MRS. BORKMAN. Yes?

ELLA. Erhart doesn't live out here with you and . . . with you, does he?

MRS. BORKMAN. Obviously Erhart cannot live out here with me. He has to live in town.

ELLA. Yes, he has told me so in his letters.

MRS. BORKMAN. He has to, for his studies. But he comes out to me for a while every evening.

ELLA. Yes—well, could I talk with him, now, then?

MRS. BORKMAN. He hasn't come yet. But I expect him any moment.

ELLA. But, Gunhild, he must be here. I can hear him up-stairs.

MRS. BORKMAN, *with a quick glance*. Up in the great room?

ELLA. Yes. I've heard him walking up there ever since I ar-rived.

MRS. BORKMAN. That isn't Erhart, Ella.

ELLA. Not Erhart?

Beginning to suspect.

Who is it, then?

MRS. BORKMAN. He.

ELLA, *quietly*. Borkman. John Gabriel Borkman.

MRS. BORKMAN. He walks up and down like that. From morn-ing till night. Day after day.

ELLA. I had heard rumours, of course——

MRS. BORKMAN. I daresay people talk a good deal about us.

ELLA. Erhart hinted in his letters that his father spends most of his time alone up there, and you down here.

MRS. BORKMAN. Yes. That's how we've lived, Ella. Ever since they let him out, and sent him home to me. Eight years.

ELLA. But—I didn't think it could be possible——

MRS. BORKMAN. That is how it is. And it can never be otherwise.

ELLA. It must be a terrible existence, Gunhild.

MRS. BORKMAN. I don't think I can stand it much longer.

ELLA. I can imagine——

MRS. BORKMAN. Hearing his footsteps up there the whole time. From early morning until late at night. They sound so loud down here.

ELLA. Yes.

MRS. BORKMAN. I often feel as though I had a sick wolf padding in a cage up there in the great room. Right above my head.

Listens and whispers.

Listen, Ella! Listen! To and fro, to and fro, the wolf pads.

ELLA, *gently.* Couldn't you do something about it, Gunhild?

MRS. BORKMAN. He has never made any move towards me.

ELLA. Couldn't you make the first move?

MRS. BORKMAN. I? After all he has done to me? No, thank you. Let the wolf pad in his cage.

ELLA. It's too hot for me in here. I will take my coat off after all.

ELLA *takes off her hat and coat.*

MRS. BORKMAN. Well, I did ask you.

ELLA. Don't you ever meet him outside the house?

MRS. BORKMAN *laughs bitterly.* At parties, you mean?

ELLA. I mean when he goes for a walk.

MRS. BORKMAN. He never goes out.

ELLA. Not even when it's dark?

MRS. BORKMAN. No. His cape and hat hang there in the cupboard. In the hall—you know——

ELLA, *to herself*. The cupboard we used to play in as children——

MRS. BORKMAN *nods*. Sometimes—late at night—I hear him come down to put them on and go out. But he always stops halfway down the stairs—and turns—and goes back to his room.

ELLA, *quietly*. Don't any of his old friends ever come to see him?

MRS. BORKMAN. He has no old friends.

ELLA. He had so many.

MRS. BORKMAN. Ha! He rid himself of them all right. He was dear to his friends, was John Gabriel Borkman.

ELLA. Yes, I suppose so.

MRS. BORKMAN, *vehemently*. Though I must say it's mean and paltry and contemptible of people to attach so much importance to the little loss they sustained through him. After all, it was only money.

ELLA. So he lives up there, completely alone.

MRS. BORKMAN. I have heard there's an old copyist or bank clerk who visits him now and again.

ELLA. Ah yes. That must be Foldal. I know they've been friends since boyhood.

MRS. BORKMAN. I believe so. I don't know anything else about him. He never mixed with us. In the days when we mixed with people.

ELLA. But now he comes to see Borkman?

MRS. BORKMAN. Yes, he can't afford to be particular. Of course, he only comes after dark.

ELLA. Foldal—wasn't he one of the people who lost their money when the bank failed?

MRS. BORKMAN. I seem to remember he did lose some money. Nothing to talk about.

ELLA. It was all he had.

MRS. BORKMAN *smiles*. Oh, but dear God, what he had! It was nothing—only a few pounds. Not worth mentioning.

ELLA. It wasn't mentioned, either, was it, at the trial? By Foldal, I mean.

MRS. BORKMAN. Anyway, I can tell you Erhart has more than compensated him for the little he lost.

ELLA. Erhart! How did he manage to do that?

MRS. BORKMAN. He's taken Foldal's youngest daughter under his wing. Helped her with her reading, so that she'll be able to make something of herself, and support herself when she's older. You see! That's a great deal more than her father could ever have done for her.

ELLA. Yes, her father must be having a hard time of it now.

MRS. BORKMAN. And Erhart's arranged for her to study music. She's already become so good at it that she's able to come up—go upstairs and play for him.

ELLA. So he still likes music?

MRS. BORKMAN. I suppose he does. And he has the piano you sent out here when—before he came back.

ELLA. And she plays to him?

MRS. BORKMAN. Yes, now and again. In the evenings. Erhart arranged that, too.

ELLA. But doesn't that mean the poor girl has to walk all the way from town and back again?

MRS. BORKMAN. No, Erhart's arranged for her to lodge with a lady who lives near here. A Mrs. Wilton——

ELLA, *suddenly alert.* Mrs. Wilton?

MRS. BORKMAN. A very rich lady. You don't know her.

ELLA. I've heard her name. Mrs. Fanny Wilton, isn't it?

MRS. BORKMAN. Yes, that's right.

ELLA. Erhart's mentioned her several times in his letters. Does she live out here now?

MRS. BORKMAN. Yes, she's rented a villa here. She moved out of town some while ago.

ELLA. They say—she's said to be divorced.

MRS. BORKMAN. I believe her husband died several years ago.

ELLA. Yes, but they were divorced. He divorced her.

MRS. BORKMAN. He left her. It wasn't her fault.

ELLA. Do you know her well, Gunhild?

MRS. BORKMAN. Yes, quite well. She lives nearby and calls occasionally.

ELLA. And you like her?

MRS. BORKMAN. She's a woman of very shrewd judgment. She understands Erhart. All his thoughts, all his feelings. And of course she's come to idolise him—as one must.

ELLA. Perhaps she knows Erhart even better than she knows you?

MRS. BORKMAN. Yes, he used to meet her quite often in town. Before she came to live out here.

ELLA, *involuntarily.* And yet she moved away from town?

MRS. BORKMAN *looks sharply at her.* Yet——? What do you mean?

ELLA. Mean? Why, good heavens——!

MRS. BORKMAN. You said that in such a curious way. You meant something, Ella.

ELLA. Yes, Gunhild. I did mean something.

MRS. BORKMAN. Well?

ELLA. First I want to tell you that I think I, too, have a kind of claim on Erhart. Perhaps you don't agree?

MRS. BORKMAN. I am hardly in a position to disagree. After all the money you have spent on him——

ELLA. Oh, not because of that, Gunhild. Because I love him.

MRS. BORKMAN *smiles.* Can you really love my son? In spite of everything.

ELLA. Yes, in spite of everything, I do. I love Erhart. As dearly as I can love any human being, now that I am old.

MRS. BORKMAN. Yes, yes, but——

ELLA. So, you see, as soon as I feel that anything threatens him I become worried.

MRS. BORKMAN. Threatens Erhart? What threatens him? Or—who threatens him?

ELLA. You, for one. In your way.

MRS. BORKMAN. I!

ELLA. And this Mrs. Wilton—I'm afraid of her, too——

MRS. BORKMAN *looks at her, speechless.* You can believe such a thing of Erhart! Of my own son! He has a great mission to fulfil——

ELLA, *contemptuously.* Mission!

MRS. BORKMAN. How dare you refer to it in that tone!

ELLA. Do you think a healthy, gay young man of Erhart's age is going to sacrifice himself for any mission?

MRS. BORKMAN. Erhart will. I know it. I am sure.

ELLA. You don't know it. You don't even believe it, Gunhild.

MRS. BORKMAN. *I* don't believe it?

ELLA. It's simply something you dream of, because if you didn't have that hope to cling to you know you would despair utterly.

MRS. BORKMAN. Yes. Then I would utterly despair. Perhaps that's what you really want, Ella dear.

ELLA. Yes—if you can't find freedom except by making Erhart suffer.

MRS. BORKMAN. You want to come between us. Between mother and son. You!

ELLA. I want to get him out of your clutches.

MRS. BORKMAN. You can't do that any longer. You had him in your clutches till he was fifteen. But now I've won him back.

ELLA. Then I will win him again. We two have fought for a man before, Gunhild.

MRS. BORKMAN. Yes, and I won.

ELLA. Do you still think you gained by your victory?

MRS. BORKMAN. My God, no.

ELLA. You won't gain anything this time, either.

MRS. BORKMAN. No gain—to keep a mother's hold over her son?

ELLA. No. It's only the power you want.

MRS. BORKMAN. What about you?

ELLA. I want his heart—his mind—his whole soul——

MRS. BORKMAN. That you will never have again.

ELLA. You've seen to that, have you?

MRS. BORKMAN *smiles.* Couldn't you tell from his letters?

ELLA *nods slowly.* I recognised your hand in those last letters of his.

MRS. BORKMAN. I have used these eight years while I have had him under my eyes, you may be sure.

ELLA. What have you told Erhart about me? Dare you tell me?

MRS. BORKMAN. Oh yes, I am not afraid to tell you. I have simply told him the truth.

ELLA. Well?

MRS. BORKMAN. I have continually impressed upon him that it is you we have to thank for the fact that we are able to live as comfortably as we do. That we are able to live at all.

ELLA. But Erhart knew this already.

MRS. BORKMAN. He used to be under the impression that you had done it all simply out of kindness. He doesn't believe that any longer, Ella.

ELLA. What does he believe now?

MRS. BORKMAN. The truth. I asked him how he could explain why Aunt Ella never came to visit us.

ELLA. He already knew.

MRS. BORKMAN. He knows better now. You'd led him to believe that you'd stayed away to spare my feelings and—those of that man who walks upstairs.

ELLA. So I did.

MRS. BORKMAN. Erhart doesn't believe that any longer.

ELLA. What have you got him to believe about me now?

MRS. BORKMAN. He believes the truth—that you're ashamed of us—that you despise us. Or don't you? Didn't you once consider taking him away from me for good? Think, Ella. You haven't forgotten.

ELLA. That was when the scandal was at its height. When the case was before the court. I don't want that any longer.

MRS. BORKMAN. It wouldn't be any good if you did. Erhart needs me, not you. As far as you're concerned, he's dead; and as far as he's concerned, you're dead.

ELLA. We shall see. I have decided to stay here.

MRS. BORKMAN. In this house?

ELLA. Yes.

MRS. BORKMAN. Overnight, you mean?

ELLA. For the rest of my life, if need be.

MRS. BORKMAN. Yes, yes, Ella. The house is yours, of course.

ELLA. Oh, Gunhild——

MRS. BORKMAN. Everything here is yours. The chair I am sitting on is yours. The bed in which I toss sleeplessly at night belongs to you. The food we eat comes to us by your good grace.

ELLA. It can't be done any other way. Borkman can't own anything. Someone or other would very quickly come and claim it.

MRS. BORKMAN. Yes, I know. We have to exist on your charity, and be grateful.

ELLA. If you want to look at it that way, I can't stop you.

MRS. BORKMAN. No, you can't. When do you want us to move out?

ELLA. Move out?

MRS. BORKMAN. Yes. You don't imagine for a moment, do you, that I will live under the same roof as you? I'd rather go to the workhouse, or tramp the roads.

ELLA. Very well. Then let Erhart come with me.

MRS. BORKMAN. Erhart! My son! My own child!

ELLA. Yes. If you do, I shall go straight home again.

MRS. BORKMAN. Erhart shall choose between us.

ELLA. Dare you let him, Gunhild?

MRS. BORKMAN *laughs.* Dare I let my son choose between his mother and you?

ELLA, *listening.* Is someone coming? I think I can hear——

MRS. BORKMAN. It must be Erhart!

There is a sharp rap on the door leading from the hall, and it is at once opened. MRS. WILTON, *in evening dress and overcoat, enters. Behind her the* MAID, *who has not had time to announce her, stands confused. The door remains half open.* MRS. WILTON *is a strikingly handsome woman in*

*her thirties, with a fine figure, broad, red smiling lips,
playful eyes and rich, dark hair.*

MRS. WILTON. Dear Mrs. Borkman, good evening.

MRS. BORKMAN, *drily.* Good evening.

To MAID, *pointing to garden room.*

Take that lamp out, and light it.

MAID *takes lamp and goes out.*

MRS. WILTON, *noticing* ELLA. Oh, forgive me. I see you have
a visitor——

MRS. BORKMAN. Only my sister. She's come to visit me——

ERHART BORKMAN *throws the half-open door wide, and
rushes in. He is a young man with shining, gay eyes. Elegantly dressed. The beginnings of a moustache.*

ERHART, *joyfully, as he stands in the doorway.* Has Aunt Ella
come?

Runs to her, and seizes her hands.

Aunt Ella! It can't be possible! Are you here?

ELLA, *embracing him.* Erhart! My dear, dear boy! How tall
you've grown! Oh, how good it is to see you again!

MRS. BORKMAN. What does this mean, Erhart? Have you
been hiding in the hall?

MRS. WILTON. Erhart—Mr. Borkman came with me.

MRS. BORKMAN. I see, Erhart. You visit other people before
your mother?

ERHART. I had to call in on Mrs. Wilton for a few minutes to
collect Frida.

MRS. BORKMAN. Is—Miss Foldal with you too, then?

MRS. WILTON. Yes, she's standing out in the porch.

ERHART, *speaking through the open door.* You can go upstairs now, Frida.

Pause. ELLA *watches* ERHART. *He seems embarrassed and
rather impatient. His face has become tense and colder.
The* MAID *brings the lighted lamp into the garden room,
goes out, and closes the door behind her.*

MRS. BORKMAN, *with forced politeness.* Well, Mrs. Wilton—if
you'd care to join us for the evening, please——

MRS. WILTON. Thank you so much, dear Mrs. Borkman. We have another engagement—we are going to visit Mr. Hinkel, the lawyer.

MRS. BORKMAN. We? Whom do you mean by we?

MRS. WILTON, *smiling*. Well, I only really mean myself. But Mrs. Hinkel and her daughters made me promise to bring your son with me if I should happen to meet him.

MRS. BORKMAN. As you apparently have done.

MRS. WILTON. Yes, as luck would have it—since he was so kind as to look in on me—on little Frida's account.

MRS. BORKMAN, *drily*. Erhart, I wasn't aware you knew these people, the—Hinkels.

ERHART. I don't really know them. You know best, Mother, whom I know or don't know.

MRS. WILTON *laughs*. There is no formality in that house. They are gay, friendly, hospitable people. Plenty of young ladies.

MRS. BORKMAN. If I know my son, that is hardly the right company for him, Mrs. Wilton.

MRS. WILTON. But, good heavens, dear Mrs. Borkman, he is young, too.

MRS. BORKMAN. Yes, I am glad to say, he is young.

ERHART, *concealing his impatience*. Oh, all right, Mother. Of course I won't visit the Hinkels this evening. I'll stay with you and Aunt Ella.

MRS. BORKMAN. I knew you would, Erhart dear.

ELLA. No, Erhart—please don't put it off for my sake.

ERHART. Yes, Aunt Ella, of course I will.

Glances uncertainly at MRS. WILTON.

But will it be all right? Can we get out of it? You've already accepted on my behalf.

MRS. WILTON. What nonsense you talk! "Can we get out of it?" When I come down to those bright, festive rooms, alone, abandoned—think of it!—I shall simply say: "No" —on your behalf.

ERHART, *reluctantly*. Oh well, if you think it'll be all right——

MRS. WILTON. I'm quite used to saying "no" to people; as I am to saying "yes." And how can you think of abandoning your aunt now, just when she's arrived? Shame on you, Monsieur Erhart—is that a way to behave towards your mother?

MRS. BORKMAN. Mother?

MRS. WILTON. Foster mother, I should have said, Mrs. Borkman.

MRS. BORKMAN. That would be more correct.

MRS. WILTON. Oh, I think one has more reason to be grateful to a good foster mother than to one's real mother. *I* think.

MRS. BORKMAN. Is that your own experience?

MRS. WILTON. Heaven bless you, no, I hardly knew my mother. But if I had had such a wonderful foster mother as Erhart, I might not have become such a wicked woman as they say I am.

Turns to ERHART.

You stay at home with your mother and aunt and have a nice cup of tea, young man.

To the ladies.

Goodbye, goodbye, dear Mrs. Borkman. Goodbye, Miss Rentheim.

They bow silently. She goes towards the door.

ERHART, *going after her.* Let me see you on your way.

MRS. WILTON, *at the door.* Not a yard. I am quite used to finding my way alone. But, be careful, Master Borkman— I am warning you.

ERHART. Why should I be careful?

MRS. WILTON. Because while I am going down the road— alone and abandoned—I shall try to cast a spell on you.

ERHART *laughs.* Are you going to try that again?

MRS. WILTON. Yes; so take care. While I walk down to the house, I shall say to myself, with all the magic I can command; "Master Erhart Borkman, put on your hat."

MRS. BORKMAN. And you think he will?

MRS. WILTON, *laughing.* Bless you, yes—he'll pick it up at once.

Then I shall say: "Put on your overcoat, Erhart Borkman! And your galoshes. Please don't forget your galoshes. And come after me. Obey. Obey. Obey."

ERHART. I shall do as you command me.

MRS. WILTON, *with raised forefinger.* Obey! Obey! Goodnight!

Laughs, nods to the ladies, and closes the door behind her.

MRS. BORKMAN. Does she really practise such tricks?

ERHART. No, how can you think that? It was only a joke. Don't let's talk about Mrs. Wilton, now.

He indicates to ELLA *to seat herself in the easy chair by the stove, and stands for a moment looking at her.*

So you've really come all the way to see us, Aunt Ella? And in winter!

ELLA. I had to in the end, Erhart.

ERHART. Had to? Why?

ELLA. I had to come and have a word with the doctors.

ERHART. Well, that's good.

ELLA *smiles.* Good?

ERHART. Yes, that you finally made up your mind to see them.

MRS. BORKMAN, *on the sofa, coldly.* Are you not well, Ella?

ELLA. You know I'm not well.

MRS. BORKMAN. Well, you've been ailing for years——

ERHART. When I was staying with you, I told you you ought to see a doctor.

ELLA. Oh, there isn't anybody I have any faith in out there. Besides, I didn't feel too bad in those days.

ERHART. Are you worse now, Aunt Ella?

ELLA. Yes, my boy. I am rather worse now.

ERHART. Not dangerously?

ELLA. It depends on what you think of as dangerous.

ERHART. Then you mustn't go home too soon.

ELLA. No, I don't think I shall.

ERHART. You must stay here in the town. Here you have all
the best doctors to choose from.

ELLA. Yes, I had that in mind when I left home.

ERHART. And you must take care to find yourself somewhere
really nice to stay—some hotel where it's cosy and peaceful.

ELLA. I booked in this morning at that old hotel I used to
stay at.

ERHART. Yes, you'll enjoy it there.

ELLA. Well, I don't think I shall be staying there after all.

ERHART. Oh? Why not?

ELLA. I changed my mind when I came out here.

ERHART. You—changed your mind?

MRS. BORKMAN, *crocheting, without looking up.* Your aunt
wants to live here, on her estate, Erhart.

ERHART. Here? With us? With *us?* Is this true, Aunt Ella?

ELLA. Yes. I have decided to do that now.

MRS. BORKMAN. It all belongs to your aunt, you know.

ELLA. Yes. So I shall be staying out here, Erhart. For a while.
I shall manage for myself. Over in the bailiff's wing——

ERHART. What a good idea! Your things are still there, aren't
they? But, I say, Aunt Ella, aren't you very tired after your
journey?

ELLA. Well, yes, I am a little.

ERHART. Then I think you ought to go to bed early. Really
early.

ELLA *looks at him, smiling.* Yes, I think I shall.

ERHART. Then we can have a real talk tomorrow—or some
time. About everything. You and Mother and I. That would
be much better, wouldn't it, Aunt Ella?

MRS. BORKMAN, *rising from the sofa.* Erhart, you want to
leave me, don't you?

ERHART. What do you mean?

MRS. BORKMAN. You want to go down to the Hinkels'.

ERHART. Oh, that. Well, you don't want me to keep Aunt Ella

up half the night, do you? She's ill, Mother. Remember that.

MRS. BORKMAN. You want to go to the Hinkels', Erhart?

ERHART, *impatiently*. But good heavens, Mother, I don't see how I can *not* go. Or what do you think, Aunt Ella?

ELLA. You must do what you want to, Erhart.

MRS. BORKMAN. You want to get him away from me!

ELLA, *rising*. Yes, Gunhild. If it's possible.

Music is heard from above.

ERHART. I can't stand this any longer. Where is my hat?

To ELLA.

Do you recognise that music from upstairs?

ELLA. No. What is it?

ERHART. It is the *Danse Macabre*. The dance of death. Don't you recognise the dance of death, Aunt Ella?

ELLA *smiles sadly*. Not yet, Erhart.

ERHART. Mother—I beg you, please—let me go.

MRS. BORKMAN. You want to leave your mother?

ERHART. I'll be back again. Tomorrow, perhaps.

MRS. BORKMAN. You want to leave me! You prefer to be with strangers! With—no, I won't think about it.

ERHART. There are lights down there, and young faces, happy faces—and music, Mother.

MRS. BORKMAN, *pointing up to the ceiling*. There is music up there too, Erhart.

ERHART. Yes, and that music is driving me out of the house.

ELLA. Do you grudge your father his few moments of forgetfulness?

ERHART. I don't grudge him anything. Let him enjoy his music. As long as I don't have to listen to it.

MRS. BORKMAN. Be strong, Erhart! Strong, my son. Never forget that you have a mission in life. A great mission.

ERHART. Oh, Mother, stop preaching. I wasn't made to be a missionary. Goodnight, Aunt Ella. Goodnight, Mother.

Runs quickly out through the door.

MRS. BORKMAN, *after a short silence.* You got him back quickly, didn't you, Ella?

ELLA. I wish I could believe that.

MRS. BORKMAN. But you won't keep him for long. You'll see.

ELLA. Because of you?

MRS. BORKMAN. Because of me. Or—her.

ELLA. I'd rather she had him than you.

MRS. BORKMAN *nods slowly.* That I can understand. I'd rather she had him than you.

ELLA. However it might end for him——

MRS. BORKMAN. I hardly think I care about that any longer.

ELLA *takes her overcoat over her arm.* For the first time in our lives, we twins agree. Goodnight, Gunhild.

Goes out through the hall.

The music sounds louder from upstairs.

MRS. BORKMAN. The wolf howls again. The sick wolf.

Stands for a moment, then throws herself to the floor, and moans softly.

Erhart, Erhart! Be loyal to me. Come home and help your mother. I can't bear this life any longer.

ACT TWO

The great drawing room—or rather, what was formerly the drawing room—upstairs in the Rentheim house. The walls are covered with old tapestries, portraying hunting scenes, shepherds and shepherdesses, all in faded colours. In the left-hand wall are folding doors. Downstage a piano. In the corner of the rear wall, left, a concealed door flush with the wall. In the middle of the right-hand wall, a large, carved oak desk, covered with many books and papers. Further downstage right is a sofa, with table and chairs. All the furniture is severe Empire style. On the desk and the table stand lighted lamps.

JOHN GABRIEL BORKMAN stands with his hands behind his back by the piano, listening to FRIDA FOLDAL who, seated, is playing the last bars of the Danse Macabre.

BORKMAN is of medium height, trimly and strongly built, in his sixties. Distinguished appearance, finely carved profile, sharp eyes and grey-white, curling hair and beard. He is dressed in a black, rather old-fashioned suit, with a white cravat. FRIDA FOLDAL is a pretty, pale girl of fifteen, with a somewhat tired and strained expression, cheaply dressed in a light-coloured frock.

The music ends. Silence.

BORKMAN. Can you guess where I first heard music like that?

FRIDA, *looking up at him.* No, Mr. Borkman.

BORKMAN. Down in the mines.

FRIDA, *not understanding.* Really? Down in the mines?

BORKMAN. I am a miner's son, as you know. Or perhaps you didn't know that?

FRIDA. No, Mr. Borkman.

BORKMAN. A miner's son. And sometimes my father took me down with him into the mines. Down there, the iron ore sings.

FRIDA. It sings?

BORKMAN *nods.* When it is broken loose. The hammer blows that loosen it are the midnight bell that sets it free. And then, in its own way, the iron sings—for joy.

FRIDA. Why does it do that, Mr. Borkman?

BORKMAN. It wants to be taken up into the daylight, and serve humanity.

He walks up and down the floor of the room, keeping his hands behind his back.

FRIDA *sits for a moment, waiting; glances at her watch, and gets up.* If you'll excuse me, Mr. Borkman, I'm afraid I must go now.

BORKMAN *stops in front of her.* Are you going already?

FRIDA, *putting her music in her portfolio.* Yes, I have to.
Embarrassed.

I've been engaged to play somewhere else this evening.

BORKMAN. At a party?

FRIDA. Yes.

BORKMAN. And you are to play for the guests?

FRIDA. No. I'm to provide the dance music.

BORKMAN. Only dance music?

FRIDA. Yes—they want to dance after supper.

BORKMAN *stands gazing at her.* Do you like that—playing dance music in people's houses?

FRIDA, *putting on her overcoat.* Well, yes, when I can get an engagement. They always pay me something.

BORKMAN. And that is what you think about while you play and they dance?

FRIDA. No, most of the time I think how nice it would be if I could join in the dance, too.

BORKMAN *nods.* I thought as much.

Begins to walk restlessly across the floor again.

Yes, yes, yes. Not be able to join in oneself—that is the heaviest burden of all.

Stops.

But there is one thought that should compensate you, Frida.

FRIDA. What's that, Mr. Borkman?

BORKMAN. The fact that you have ten times more music in you than all the dancers put together.

FRIDA *smiles.* Oh, I'm not so sure about that.

BORKMAN *points his finger at her.* Don't be foolish, girl. Never doubt yourself.

FRIDA. Even if nobody else believes in you?

BORKMAN. As long as you yourself are sure, that is enough. Where are you to play this evening?

FRIDA. Over at Mr. Hinkel's.

BORKMAN *looks sharply at her.* Hinkel—the lawyer?

FRIDA. Yes.

BORKMAN. Do people visit that man's house? Does he have guests?

FRIDA. Yes, a lot of people are going to be there, I heard Mrs. Wilton say.

BORKMAN. But what kind of people? Can you tell me that?

FRIDA. No, I don't really know. Oh yes—I know young Mr. Borkman will be there this evening.

BORKMAN. Erhart? My son?

FRIDA. Yes. He's going.

BORKMAN. Where did you hear that?

FRIDA. He said so himself. An hour ago.

BORKMAN. Is he out here today?

FRIDA. Yes, he's been at Mrs. Wilton's all afternoon.

BORKMAN. Do you know if he has been here, too? I mean, if he has come to speak to anyone downstairs?

FRIDA. Yes, I think he looked in on Mrs. Borkman.

BORKMAN. Aha. I see.

FRIDA. But she had a strange lady with her, I think.

BORKMAN. Had she? Indeed. Oh well, I suppose people visit her now and then.

FRIDA. If I meet Mr. Erhart this evening, shall I tell him to come up here and see you too?

BORKMAN, *gruffly.* No. Don't tell him any such thing. If anyone wants to visit me, let him come. I ask favours of no-one.

FRIDA. Oh well, then, I won't say anything. Goodnight, Mr. Borkman.

BORKMAN *starts walking again, growling to himself.* Goodnight.

FRIDA. May I run down the back stairs? It's quicker.

BORKMAN. Great heavens, run down what staircase you like. Goodnight to you.

FRIDA. Goodnight, Mr. Borkman.

Goes out through the small concealed door upstage left.

BORKMAN *goes meditatively over to the piano and makes to close it, but does not bother. Looks at the emptiness around him, and begins again to pace up and down the floor from the corner by the piano to the corner upstage right. Restless and uneasy the whole time. At length he goes to the desk, cocks an ear towards the folding doors, picks up a hand-mirror quickly, looks in it and arranges his cravat. There is a knock on the door.* BORKMAN *listens, gives a quick glance towards the door, but remains silent. After a moment, the knock is repeated, more loudly.*

BORKMAN, *standing at the desk, his left hand resting on the desk top and his right hand thrust into the breast of his coat.* Come in.

VILHELM FOLDAL *cautiously enters the room. He is a bent, worn-out man with mild blue eyes and long, thin grey hair which hangs down over his coat collar. He carries a port-*

folio under his arm, a soft felt hat in his hand, and big horn spectacles pushed up on his forehead.

BORKMAN *changes position and gives the newcomer a disappointed yet friendly look.* Oh, it's you.

FOLDAL. A good evening to you, John Gabriel. Yes, indeed it's me.

BORKMAN. Anyway, you're very late.

FOLDAL. Well, it's quite a distance. Especially on foot.

BORKMAN. But why do you always walk, Vilhelm? The tram goes practically by your door.

FOLDAL. Walking's healthier. And saves twopence. Well, has Frida been up to play for you this evening?

BORKMAN. She left this very moment. I'm surprised you didn't meet her outside.

FOLDAL. No. I haven't seen her for a long time. Ever since she went out to live with Mrs. Wilton.

BORKMAN *sits on the sofa and waves his hand towards a chair.* Do take a chair, Vilhelm.

FOLDAL *sits on the edge of a chair.* Thank you very much. *Looks gloomily at him.* You can't imagine how lonely I've been since Frida left home.

BORKMAN. What nonsense. You've still got all the others.

FOLDAL. God knows I have. Five of them. But Frida was the only one who understood me a little. *Shakes his head miserably.* None of the others understand me at all.

BORKMAN *darkly, looks into space and drums his fingers on the table.* Yes. That is the curse, the burden we chosen men have to bear. The masses, the mediocre millions—they do not understand us, Vilhelm.

FOLDAL. I could do without being understood. If one's patient, that may come. But there's something worse.

BORKMAN. Nothing can be worse than that.

FOLDAL. Well, I don't agree with you, John Gabriel. I've had a dreadful scene at home, just before I came here.

BORKMAN. Indeed? Why?

FOLDAL. My family—they despise me.

BORKMAN. Despise you?

FOLDAL *wipes his eyes.* I've been aware of it for some time. But today it all came out.

BORKMAN *is silent for a moment.* You didn't make a very good choice when you married, did you, Vilhelm?

FOLDAL. I didn't have much choice. Besides, one wants to get married when one's getting on in years. Especially when you're in such straitened circumstances as I was——

BORKMAN *springs up in anger.* What is this? An accusation? A reproach?

FOLDAL. Oh no, for God's sake, John Gabriel——

BORKMAN. You're harping on the bank disaster, aren't you?

FOLDAL. But I don't blame you for that. God forbid——

BORKMAN *sits down again, growling.* Well, I'm glad to hear it.

FOLDAL. You mustn't think it's my wife I complain about. She hasn't much education, poor thing, I must admit. But she's a good soul. No, it's the children——

BORKMAN. I might have known.

FOLDAL. The children—they're educated, you see. They expect more from life.

BORKMAN *looks at him sympathetically.* So your children despise you, Vilhelm?

FOLDAL *shrugs his shoulders.* Well, I haven't made much of a career, I must admit.

BORKMAN *leans closer and places his hand on* FOLDAL's *arm.* Don't they know that you wrote a play when you were young—a tragedy?

FOLDAL. Yes, of course they know. But that doesn't seem to impress them very much.

BORKMAN. Then they lack judgment, Vilhelm. Your tragedy is good. I believe that sincerely.

FOLDAL. Yes, there is quite a lot of good stuff in it, don't you think, John Gabriel? Oh dear, if I could only get it put on! *Opens the portfolio and fumbles eagerly in it.*

Look! I want to show you a change I've made——

BORKMAN. You have it with you?

FOLDAL. Yes, I brought it along. It's so long since I read it to you, I thought it might entertain you to listen to an act or two——

BORKMAN, *getting up*. No, no, some other time.

FOLDAL. Well, well. As you like.

BORKMAN *walks to and fro across the floor*. FOLDAL *puts the manuscript back into the portfolio*.

BORKMAN *stops in front of him*. You were right just now, when you said you hadn't made a career. But this I promise you, Vilhelm—the day I am rehabilitated——

FOLDAL *begins to rise*. Oh, thank you very much.

BORKMAN, *with a wave of his hand*. Sit down, please, Vilhelm. The day I am rehabilitated—when they realise they cannot do without me—when they come up to me in this room and get down on their knees and implore me to take over control of the bank again—the new bank they have founded—but cannot run——

Stops by the desk as before, and strikes his chest.

I shall stand *here* to receive them. And throughout the land men will ask and learn what conditions John Gabriel Borkman lays down——

Pauses suddenly and stares at FOLDAL.

You look doubtingly at me. Perhaps you don't believe they will come? They must—must—must come to me—sometime. You do believe that, don't you?

FOLDAL. Yes, yes, God knows I do, John Gabriel.

BORKMAN *sits on the sofa again*. I am sure of it. Absolutely certain—that they will come. Were I not certain—I should have put a bullet through my head long ago.

FOLDAL. No, for heaven's sake——

BORKMAN. But they will come! Oh, they will come! You'll see. I expect them any day, any hour. And as you see, I hold myself perpetually in readiness to receive them.

FOLDAL, *with a sigh*. If only they would come soon.

BORKMAN, *restlessly*. Yes, Vilhelm. Time passes; the years pass; life—no, I dare not think of it.

Looks at him.

Do you know how I sometimes feel?

FOLDAL. How?

BORKMAN. Like a Napoleon, maimed in his first battle.

FOLDAL *puts his hand on his portfolio.* Ah—I know that feeling.

BORKMAN. You can hardly compare the two situations.

FOLDAL. My little world of poetry means much to me, John Gabriel.

BORKMAN. Yes, but I—I could have created millions! Think of all the mines I could have brought under my control, the shafts I could have sunk. I would have harnessed cataracts —hewn quarries. My ships would have covered the world, linking continent to continent. All this I would have created alone.

FOLDAL. Yes, I know. Nothing was too big for you.

BORKMAN. And now I have to sit here like a wounded eagle, watching other men sneak in and steal it from me, piece by piece.

FOLDAL. It's just the same for me.

BORKMAN. I was so close to my goal. I only needed eight days' grace to consolidate my position. Every deposit would have been redeemed. All the money I had used so boldly would have been back in its place. All the stupendous enterprises I had planned were within a hair's breadth of being re-alised. No one would have lost a penny.

FOLDAL. My word, yes, how nearly you succeeded.

BORKMAN. And then, in those last crucial days, I was betrayed.

Looks at FOLDAL.

Do you know what I hold to be the ultimate treachery a man can commit?

FOLDAL. No, tell me.

BORKMAN. Not murder. Not robbery or perjury. Those are crimes one commits against people one hates or is indiffer-ent to.

FOLDAL. What is it then, John Gabriel?

BORKMAN. The ultimate crime is to abuse the trust of a friend.

FOLDAL. Yes, but wait a moment——

BORKMAN. You don't have to say it—I can see it in your face. But you're wrong. All those who had their money in the bank would have got it back. To the last farthing. No, Vilhelm—the ultimate crime a man can commit is to abuse the trust of a friend, publish his letters to the world, letters written in confidence, to be read by one person only, like a whisper in an empty, dark, locked room. The man who can stoop to such means is poisoned through and through, and rotted by evil. But such a friend I had. And it was he who broke me.

FOLDAL. I think I know whom you mean.

BORKMAN. There wasn't a detail of my affairs I didn't reveal to him. And then, when the moment was ripe, he turned against me the weapon I had placed in his hand.

FOLDAL. I've never been able to understand why he—of course, there was a rumour at the time.

BORKMAN. Rumour? What rumour? Tell me. I never heard anything. I was . . . confined at once. What was this rumour, Vilhelm?

FOLDAL. I heard they wanted to make you a Cabinet Minister.

BORKMAN. It was offered to me. But I refused.

FOLDAL. Then you didn't stand in his way there?

BORKMAN. Oh no. That wasn't why he betrayed me.

FOLDAL. Well, then I simply don't understand.

BORKMAN. I may as well tell you. There was a woman, Vilhelm.

FOLDAL. A woman? But, John Gabriel——?

BORKMAN. A stupid business. Finished—we won't say any more about it.

Sardonically.

Neither of us became a Cabinet Minister in the end.

FOLDAL. But he climbed.

BORKMAN. And I sank.

FOLDAL. Yes, what a tragedy——

BORKMAN. Yes. When I think about it, it seems almost as tragic as your play.

FOLDAL, *innocently.* Quite as tragic.

BORKMAN *laughs quietly.* But if you look at it another way, it is really a kind of comedy.

FOLDAL. A comedy?

BORKMAN. You didn't meet Frida when you came this evening?

FOLDAL. No.

BORKMAN. While we two sit here, she is sitting down there playing dance music for the man who betrayed and ruined me.

FOLDAL. Believe me, John Gabriel, I had no idea.

BORKMAN. Yes. She gathered up her music and left me—for that fine house.

FOLDAL, *apologetically.* Yes, yes, poor child——

BORKMAN. And can you guess for whom she will be playing there?

FOLDAL. Who?

BORKMAN. My son, Vilhelm.

FOLDAL. What?

BORKMAN. Yes, Vilhelm; what do you think of that? My son is dancing in his house tonight. Is not that a comedy?

FOLDAL. Yes, but—he doesn't know, surely.

BORKMAN. What doesn't he know?

FOLDAL. He doesn't know how he—how this man—er——

BORKMAN. You may use his name. I can endure it now.

FOLDAL. I'm sure your son doesn't know what happened between you, John Gabriel.

BORKMAN. He knows, Vilhelm. As surely as I sit here.

FOLDAL. If he did, do you think he'd go there?

BORKMAN. I don't suppose my son sees things with my eyes. I dare swear he sides with my enemies. Doubtless he believes, as they do, that Hinkel only did his damned duty as a lawyer when he came forward and betrayed me.

FOLDAL. But, John Gabriel, who could have put that idea into his head?

BORKMAN. Who? You forget who brought him up. First his aunt—from the time when he was six or seven years old. And now his mother.

FOLDAL. I think you're being unjust.

BORKMAN. I am never unjust. Both those women have turned him against me, I tell you!

FOLDAL, *meekly*. Yes, yes, if you say so.

BORKMAN. Women! They corrupt and pervert our lives. They deflect us from our destinies, rob us of our triumphs.

FOLDAL. Not all women.

BORKMAN. Indeed? Name me one who is worthy.

FOLDAL. No, it's true. The few I know aren't worth much.

BORKMAN. What's the use then—if such women exist, but one does not know them?

FOLDAL. Yes, John Gabriel, it makes a world of difference. It's a rare and blessed thought that somewhere on earth, far away perhaps, there lives the true woman.

BORKMAN. Oh, spare me your poet's twaddle.

FOLDAL. Do you call my most sacred belief poet's twaddle?

BORKMAN. I do! That's why you've never got anywhere. If you would only forego all this nonsense, I could still help you back on to your feet again—help you to make a career.

FOLDAL. Oh, you couldn't do that.

BORKMAN. I can. Once I am returned to power.

FOLDAL. But that's a very remote prospect.

BORKMAN. Perhaps you think the time will never come? Answer me!

FOLDAL. I don't know what to say.

BORKMAN *rises, cold and aloof, and waves his hand towards the door*. Then I have no further use for you.

FOLDAL, *rising from his chair*. No use——!

BORKMAN. If you do not believe that my fortunes will change——

FOLDAL. But that would be against all reason—you'd have to be rehabilitated first——

BORKMAN. Go on. Go on.

FOLDAL. I never sat for my degree, I admit, but I've read enough to know——

BORKMAN. You think it's impossible?

FOLDAL. There's no precedent.

BORKMAN. Precedents are for ordinary people.

FOLDAL. The law doesn't discriminate.

BORKMAN, *with harsh finality.* You are no poet, Vilhelm.

FOLDAL. Do you really mean that?

BORKMAN. We are simply wasting each other's time. You had better not come again.

FOLDAL. You want me to go, then?

BORKMAN, *without looking at him.* I have no further use for you.

FOLDAL, *humbly, taking his portfolio.* No, no. As you wish.

BORKMAN. In other words, you have been lying to me all these years.

FOLDAL. Never lied, John Gabriel.

BORKMAN. Haven't you sat here and built up my hopes and beliefs with lies?

FOLDAL. It wasn't a lie, as long as you believed in my vocation. As long as you believed in me, I believed in you.

BORKMAN. Then we have deceived each other. And perhaps we have deceived ourselves too.

FOLDAL. But isn't that what friendship really is, John Gabriel?

BORKMAN. Yes. To deceive; that is friendship. You are right there. I have had this experience once before.

FOLDAL. No poet. That you could be so brutal.

BORKMAN, *more gently.* Well, I am no expert.

FOLDAL. More than you realise, perhaps.

BORKMAN. How?

FOLDAL. I have had doubts myself—now and again. A horrible doubt—that I have frittered away my life for the sake of an illusion.

BORKMAN. If you doubt yourself, you stand on feet of clay.

FOLDAL. You believed in me. That's why it was so comforting for me to come here.

Takes his hat.

But now you are a stranger to me.

BORKMAN. And you to me.

FOLDAL. Goodnight, John Gabriel.

BORKMAN. Goodnight, Vilhelm.

FOLDAL exits left. BORKMAN stands for a moment, staring at the closed door. He makes a movement as though he would call FOLDAL back, but thinks better of it and begins to pace up and down the floor with his hands behind his back. Then he stops by the sofa table and extinguishes the lamp. The room becomes half dark. Shortly afterwards, there is a knock on the concealed door.

Who's that knocking?

No answer. There is another knock.

Who is it? Come in.

ELLA RENTHEIM, with a lighted candle in her hand, appears in the doorway. She is wearing the same dress as before, with her coat thrown over her shoulders.

BORKMAN, *staring at her.* Who are you? What do you want?

ELLA *closes the door behind her and walks towards him.* It is I, Borkman.

She sets the candle down on the piano and remains standing there.

BORKMAN *stares at her and whispers.* Is it—is it Ella? Is it Ella Rentheim?

ELLA. Yes. It is "your" Ella—as you used to call me. Once. Many, many years ago.

BORKMAN. Yes, it is you, Ella—I see it now.

ELLA. Can you recognise me?

BORKMAN. Yes—now I begin to——

ELLA. The years have been unkind to me, Borkman. Don't you think so?

BORKMAN. You have changed somewhat. At first sight, I didn't——

ELLA. I don't have dark curls now, falling over my shoulders. Do you remember how you loved to twist them round your fingers?

BORKMAN. That's it! You wear your hair differently. I see it now, Ella.

ELLA *smiles sadly.* Exactly. I wear it differently.

BORKMAN. I didn't know you were in this part of the country.

ELLA. I've only just come.

BORKMAN. Why have you come here—now, in winter?

ELLA. I'll tell you.

BORKMAN. Is there something you want from me?

ELLA. From you too, yes. But if we are going to talk about that, I shall have to begin at the beginning—a long time ago.

BORKMAN. You must be tired.

ELLA. Yes, I am tired.

BORKMAN. Won't you sit down?

ELLA. Thank you. I need to sit down.

Goes right, and seats herself on the corner of the sofa. BORKMAN *stands by the table with his hands behind his back, looking at her. Short silence.*

It's a long time since we met face to face, Borkman.

BORKMAN. A long, long time.

ELLA. A whole lifetime has passed. A wasted life.

BORKMAN. Wasted?

ELLA. Yes. For both of us.

BORKMAN. I do not regard my life as wasted—yet.

ELLA. But my life? What about that?

BORKMAN. You have only yourself to blame for that, Ella.

ELLA. *You* say that?

BORKMAN. You could have been happy without me.

ELLA. Do you think so?

BORKMAN. If you'd wanted to.

ELLA. Oh yes; I knew of course that there was someone else ready to receive me——

BORKMAN. But you turned your back on him.

ELLA. Yes.

BORKMAN. Again and again you rejected him. Year after year——

ELLA. Year after year I rejected happiness. Is that what you mean?

BORKMAN. You could have been as happy with him. And I would have been saved.

ELLA. You——?

BORKMAN. Yes. You would have saved me, Ella.

ELLA. How?

BORKMAN. He thought you had rejected him because of me. So—he took his revenge. It was easy for him. He had all my secret and confidential letters in his care. He used them —and that was the end of me, for the time being. You see; that is your fault, Ella.

ELLA. Why, yes, Borkman—when we look at it closely, perhaps it is I who have betrayed you, and stand in your debt.

BORKMAN. If you like. I know well enough what I have to thank you for. At the auction you bought the estate, and gave me and—and your sister the use of this house. You took Erhart, and cared for him in every way——

ELLA. For as long as I was allowed to.

BORKMAN. Allowed by your sister, yes. I have never interfered in domestic matters. As I was saying—I know the sacrifices you have made for me and for your sister. But remember, it was I who put you in a position to make those sacrifices, Ella.

ELLA. You're wrong, Borkman! It was love that forced me to act as I did—my devotion to Erhart—and to you, too.

BORKMAN. My dear, let's not drag our emotions into this. I mean of course that when you acted as you did, it was I who had provided you with the means to do so.

ELLA *smiles*. Hm. The means——

BORKMAN. Yes, exactly, the means! When the time came for

the decisive battle—when I could spare neither family nor friend—when I had to *take,* and took, the millions which had been entrusted to me—I spared everything that was yours, everything you had—though I could have taken that too, and used it—like everything else.

ELLA, *cold and calm.* That is perfectly true, Borkman.

BORKMAN. It is. But when they came and took me, everything of yours lay there untouched, in the vaults of the bank.

ELLA *looks at him.* I've so often wondered about that—why did you spare everything that belonged to me? And nothing else?

BORKMAN. Why?

ELLA. Yes, why? Tell me that.

BORKMAN, *scathingly.* You think I wanted something to fall back on, if everything should fail?

ELLA. Oh no. You never feared that. In those days.

BORKMAN. No, never! I was so unshakably certain of victory.

ELLA. Exactly; then why——?

BORKMAN *shrugs his shoulders.* Great heavens, Ella—it isn't so easy to remember one's motives of twenty years ago. I only remember that, as I walked there alone, wrestling with all the great projects I intended to launch, I felt—almost like an aeronaut. Walking the sleepless nights—filling, as it were, some giant balloon in which I was about to sail across an uncharted and perilous ocean.

ELLA *smiles.* You, who never doubted victory?

BORKMAN, *impatiently.* People are like that, Ella. They doubt and believe in the same breath.

To himself.

That was why I did not want to have you and your money with me in the balloon.

ELLA. Why? Tell me why?

BORKMAN, *without looking at her.* One does not take what one loves most dearly on such a journey.

ELLA. But you had what you loved most dearly on board with you. Your future. Your own life.

BORKMAN. Life is not always the most precious thing.

ELLA. Is that how you felt then?

BORKMAN. Yes. So it seems to me now.

ELLA. I was dearer to you than your life?

BORKMAN. I—seem to remember—I felt—something of the kind.

ELLA. But this was years after you had betrayed me, and married—someone else!

BORKMAN. Betrayed you, you say? You know quite well that it was higher motives—well, other motives, that compelled me. Without him, I could get nowhere.

ELLA, *controlling herself.* So you betrayed me from—higher motives?

BORKMAN. I could not do without his help. And you were the price he named.

ELLA. And you paid. In full; without bargaining.

BORKMAN. There was no choice. I had to conquer or be destroyed.

ELLA. And yet you can truthfully say that to you I was the most precious thing in the world!

BORKMAN. Yes, and afterwards too. Long, long afterwards.

ELLA. And yet you bartered me! Traded your love to another man! Sold my love for the chairmanship of a bank.

BORKMAN, *dark, bowed.* It was an absolute necessity, Ella.

ELLA *rises passionately from the sofa, trembling.* You criminal!

BORKMAN. I have heard that word before.

ELLA. Oh, don't think I'm talking about your crimes against the law. Do you think I care what use you made of those stocks and bonds? If I had been beside you when everything collapsed——

BORKMAN. Yes?

ELLA. I would have borne it all so gladly with you. The shame, the ruin, everything, everything—and helped you to bear it too.

BORKMAN. Would you have done that? Could you?

ELLA. I could and would have done it. Because then I didn't know about the monstrous crime you had committed.

BORKMAN. Which crime? What do you mean?

ELLA. I mean the crime for which there is no forgiveness—

BORKMAN. You must be out of your mind.

ELLA, *moving closer to him.* You are a murderer! You have committed the mortal sin!

BORKMAN *retreats towards the piano.* You are raving, Ella!

ELLA. You have killed love in me!

Goes towards him.

Do you understand what that means? The Bible speaks of a mysterious sin for which there is no forgiveness. I've never understood what that meant before. Now I understand. The sin for which there is no forgiveness is to murder love in a human being.

BORKMAN. And—*that* you say I have done?

ELLA. You have. I never really understood what had happened to me until this evening. That you betrayed me and turned to Gunhild instead I just accepted as male inconstancy on your part—a result of callous tricks on hers. And I think I despised you a little—in spite of everything. But now I see it! You betrayed the woman you loved! Me, me, me! The thing you held most precious in the world, you were willing to dispose of at a profit. You are guilty of double murder. The murder of your own soul, and mine.

BORKMAN, *cold and controlled.* How well I recall your passionate nature, Ella. It is only natural for you to see it like that. You are a woman. Consequently, nothing else in the whole world matters to you. You can only think about this one thing.

ELLA. Exactly. Only this one thing.

BORKMAN. Only what is nearest to your own heart.

ELLA. Only that! Only that!

BORKMAN. But you must remember that I am a man. As a woman, you were, to me, the most precious thing in the world. But if need be, one woman can be replaced by another——

ELLA *smiles.* Did you find that out after you had married Gunhild?

BORKMAN. No. But my mission in life helped me to bear that too. I wanted all the sources of power in this country to serve me. The earth, the mountains, the forests, the sea. So that I might create a kingdom for myself, and prosperity for thousands and thousands of others.

ELLA. I know. The evenings we spent talking about your plans——

BORKMAN. Yes. I was able to talk to you, Ella.

ELLA. I used to make fun of your dreams, and ask if you wanted to release the spirits that slumber in the mines.

BORKMAN *nods.* I remember that phrase.

Slowly.

The spirits that slumber in the mines.

ELLA. But you took it seriously. You said: "Yes, yes, Ella, that is exactly what I want to do."

BORKMAN. So it was. I only needed to get my foot on the ladder and that depended on this one man. He was able and willing to obtain for me the key position in the bank —provided that I on my part——

ELLA. Renounced the woman you loved—and who was so consumingly in love with you.

BORKMAN. I knew how insatiable his passion for you was. I knew no other condition would induce him to——

ELLA. So you struck the bargain.

BORKMAN. Yes, Ella, I did! My lust for power was so overwhelming, can't you understand? So I—struck the bargain. I had to. And he helped me up towards the heights—halfway towards the heights that drew me—and I climbed and climbed—year after year I climbed——

ELLA. And I passed out of your life.

BORKMAN. But he threw me back into the abyss. Because of you, Ella.

ELLA. Borkman—don't you feel as if our relationship had been cursed in some way?

BORKMAN. Cursed?

ELLA. Yes. Don't you think so?

BORKMAN, *uneasily.* Yes. But why? Oh, Ella—I don't know any longer who is right—you or I.

ELLA. You are the one who sinned. You destroyed my capacity for love.

BORKMAN. Don't say that, Ella.

ELLA. At least you made it impossible for me to love as a woman. From the time your image began to fade, I have lived as though under an eclipse. All these years it has become more and more difficult, until finally it became impossible for me to love any living thing. People, animals, flowers—only this one person——

BORKMAN. Who?

ELLA. Erhart, of course.

BORKMAN. Erhart?

ELLA. Your son, Borkman.

BORKMAN. Has he really meant so much to you?

ELLA. Why else do you suppose I took him to live with me? And kept him for as long as I could? Why else?

BORKMAN. I thought it was simply out of charity. Like all the other things you've done.

ELLA. Charity, did you say?

Laughs.

I've never felt charity towards anyone, not since you betrayed me. If a poor, starving child came into my kitchen, frozen and crying, and asked for a little food, I told the cook to see to it. I never felt any compulsion to take the child into my own room, warm it at my own fire, enjoy watching it eat its fill. And I was never like that when I was young—I remember so well—it's you who've created this emptiness and sterility in me, and all around me.

BORKMAN. But not towards Erhart.

ELLA. No. Not towards your son. But towards all other living things. You cheated me of the joy of being a mother—and of the sorrow and tears of motherhood, too. And that is perhaps the cruellest thing you've done to me, Borkman.

BORKMAN. Ella!

ELLA. Who knows? Perhaps the sorrow and tears were what

I needed most. But I couldn't accept that loss. So I took Erhart—and won his confidence, his love—until——

BORKMAN. Until what?

ELLA. Until his mother took him from me again.

BORKMAN. Well, he had to come back and live in town.

ELLA. Yes, but I can't stand the desolation—the emptiness— the loss of Erhart's love.

BORKMAN. Hm! I don't think you've lost him, Ella. It isn't easy to lose one's heart to anyone downstairs.

ELLA. I have lost him. And she has won him back. Or some-one else has. I can tell that from the letters he writes to me.

BORKMAN. Did you come here to take him away with you?

ELLA. If only I could——

BORKMAN. Certainly you can, as far as I'm concerned. You have the greater claim on him.

ELLA. Claim, claim! If he doesn't come of his own free will, he won't belong to me. And that's what I must have! I must have my child—he must belong to me. I won't share him with anyone.

BORKMAN. Well, we must remember that Erhart is a grown man. You couldn't expect to retain his undivided affec-tions for long.

ELLA. It needn't be for long.

BORKMAN. Oh? I thought when you want anything, you want it for life.

ELLA. I do. But that needn't be very long.

BORKMAN. What do you mean?

ELLA. You know I have been ill these last years?

BORKMAN. Have you?

ELLA. Didn't you know?

BORKMAN. No, I don't think so.

ELLA. Hasn't Erhart told you?

BORKMAN. Not that I remember.

ELLA. Perhaps he doesn't talk about me to you?

BORKMAN. Oh, I'm sure he's mentioned you. I hardly ever see

him. There is someone downstairs who keeps him away from me. Well away—you understand?

ELLA. Are you sure of that, Borkman?

BORKMAN. I am sure. But—you said you have been ill, Ella?

ELLA. Yes, I have. This autumn it became so bad that I've had to come over here and see a specialist.

BORKMAN. And you have talked to him?

ELLA. Yes. This morning.

BORKMAN. What does he say?

ELLA. He confirmed what I had long suspected——

BORKMAN. Yes?

ELLA, *calmly.* I shan't live for long, Borkman.

BORKMAN. You mustn't believe that, Ella.

ELLA. It's a disease for which the doctors know no cure. They can only let it run its course. And reduce the pain a little, perhaps. That at least is something.

BORKMAN. Oh, but—it may be a long time yet, I'm sure——

ELLA. I may get through the winter, they say.

BORKMAN, *without thinking.* Well, the winters are long here.

ELLA, *quietly.* Long enough for me, anyway.

BORKMAN. But what on earth can have been the cause of this disease? You've always lived such a healthy life.

ELLA *looks at him.* The doctor suggested that perhaps I had at some time gone through some violent emotional crisis.

BORKMAN. Oh, I understand. *I* am to blame for this?

ELLA. It's too late to talk about that now. But I must have my child again, before I go. It's so hateful for me to think that I must lose everything, leave the sunshine and light and air, without leaving behind me a single person who will remember me and love me and be sad that I have gone—the way a son remembers a mother he has lost.

BORKMAN, *after a brief pause.* Take him, Ella—if you can win him.

ELLA. You agree?

BORKMAN. Yes. But it's not much of a sacrifice. He isn't mine to give away.

ELLA. Thank you—thank you. But there is another thing I want to ask you. Something that means very much to me, Borkman.

BORKMAN. Name it.

ELLA. You will probably think it childish of me.

BORKMAN. Name it. Name it.

ELLA. When I die, I shall leave a considerable fortune——

BORKMAN. Yes. It must be considerable.

ELLA. I intend to leave it all to Erhart.

BORKMAN. I don't suppose you have anyone closer.

ELLA. No. No-one closer.

BORKMAN. There are no other members of your family left. You are the last.

ELLA. Yes. When I die, the name of Rentheim will die too. I hate that thought. To be obliterated so utterly that even one's name will die.

BORKMAN. Ah, I see what you want!

ELLA. Don't let it happen. Let Erhart bear my name after me.

BORKMAN. I understand you. You want to free my son from the burden of his father's name. That's it, isn't it?

ELLA. No. I would gladly and defiantly have borne your name with you. But when a mother is about to die—a name binds her to her son more closely than you know, Borkman.

BORKMAN, *coldly and proudly.* It shall be as you wish, Ella. I am man enough to bear my name alone.

ELLA *seizes his hands.* Thank you, thank you. All debts are paid between us, now. Yes, yes! You have made amends as far as you could. When I am dead, Erhart Rentheim will live.

The concealed door is thrown open, MRS. BORKMAN, *her big shawl over her head, stands in the doorway.*

MRS. BORKMAN. Never! Erhart shall never bear that name!

ELLA. Gunhild!

BORKMAN. No-one has leave to come up here!

MRS. BORKMAN *takes a step into the room.* I have given myself leave.

BORKMAN. What do you want with me?

MRS. BORKMAN. I want to fight for you—protect you!

ELLA. It is you he needs to be protected against, Gunhild.

MRS. BORKMAN. I hardly think so. I tell you he shall bear his father's name. And restore it to honour. And I alone shall be his mother! My son's love shall belong to me, and to no-one else.

She goes out through the concealed door and closes it behind her.

ELLA. Borkman—this will destroy Erhart. You and Gunhild *must* come to an understanding. We must go down to her. At once.

BORKMAN. We? You mean I should go down there?

ELLA. You and I, together.

BORKMAN *shakes his head.* She is hard, Ella. As hard as the iron I once dreamed of quarrying out of the mountains.

ELLA. Try. Try now.

BORKMAN *does not reply. He stands looking at her, uncertainly.*

ACT THREE

MRS. BORKMAN's *sitting room. The lamp is still burning on the sofa table. Inside the garden room the lamp is out and it is dark.* MRS. BORKMAN, *her shawl over her head, enters through the hall door, greatly agitated. She goes to the window and pushes the curtain slightly to one side. Then she moves away and sits by the stove, but soon jumps to her feet again, walks across the room and pulls the bell-rope. Stands by the sofa and waits a moment. Nobody comes. Then she rings again, this time more violently. A few seconds later, the* MAID *comes in from the hall. She looks bad-tempered and sleepy and has obviously dressed in a hurry.*

MRS. BORKMAN, *impatiently.* Where have you been, Malene? I've rung for you; twice.

MAID. Yes, madam, I heard you.

MRS. BORKMAN. Well, why didn't you come?

MAID. I had to get some clothes on first, didn't I?

MRS. BORKMAN. Now dress yourself warmly and run down and fetch my son at once.

MAID, *surprised.* You want me to fetch Mr. Erhart?

MRS. BORKMAN. Yes. Tell him to come at once, I want to speak to him.

MAID, *sulkily.* Well. I suppose I'd better go across to the bailiff's and wake the coachman.

MRS. BORKMAN. Why should you do that?

MAID. So that he can harness the sleigh. There's a terrible snowstorm outside tonight.

MRS. BORKMAN. Oh, never mind that. Hurry up and run down there. It's only just round the corner.

MAID. No, but madam, it's not just round the corner.

MRS. BORKMAN. Of course it is. Don't you know where Mr. Hinkel lives?

MAID, *maliciously.* Oh, that's where he is this evening, is it?

MRS. BORKMAN. Where else?

MAID *smirks.* No, no. I only thought he'd be in the usual place.

MRS. BORKMAN. Where do you mean?

MAID. At that Mrs. Wilton's, or whatever her name is.

MRS. BORKMAN. Mrs. Wilton? But my son doesn't go there very often.

MAID. I've heard he's there every day.

MRS. BORKMAN. That is just gossip, Malene. Now run down to Mr. Hinkel's and get hold of him.

MAID, *tossing her head.* Very good, madam. I'll go, I'll go.
She is about to go out through the hall, but at that moment the door opens and ELLA RENTHEIM *and* BORKMAN *appear in the doorway.*

MAID, *terrified, clasps her hands.* Oh, Jesus!

MRS. BORKMAN *whispers to the* MAID. Tell him to come at once.

MAID. Yes, madam.

ELLA and, after her, BORKMAN, *enter the room. The* MAID *sidles behind them through the door, and closes it after her. There is a short silence.*

MRS. BORKMAN *turns to* ELLA. What does he want down here?

ELLA. He wants to try to come to an understanding with you, Gunhild.

MRS. BORKMAN. He has never tried to do so before.

ELLA. He wants to now.

MRS. BORKMAN. The last time we stood facing each other was

in the court. When I had been summoned to defend myself——

BORKMAN. And tonight it is I who shall defend myself.

MRS. BORKMAN. You?

BORKMAN. Not against the charge I was convicted on. I did
what they said I did.

MRS. BORKMAN. Yes. All the world knows that.

BORKMAN. But they do not know why I did it. Why I had to
do it. People don't understand that I had to because I was
myself—because I was John Gabriel Borkman—and no-one
else. That's what I want to try to explain to you.

MRS. BORKMAN. It's no use explaining what drove you to it.
That won't acquit you.

BORKMAN. It can, in my own eyes.

MRS. BORKMAN. Oh, let us leave the subject. I have brooded
long enough over these things.

BORKMAN. So have I. Five endless years in the prison cell,
and three before the trial, gave me time. And during the
eight years in the room upstairs, I have had even more
time to brood. Again and again I have gone through the
trial, retrying it—before myself. I have been my own prose-
cutor, my own counsel, and my own judge. I have been
more impartial than anyone else could have been—anyone.
I think I may say that. I have walked up there on the floor
of that room, turning every one of my actions inside out,
and upside down. I have examined them from every an-
gle as ruthlessly and mercilessly as any advocate. And the
verdict I reach is always the same; that the only person
against whom I have committed any crime is myself.

MRS. BORKMAN. What about me? And your son?

BORKMAN. I include my family when I say myself.

MRS. BORKMAN. What about the hundreds of others whom
you ruined?

BORKMAN. I had the power! And the irresistible calling within
me! The buried millions lay there all over the country,
deep in the mountains, crying out to me, crying to be released! But no-one else heard them. I alone.

MRS. BORKMAN. Yes, and branded the name of Borkman with shame for ever.

BORKMAN. If the others had had the power, wouldn't they have acted exactly as I did?

MRS. BORKMAN. No-one but you would have done it.

BORKMAN. Then it was because no-one had my ability. And if they had done as I did, it would have been for selfish reasons. The case would have been quite different. In short, I have acquitted myself.

ELLA. Dare you say that so confidently, Borkman?

BORKMAN *nods.* I have dismissed the charges that were brought against me. But now comes the great and dreadful charge I bring against myself.

MRS. BORKMAN. What is that?

BORKMAN. Up there, I have wasted eight precious years of my life! The day I was released, I should have walked out into reality—reality hard as iron, free of dreams. I should have begun from the bottom and worked myself up to the heights again—higher than ever before—in spite of all that had happened.

MRS. BORKMAN. Oh, you would only have done it all over again, believe me.

BORKMAN *shakes his head and looks magisterially at her.* Nothing new happens. But equally, that which has happened never happens in quite the same way again. The vision transforms the deed. The new vision transforms the old deed. No, you don't understand that.

MRS. BORKMAN. No, I don't understand that.

BORKMAN. No, that is the curse upon me—I have never been understood by anyone.

ELLA. Never, Borkman?

BORKMAN. Except once, perhaps. Long ago. When I didn't think I needed it. Since then I have never had anyone at my side, vigilant enough to keep me continually alert and urge me forward, challenging me to take up my work again, with renewed strength. To assure me that I have not failed—irrevocably.

MRS. BORKMAN. So you need to be assured about that?

BORKMAN. Yes. The whole world proclaims that I am finished, and there are moments when I almost believe it. But then a voice within me reminds me who I am. And that acquits me.

MRS. BORKMAN. Why did you never come to me and ask for —understanding?

BORKMAN. Would it have been any use?

MRS. BORKMAN. You have never loved anything outside yourself—that is the real truth.

BORKMAN, *proudly*. I have loved power——

MRS. BORKMAN. Power, yes.

BORKMAN. The power to create happiness all around me.

MRS. BORKMAN. Once you had the power to make me happy. Why did you never use it?

BORKMAN, *without looking at her*. In a shipwreck, casualties cannot always be avoided.

MRS. BORKMAN. And your own son! Have you used your power to create happiness for him?

BORKMAN. I do not know him.

MRS. BORKMAN. No. You don't even know him.

BORKMAN. His mother saw to that.

MRS. BORKMAN. If you only knew what I have seen to!

BORKMAN. Well, tell me.

MRS. BORKMAN. I have seen to your epitaph.

BORKMAN, *with a short, dry laugh*. My epitaph! Listen to her! She speaks as though I were dead.

MRS. BORKMAN. You are.

BORKMAN, *slowly*. Yes, perhaps you're right.

Flares up.

No! Not yet! I came very close, so close to dying. But now I am awake. I am well again. Life still lies ahead of me. I can see it—my new life—waiting for me—new and shining. And you shall see it too. You too!

MRS. BORKMAN, *raising her hand*. Never dream of life again! Rest in peace where you lie!

ELLA. Gunhild! Gunhild!

MRS. BORKMAN. I shall raise a monument over your grave.

BORKMAN. Suitably inscribed, no doubt.

MRS. BORKMAN. Oh no. It won't be any monument of stone or metal. And no-one shall carve any scornful inscription on the monument I shall raise. There shall be planted as it were a living screen of trees and bushes, over the dead man walking in his tomb, shrouding his shame; consigning for ever to oblivion the name of John Gabriel Borkman.

BORKMAN. And you will perform this labour of love?

MRS. BORKMAN. No. I cannot. But I have brought up some-one who will dedicate his life to this work. And he shall be so clear and bright and shining that your dark life of the pit will be obliterated and forgotten.

BORKMAN. Is it Erhart you mean?

MRS. BORKMAN. Yes, Erhart. My son, whose name you are willing to sacrifice as a penance for your own misdeeds.

BORKMAN, *with a glance at* ELLA. As a penance for my greatest sin.

MRS. BORKMAN. That was a sin against a stranger. What about your sin against me? But he won't obey you. When I cry to him in my need, he will come! Because it's with me he wants to live! With me, and no-one else.

Listens suddenly, and cries.

There he is—there he is! Erhart!

ERHART BORKMAN *flings the door open and enters the room. He is wearing an overcoat and a hat.*

ERHART, *pale and worried.* Mother—what in God's name——?

He sees BORKMAN, *standing in the doorway of the garden room, stops, and takes off his hat. Is silent for a moment, then asks.*

Why do you want me, Mother? What has happened here?

MRS. BORKMAN *stretches out her arms towards him.* I want to see you, Erhart. I want to keep you with me—always.

ERHART. Always! What do you mean?

MRS. BORKMAN. Keep you, keep you, that's what I want! Because there's someone who wants to take you away from me.

ERHART. Ah—you know that?

MRS. BORKMAN. Yes. Do you know it too?

ERHART. Do I know it? Yes, of course——

MRS. BORKMAN. Ah, you've been plotting! Behind my back! Erhart, Erhart!

ERHART. Mother, tell me what you know.

MRS. BORKMAN. I know everything. I know your aunt has come here to take you away from me.

ERHART. Aunt Ella!

ELLA. Please listen to what I have to say first, Erhart.

MRS. BORKMAN. She wants me to give you to her. She wants to take your mother's place, Erhart. From now on, she wants you to be her son, and not mine. Wants you to inherit everything when she dies—to renounce your name and take her name instead.

ERHART. Aunt Ella, is this true?

ELLA. Yes, it's true.

ERHART. I had no idea. Why do you want me to come back and live with you again?

ELLA. Because I feel I'm losing you.

MRS. BORKMAN. Yes, to me. And that is as it should be.

ELLA. Erhart, I can't be without you. I am a—lonely, dying woman.

ERHART. Dying?

ELLA. Yes, dying. Will you stay with me till the end? As though you were my own child——?

MRS. BORKMAN. And betray your mother and perhaps your mission in life?

ELLA. I haven't much time left, Erhart.

ERHART. Aunt Ella—you have been so wonderfully good to me. You gave me as happy a childhood as anyone could have——

MRS. BORKMAN. Erhart!

ELLA. You still remember——!

ERHART—but I can't give up my life to you now. I can't—I can't possibly put everything aside and try to be a son to you——

MRS. BORKMAN. I knew it! You won't get him! You won't get him, Ella!

ELLA. No. You have won him back.

MRS. BORKMAN. Yes, yes! He is mine, and he'll always be mine. Erhart—it's true, isn't it?—we two shall stay together for a while yet?

ERHART. Mother—I'd better tell you now——

MRS. BORKMAN. Yes?

ERHART. You and I won't be together for much longer.

MRS. BORKMAN. What are you trying to tell me?

ERHART. Good God, Mother, I'm young! I'm suffocating in this house! I can't breathe here!

MRS. BORKMAN. Here? Living with me?

ERHART. Yes, living with you, Mother.

ELLA. Oh, Erhart, come with me!

ERHART. No, Aunt Ella, it's no better with you. It's different— but no better. It's roses and lavender—it's airless, the same as here.

MRS. BORKMAN. Airless, did you say?

ERHART, *with rising impatience.* Yes—I don't know what else to call it. Your sickly pampering, and—I don't know how to put it—the way you idolise me—I can't stand it any longer.

MRS. BORKMAN. Have you forgotten what you have dedicated your life to, Erhart?

ERHART, *explosively.* You mean, what *you* have dedicated it to! You, Mother, you've been my will—I've never been allowed to have any of my own. But now—I can't bear this strait jacket any longer! I'm young! Remember that, Mother!

With a respectful glance at BORKMAN.

I can't dedicate my life to atoning for what someone else has done. Whoever it may be.

MRS. BORKMAN. Erhart! Who has made you change your mind?

ERHART, *stung.* Who——? Couldn't I have done it myself?

MRS. BORKMAN. No, no, no! You are not under your mother's influence any longer. Nor your foster mother's. There is someone else.

ERHART, *trying to seem confident.* I stand on my own feet now, Mother. I have a will of my own.

BORKMAN *takes a step towards* ERHART. Then perhaps my turn has come at last.

ERHART, *distantly respectful.* What do you mean by that, Father?

MRS. BORKMAN. Yes, that I should like to know.

BORKMAN. Listen, Ehrart—will you come with your father? You cannot redeem another man's failure. That is only an empty dream, which has been instilled into you in this airless room. Even if you were to live like all the saints put together, it would not help me one whit.

ERHART, *respectfully.* Yes. That is true.

BORKMAN. Nor would it help if I were to moulder up there, contrite and penitent. All these years I have tried to keep alive on hopes and dreams. Now I want reality.

ERHART, *with a slight bow.* And where—what will you do, Father?

BORKMAN. I shall rehabilitate myself. I shall start at the bottom again. It is only through his present and his future that a man can redeem his past. Through work; untiring work for the ideal that inspired me when I was young, and inspires me a thousand times more strongly today. Erhart—will you come with me, and help me with this new life?

MRS. BORKMAN. Don't do it, Erhart!

ELLA, *warmly.* Yes, yes, Erhart, help him!

BORKMAN. Will you?

ERHART. Father—I can't now. It's impossible!

BORKMAN. Well, Erhart. What do you propose to do?

ERHART. I'm young! I want to live! I want to live my own life!

ELLA. And you won't sacrifice a few short months to brighten the last days of my life?

ERHART. Aunt Ella, I can't. I'd gladly do it, but I can't.

MRS. BORKMAN. And you feel no duty towards your mother any longer?

ERHART. I shall always love you, Mother. But I can't live just for you.

BORKMAN. Then come with me. Life is work, Erhart! Come; we two will go out into life and work together.

ERHART, *passionately*. Yes, but I don't want to work now! I'm young! I never knew what it was to be young before. But now—I feel it in my veins. I don't want to work! I just want to live, live, live!

MRS. BORKMAN, *sensing the truth*. Erhart—what do you want to live for?

ERHART. For happiness, Mother.

MRS. BORKMAN. And where do you expect to find it?

ERHART. I have found it!

MRS. BORKMAN, *with a cry*. Erhart——!

ERHART *goes quickly to the hall door and opens it*.

ERHART *calls*. Fanny, you can come in now.

MRS. WILTON, *wearing her overcoat, appears in the doorway*.

MRS. BORKMAN, *clasping her hands*. Mrs. Wilton!

MRS. WILTON, *shyly, with a questioning glance at* ERHART. May I——?

ERHART. Yes, you can come in now. I have told them everything.

MRS. WILTON *comes into the room*. ERHART *closes the door behind her. She bows respectfully to* BORKMAN, *who acknowledges her greeting silently. Short pause*.

MRS. WILTON. You have heard the news, then. I fear I am the cause of much unhappiness in this house.

MRS. BORKMAN. You have destroyed the little I had left to live for. But this is all utterly impossible!

MRS. WILTON. I appreciate how impossible it must seem to you, Mrs. Borkman.

MRS. BORKMAN. Surely you yourself must admit that it is impossible.

MRS. WILTON. Incredible is the word I would use. Nevertheless it is true.

MRS. BORKMAN. Do you mean this seriously, Erhart?

ERHART. This is the happiness I have found, Mother. That is all I can say.

MRS. BORKMAN, *to* MRS. WILTON. You have infatuated and seduced my unfortunate son!

MRS. WILTON, *tossing her head proudly*. I have not.

MRS. BORKMAN. Do you dare to deny it?

MRS. WILTON. Yes. I have neither infatuated nor seduced him. Erhart has come to me of his own free will. And I have met him halfway, of my free will.

MRS. BORKMAN. Oh yes! I can well believe that!

MRS. WILTON. Mrs. Borkman—there are forces in life of the existence of which you seem to be unaware.

MRS. BORKMAN. What forces, if I may ask?

MRS. WILTON. Those forces which command two human beings to join their lives together regardless of other people.

MRS. BORKMAN *smiles*. I thought you were already joined to someone else.

MRS. WILTON. He left me.

MRS. BORKMAN. But he is still alive, I am told.

MRS. WILTON. He is dead to me.

ERHART. Yes, Mother, as far as Fanny is concerned he is dead. And he's no concern of mine.

MRS. BORKMAN. Then you know about him?

ERHART. Yes, Mother, of course I know about him.

MRS. BORKMAN. And yet you say he's no concern of yours?

ERHART. I tell you I want happiness, Mother! I'm young! I want to live, live, live!

MRS. BORKMAN. Yes, you are young, Erhart. Much too young for—this.

MRS. WILTON. Don't think I haven't told him so, Mrs. Borkman. I've told him everything about myself. I have continually reminded him that I am a full seven years older than he——

ERHART. Oh, Fanny, I knew that from the beginning.

MRS. WILTON. But nothing—nothing could make him change his mind.

MRS. BORKMAN. Indeed? Nothing? Why didn't you tell him to stop seeing you? Keep your doors closed to him? That is what you should have done while there was still time.

MRS. WILTON. I couldn't do that, Mrs. Borkman.

MRS. BORKMAN. Why not?

MRS. WILTON. Because my happiness, too, depended on it.

MRS. BORKMAN, *scornfully.* Hm—happiness!

MRS. WILTON. I have never known till now what happiness is. And I cannot turn my back on it, merely because it comes so late.

MRS. BORKMAN. And how long do you suppose this happiness will last?

ERHART. A few months or a lifetime, Mother—what does it matter?

MRS. BORKMAN. Oh, you are blind! Don't you see where all this is going to end?

ERHART. I don't want to think about the future. I only want the chance to live.

MRS. BORKMAN. And you call that living, Erhart?

ERHART. Yes—don't you see how beautiful she is?

MRS. BORKMAN. Now I shall have to bear the shame of this too.

BORKMAN. Well, you are used to that, Gunhild.

ELLA. Borkman——

ERHART. Father——

MRS. BORKMAN. I shall have to live here and see my son every day together with a——

ERHART. You won't have to see anything, Mother. You needn't worry about that. I shall not be staying here.

MRS. WILTON. We are going away, Mrs. Borkman.

MRS. BORKMAN. Together?

MRS. WILTON. Yes, I am going south. I'm taking a young girl abroad. And Erhart is coming with us.

MRS. BORKMAN. With you—and a young girl?

MRS. WILTON. Yes. Little Frida Foldal, whom I have had living with me. I want her to go abroad and study music.

MRS. BORKMAN. And so you are taking her with you?

MRS. WILTON. Yes, I can't let the child go abroad alone.

MRS. BORKMAN, *repressing a smile.* What do you have to say to that, Erhart?

ERHART, *a little embarrassed, shrugs his shoulders.* Why, Mother, if that's what Fanny wants——

MRS. BORKMAN, *coldly.* When do you intend to leave, if I may ask?

MRS. WILTON. Now. Tonight. My sleigh is waiting down there, on the road—outside the Hinkels' house.

MRS. BORKMAN. Of course. The party.

MRS. WILTON *smiles.* Yes, Erhart and I were the only guests. And little Frida, of course.

MRS. BORKMAN. And where is she now?

MRS. WILTON. Sitting in the sleigh waiting for us.

ERHART. Mother, you do understand——? I wanted to spare you and—and everybody—all this.

MRS. BORKMAN. You wanted to leave me without saying goodbye?

ERHART. Yes, I thought it would be better. Better for both of us. Everything was arranged—I'd packed my clothes—but then you sent for me, so——

He makes to stretch out his hands towards her.

Goodbye, Mother.

MRS. BORKMAN. Don't touch me!

ERHART, *quietly.* Is that your last word?

MRS. BORKMAN. Yes.

ERHART, *turning.* Goodbye, Aunt Ella.

ELLA, *clasping his hands.* Goodbye, Erhart! Live your life— and be happy—as happy as you can.

ERHART. Thank you, Aunt Ella.

Bows to BORKMAN.

Goodbye, Father.

Whispers to MRS. WILTON.

Let's get away, now.

MRS. WILTON. Yes.

MRS. BORKMAN. Mrs. Wilton—do you think you are being wise in taking this young girl with you?

MRS. WILTON. Men are so unpredictable, Mrs. Borkman. And women too. When Erhart is tired of me, and I of him, it will be good for both of us that he should have someone to fall back on, poor boy.

MRS. BORKMAN. And what will you do?

MRS. WILTON. Oh, I shall manage, I promise you. Goodbye, everybody!

She inclines her head and goes out into the hall. ERHART *stands for a moment as though hesitating: then he turns and follows her.*

MRS. BORKMAN, *with lowered, folded hands.* Childless!

BORKMAN, *as though awakening to a decision.* Then out into the storm alone! My hat! My cape!

He rushes towards the door.

ELLA *stops him, frightened.* John Gabriel, where are you going?

BORKMAN. Out into the storm of life! Let me go, Ella.

ELLA, *holding him tightly.* No, no, I won't let you go. You're ill.

BORKMAN. Let me go, I tell you.

Tears himself loose and goes out through the door into the hall.

ELLA, *in the doorway.* Help me to stop him, Gunhild!

MRS. BORKMAN, *cold and hard, standing in the middle of the room.* I'm not keeping anyone. Let them all leave me. All of them. Let them go—as far as they like.

Suddenly, with a rending scream.

Erhart, don't go!

She rushes with outstretched arms towards the door. ELLA *stops her.*

ACT FOUR

An open courtyard outside the house, which stands on the right. A corner of it, with the front door and a flight of stone steps, juts out. Upstage, close to the courtyard, stretches a line of steep hills covered with pine trees. The edge of the forest, with young trees and scattered undergrowth, can be seen to the left. The snow has stopped, but the ground is covered with a deep layer of freshly fallen snow. The pines are heavily bowed with it. Dark night sky, with driving clouds. The moon can be vaguely glimpsed from time to time. The only illumination comes from the light reflected from the snow.

BORKMAN, MRS. BORKMAN *and* ELLA *stand outside on the steps.* BORKMAN, *faint and tired, is leaning against the wall of the house. He has an old-fashioned cape thrown over his shoulders, and holds a soft grey felt hat in one hand and a thick thorn stick in the other.* ELLA *has her coat on her arm.* MRS. BORKMAN'S *big shawl has fallen down over her shoulders, leaving her head bare.*

ELLA, *barring* MRS. BORKMAN'S *path.* Don't run after him, Gunhild!

MRS. BORKMAN. Let me go, Ella. He mustn't leave me.

ELLA. I tell you it's no use. You won't catch him.

MRS. BORKMAN. Let me go! I want to run down the road and

scream after him. Surely he must hear his mother's screams!

ELLA. He can't hear you. The windows of the sleigh will be closed.

MRS. BORKMAN. No, no. He can't have got to the sleigh yet.

ELLA. He reached it ages ago, believe me.

MRS. BORKMAN. If he's in the sleigh she will be there with him.

BORKMAN *laughs grimly*. And he won't hear his mother's screams, then, will he?

MRS. BORKMAN. No, he won't hear them.

Listens.

Ssh! What's that?

ELLA *listens too*. It sounds like sleigh bells——

MRS. BORKMAN. It's her sleigh!

ELLA. It might be someone else's.

MRS. BORKMAN. No, no, it's Mrs. Wilton's sleigh. I know those silver bells. Listen! Now they're driving past the house—down at the bottom of the hill.

ELLA. Gunhild, if you're going to cry after him, do it now. Perhaps he might still——

The bells sound very close, in the forest.

Quickly, Gunhild! They're right below us.

Short pause.

MRS. BORKMAN. No. I shall not cry after him. Let Erhart Borkman drive past me—to what he calls life and happiness.

The sound dies away in the distance.

ELLA, *after a moment*. I can't hear the bells any longer.

MRS. BORKMAN. They sounded to me like funeral bells.

BORKMAN *laughs dryly*. Not yet. They haven't tolled for me yet.

MRS. BORKMAN. But for me they have. And for him who has left me——

ELLA. Perhaps they ring in life and happiness for him, Gunhild.

MRS. BORKMAN. Life and happiness, did you say?

ELLA. For a while, at least.

MRS. BORKMAN. Can you really wish him happiness—with her?

ELLA. Yes, with all my heart!

MRS. BORKMAN. Then your love must be stronger than mine.

ELLA. Perhaps it is want of love that gives my love strength.

MRS. BORKMAN. In that case, mine will soon be as strong as yours.

She turns and goes into the house.

ELLA *stands for a moment, looking anxiously at* BORKMAN. *Then she puts her hand gently on his shoulder.* John, you must go in now.

BORKMAN, *as though awakening.* Me?

ELLA. Yes. The winter air is too cold for you. I can see that, John. Come now, come in with me. Into the warmth.

BORKMAN. Upstairs again?

ELLA. No; downstairs to her.

BORKMAN. I shall never again set foot under that roof.

ELLA. Where will you go? It's nighttime, and late, John——

BORKMAN *puts his hat on.* First of all I shall go out and look over my buried treasures.

ELLA. John—I don't understand you.

BORKMAN, *with a coughing laugh.* Oh, I don't mean hidden loot. You needn't be afraid of that, Ella.

Stops and points.

Over there! Who is it?

VILHELM FOLDAL, *in an old jacket covered with snow, the brim of his hat turned down and a big umbrella in his hand, enters downstage past the corner of the house, plodding laboriously through the snow. He limps badly on his left foot.*

Vilhelm! Are you here again? What do you want?

FOLDAL *looks up.* Good God! Are you out of doors, John Gabriel?

Bows.

And Mrs. Borkman, too, I see.

BORKMAN. This is not my wife.

FOLDAL. Oh, I beg your pardon. You see, I've lost my glasses in the snow. But you never go out——

BORKMAN, *recklessly hilarious.* It's time I returned to life in the open air, you see. Nearly three years before the trial; five in the cell; eight upstairs; sixteen years in prison——

ELLA. Borkman, Borkman——

FOLDAL. Ah, yes, yes, yes——

BORKMAN. But tell me, what do you want?

FOLDAL, *still standing below the steps.* I felt I wanted to come up and see you, John Gabriel. I felt I *had* to come up and talk to you in your room. Dear God, that room, John Gabriel!

BORKMAN. You wanted to come, even after I had shown you the door?

FOLDAL. Oh, that doesn't matter now.

BORKMAN. What have you done to your foot? You're limping.

FOLDAL. You'll never guess. I've been run over.

ELLA. Run over!

FOLDAL. Yes, by a sleigh——

BORKMAN. Ha!

FOLDAL. With two horses. They came galloping down the hill. I couldn't get out of the way quickly enough, and so——

ELLA. And so they ran over you?

FOLDAL. They drove right at me, Mrs.—er—or Miss. They drove right at me, so that I rolled over in the snow, and lost my glasses and got my umbrella broken.
Rubs himself.
And my foot got hurt a little, too.

BORKMAN *laughs.* Do you know who was sitting in that sleigh, Vilhelm?

FOLDAL. No, how could I? It was all closed, and the curtains were drawn. And the driver didn't stop when he saw me lying there. But that doesn't matter because—— Oh, I'm so happy!

BORKMAN. Happy?

FOLDAL. I don't know whether that's the right word. But I— I think it must be. The most extraordinary thing's happened. So I had to come up and share my happiness with you, John Gabriel.

BORKMAN, *roughly.* Well, give me my share, then.

ELLA. Take your friend inside first, Borkman.

BORKMAN. I've told you I won't enter that house again.

ELLA. But you've just heard he's been run over.

BORKMAN. We all get run over some time in life. The only thing to do is to get up again and behave as though nothing had happened.

FOLDAL. Those are wise words, John Gabriel. But I can easily tell you out here.

BORKMAN, *more gently.* Do me that favour, Vilhelm.

FOLDAL. Listen. Can you imagine what I found when I came home from seeing you this evening? A letter. And you'll never guess who it's from.

BORKMAN. Little Frida, perhaps?

FOLDAL. Yes! How did you guess? Yes, it was a long—well, quite a long letter from Frida. Brought by a servant. And can you guess what was in the letter?

BORKMAN. A farewell to her parents, perhaps?

FOLDAL. Right again! How clever of you to guess! Yes, she writes that Mrs. Wilton has become so fond of her that she's taking her abroad to carry on with her music, she writes. And Mrs. Wilton's managed to find a clever tutor to go with them, and coach Frida. Her education's been a little neglected, you see.

BORKMAN *chuckles.* Yes, yes. I understand it all so well, Vilhelm.

FOLDAL *continues eagerly.* And imagine, she wasn't told about it until tonight! At the party, you know—the—er—yes. And even so she managed to find time to write. And such a warm and tender and loving letter it was, too. No suggestion that she despises me any longer. And what a delicate gesture, to say goodbye to us in writing!

Laughs.

But I'm not going to be satisfied with that!

BORKMAN. How do you mean?

FOLDAL. She writes that they're off tomorrow. Very early.

BORKMAN. Indeed, indeed! Tomorrow? Is that what she says?

FOLDAL *laughs and rubs his hands.* Yes, but I'm too clever for her. I'm going straight up to Mrs. Wilton's——

BORKMAN. Now? Tonight?

FOLDAL. Good heavens, yes, it's not so late. And if the house is shut up, I'll ring. Without hesitation. For I must and shall see Frida before she goes. Goodnight, goodnight.

Begins to go.

BORKMAN. My poor Vilhelm, you can save yourself that long walk.

FOLDAL. Ah, you're thinking of my foot——

BORKMAN. Yes, and you won't get into Mrs. Wilton's house, anyway.

FOLDAL. Indeed I shall. I'll ring and ring till someone opens. I must see Frida.

ELLA. Your daughter has gone, Mr. Foldal.

FOLDAL, *thunderstruck.* Has she gone already? Are you sure? Where did you hear that?

BORKMAN. We heard it from her tutor——

FOLDAL. Oh? Who is he?

BORKMAN. A student by the name of Erhart Borkman.

FOLDAL, *overjoyed.* Your son, John Gabriel! Is he going too?

BORKMAN. Yes; he's the one who's going to help Mrs. Wilton to educate little Frida.

FOLDAL. God be praised! The child's in the best possible hands, then. But are you quite sure they've gone?

BORKMAN. They were in the sleigh which ran you down.

FOLDAL *claps his hands.* My little Frida in that magnificent sleigh!

BORKMAN. Yes, yes, Vilhelm. Your daughter is doing very well for herself. And Erhart Borkman too. Did you notice the silver bells?

FOLDAL. Oh yes, I—— *Silver* bells did you say? Were they silver bells? Real, solid-silver bells?

BORKMAN. You can be sure of that. Everything there was real. Inside and out.

FOLDAL. Isn't it strange the way things work out? My—my little talent for poetry has resulted in Frida being musical. So I haven't been a poet for nothing after all. For now she's able to go out into the great world and see all the things I longed to see once. Little Frida drives out into the world in a closed sleigh! With silver bells on the harness——

BORKMAN. And runs over her father.

FOLDAL, *joyfully.* Oh, that! What does it matter about me, as long as the child——? Well, I've come too late. I'll go home and console her mother, who's sitting in the kitchen crying.

BORKMAN. Is she crying?

FOLDAL. Yes. Imagine it! She was crying her heart out when I left.

BORKMAN. And you laugh, Vilhelm?

FOLDAL. I, oh yes! But, she, poor thing, she doesn't know any better. Well, goodbye! It's lucky I haven't far to go to the tram. Goodbye, goodbye, John Gabriel. Goodbye, miss. *Waves and plods painfully out the way he came.*

BORKMAN. Goodbye, Vilhelm. It's not the first time in your life you have been run over, old friend.

ELLA, *controlling her concern as she watches him.* You're so pale, John, so pale——

BORKMAN. That is because of the prison air upstairs.

ELLA. I've never seen you like this.

BORKMAN. No. You've never seen an escaped prisoner before, have you?

ELLA. Come inside with me, John.

BORKMAN. It's no good trying to wheedle me. I've told you I——

ELLA. I beg you—for your own sake.

The MAID *comes out on to the steps.*

MAID. Excuse me, Madam says I'm to lock the front door now.

BORKMAN, *quietly, to* ELLA. Listen to that! They want to shut me in again.

ELLA, *to the* MAID. The master is not feeling well. He wants a little fresh air.

MAID. Yes, but Mrs. Borkman *said*——

ELLA. I shall lock up. Leave the key in the door.

MAID. Very good, madam, I'll do as you say.

She goes back into the house.

BORKMAN *stands still for a moment listening, then goes quickly down to the courtyard.* I'm outside the wall now, Ella! They'll never catch me now!

ELLA, *down with him.* But you're free in there too, John. You can come and go as you please.

BORKMAN, *quietly, as though frightened.* I shall never go under a roof again. Out here in the night air, it's good! If I were to go up to that room now, the walls and ceiling would shrink and crush me, crush me like a fly——

ELLA. But where will you go?

BORKMAN. I shall go on, and on, and on. See if I can find my way back to freedom and life and humanity. Will you go with me, Ella?

ELLA. I? Now?

BORKMAN. Yes, yes. At once.

ELLA. But—how far——?

BORKMAN. As far as I can go.

ELLA. But, John—it's a winter night—it's wet and cold——

BORKMAN. Ah! You're concerned for your health, are you, madam? Yes, yes, it's very frail, isn't it?

ELLA. It's your health I'm concerned for.

BORKMAN *laughs.* A dead man's health! You make me laugh, Ella.

He goes on.

ELLA *goes after him and holds him back.* What did you say
you were?

BORKMAN. A dead man. Don't you remember, Gunhild said
I should rest in peace where I lay?

ELLA, *purposefully wrapping her coat around here.* I shall go
with you, John.

BORKMAN. Yes, we two belong together, Ella: you and I.
Come.

*They enter the trees left and gradually disappear from
sight. The house and courtyard fade away, and the landscape, rugged and mountainous, slowly changes, becoming wilder and wilder.*

ELLA'S VOICE, *from within the forest, right.* Where are we
going, John? I don't know where I am.

BORKMAN'S VOICE, *higher up.* Follow my footprints!

ELLA'S VOICE. But why must we climb so high?

BORKMAN'S VOICE, *nearer.* We must follow the winding path.

ELLA'S VOICE, *she is still hidden.* I haven't the strength to
go on much longer!

BORKMAN, *at the edge of the forest, right.* Come, Ella, come!
We are not far from the prospect now. There was a seat
here——

ELLA, *coming into sight through the trees.* Do you remember?

BORKMAN. There you can rest.

*They have reached a small clearing high up in the forest.
The mountain rises steeply behind them. To the left, far
down, can be seen a vast landscape, with fjords, and high
distant peaks rising one behind another. To the left of the
clearing is a dead pine tree with a seat beneath it. Snow
lies deep on the ground.* BORKMAN, *with* ELLA *following
him, wades heavily through the snow.*

BORKMAN *stops by the precipice, left.* Come, Ella, and I
shall show you!

ELLA, *joining him.* What will you show me, John?

BORKMAN, *pointing.* See how the country stretches out before
us, open and free—far, far away.

ELLA. We used to sit on that seat, and stare into the distance.

BORKMAN. It was a country of dreams we gazed into.

ELLA *nods heavily.* The country of our dreams, yes. Now it is covered with snow. And the old tree is dead.

BORKMAN, *not listening to her.* Can you see the smoke from the great steamers out on the fjord?

ELLA. No.

BORKMAN. I can. They come and go. They create a sense of fellowship throughout the world. They bring light and warmth to the hearts of men in many thousands of homes. That is what I dreamed of creating.

ELLA, *quietly.* But it remained a dream.

BORKMAN. Yes. It remained a dream.

Listens.

Listen. Down there by the river the factories hum. *My* factories. Listen how they hum. The night shifts are working. They work both night and day. Listen, listen! The wheels whirl and the pistons thud, round and round, in and out. Can't you hear them, Ella?

ELLA. No.

BORKMAN. I hear them.

ELLA, *frightened.* No, John, you can't.

BORKMAN. Ah, but these are only the outworks surrounding the kingdom.

ELLA. What kingdom?

BORKMAN. My kingdom! The kingdom I was about to take possession of when I died.

ELLA. Oh, John, John!

BORKMAN. And there it lies, defenceless, masterless, abandoned to thieves and robbers. Ella! Do you see those mountains far away? Range beyond range, rising and towering! That is my infinite and inexhaustible kingdom.

ELLA. Ah, but it's a cold wind that blows from that kingdom, John.

BORKMAN. To me it is the breath of life. It is a greeting from the spirits that serve me. I feel them, those buried millions, I see those veins of iron ore, stretching their twisting, branching, enticing arms towards me. I've seen you all before, like shadows brought to life—that night when I stood in the vaults of the bank with the lantern in my hand. You wanted to be freed. And I tried to free you. But I failed. Your treasure sank back into the darkness.

Stretching out his hands.

But let me whisper this to you now, in the stillness of the night. I love you where you lie like the dead, deep down in the dark. I love you, treasures that crave for life, with your bright retinue of power and glory. I love you, love you, love you.

ELLA. Yes, your love is still buried down there, John. It always has been. But up here, in the daylight, there was a warm, living heart beating for you, and you broke it. Worse, you sold it—for——

BORKMAN, *a cold shudder seems to go through him.* For the kingdom—and the power—and the glory, you mean?

ELLA. That is what I mean. And therefore I prophesy, John Gabriel Borkman, that you will never get the price you demanded for that murder. You will never ride triumphant into your cold kingdom.

BORKMAN *staggers to the seat and sits down heavily.* I fear you are right, Ella.

ELLA. You must not fear that, John. It will be better for you.

BORKMAN, *clutches his chest with a cry.* Ah!

Weakly.

Now it let go of me.

ELLA. What was it, John?

BORKMAN *sinks back on the seat.* A hand of ice that gripped my heart.

ELLA. John! *You've* felt that hand of ice now?

BORKMAN *mumbles.* No. Not a hand of ice. A hand of iron.

He slides down upon the seat.

ELLA *tears off her coat and covers him with it.* Rest quietly, John. I'll go for help.

She goes a few paces right. Stops, goes back and feels his pulse and his face.

No. Better so, John Borkman. Better so; for you.

She wraps her coat more tightly round him and sits down in the snow in front of the seat. MRS. BORKMAN *in her overcoat comes through the forest on the right. In front of her goes the* MAID *with a lighted lantern.*

MAID, *shining the lantern on the snow.* Yes, yes, madam. Here are their footprints.

MRS. BORKMAN, *peering round.* Yes, there they are. Over on that seat! Ella!

ELLA *rises.* Are you looking for us?

MRS. BORKMAN. What else could I do?

ELLA. Here he is, Gunhild.

MRS. BORKMAN. Asleep?

ELLA. A long, deep sleep, I am afraid.

MRS. BORKMAN. Ella!

Controls herself, and asks quietly.

Was it—deliberate?

ELLA. No.

MRS. BORKMAN, *relieved.* Not by his own hand, then?

ELLA. No. A hand of iron gripped his heart.

MRS. BORKMAN, *to* MAID. Go for help. Get some people from the farm.

MAID. Very good, madam.

To herself.

God in Heaven!

Goes out right through the forest.

MRS. BORKMAN *stands behind the seat.* So the night air killed him——

ELLA. So it seems.

MRS. BORKMAN. That strong man.

ELLA *goes in front of the seat.* Won't you look at him, Gunhild?

MRS. BORKMAN. No, no!

Quietly.

John Gabriel Borkman was a miner's son. He couldn't live in the fresh air.

ELLA. I think it was the cold that killed him.

MRS. BORKMAN. The cold? That killed him long ago.

ELLA. And turned us into shadows.

MRS. BORKMAN. Yes.

ELLA. One dead man and two shadows. See what the cold has done.

MRS. BORKMAN. Yes. The coldness of the heart. And now I think we two can join hands, Ella.

ELLA. I think we can, now.

MRS. BORKMAN. We twin sisters—over the man we both loved.

ELLA. We two shadows—over the dead man.

MRS. BORKMAN *behind the seat, and* ELLA *in front of it, join hands.*

When We Dead Awaken

INTRODUCTION

WHEN WE DEAD AWAKEN, Ibsen's last play, is the least known of all his mature works in the English-speaking world. It has long been out of print, and has only twice been professionally staged in London, both times inadequately. William Archer did not understand it, and thought it showed signs of senility.[1] C. E. Montague also found it bewildering. "The play as a whole affected us like a large, complicated machine working in a dark room; one peered in here and there, and saw part of a wheel going round with apparent purpose, or a piece of belting that seemed to imply coherence in the whole apparatus, but the next moment it whirled on undistinguishably, and even that small clue was lost. However," he added, "likely enough, when we stupid awaken, we shall find the queer, tough play a big thing, and even a clear one."

Two people, at least, had already found it big. "It shews no decay of Ibsen's highest qualities," wrote Bernard Shaw. "His magic is nowhere more potent. It is shorter than usual; that is all." And the young James Joyce, writing in the *Fortnightly Review* in 1900, proclaimed: "On the whole, WHEN WE DEAD AWAKEN may rank with the greatest of the author's work—if, indeed, it be not the greatest."

[1] "It is scabrous to a degree—if it weren't like deserting the Old Man, 'pon my soul I'd let someone else translate it." (Letter to Charles Archer, December 14, 1899.)

It is significant that WHEN WE DEAD AWAKEN should so have appealed to Joyce, for although Ibsen subtitled it "A Dramatic Epilogue," he took pains to make clear that he intended it, not as his final word, but as a declaration that he had now finished with the realistic type of drama through which he had won international recognition, and was intending to break out into new and experimental fields. When, a few days before the publication of the play in December 1899, the Danish newspaper *Politiken* assumed from the subtitle that "With this play, the author will have said his last word, and will thereby have written *finis* to his dramatic work," the correspondent of another paper, *Verdens Gang*, asked Ibsen if this were true. Ibsen replied:

"No, that conclusion has been reached too hastily. The word 'epilogue' was not meant by me to have any such implications. Whether I write any more is another question, but all I meant by 'epilogue,' in this context, was that the play forms an epilogue to the series of plays which began with *A Doll's House* and which now ends with WHEN WE DEAD AWAKEN. . . . It completes the cycle, and makes of it an entity, and now I am finished with it. If I write anything more, it will be in quite another context; perhaps, too, in another form."

Within a month, on New Year's Day, 1900, he told Ernst Motzfeldt that he wanted to begin work on a new play; and on March 5 he wrote to his French translator, Moritz Prosor: "If it be granted to me to retain the strength of body and mind which I still enjoy, I shall not be able to absent myself for long from the old battlefields. But if I return, I shall come forward with new weapons, and with new equipment."

I do not think there is much doubt that, by these remarks, Ibsen meant that he was finished with orthodox realism and was intending to move, as Strindberg had recently done, back towards poetry and symbolism. This tendency had already found expression in the final act of *John Gabriel Borkman*, which he had completed in 1896. In 1898, Strindberg had sent Ibsen a copy of his new and highly symbolic drama, *To Damascus*, and although Ibsen seldom read books ("I leave them to my wife," he once said, and most of the presentation copies in his library remain uncut), it is known that he read both volumes of *To Damascus*. Nor, surely, is it without significance that, at this time, he had an oil painting of Strindberg on his study wall. He had bought it, he explained, not because of any sympathy or friendship either with the painter or with Strindberg, but because "I am now not able to write a word without having that madman staring down at me!" One can only speculate on what Ibsen would have written if illness had not struck him down and rendered him helpless for the last years of his life; but WHEN WE DEAD AWAKEN gives us a hint, and it is interesting to ponder its possible influence on Joyce, who was to make the same decision to abandon realism in favour of symbolism barely a dozen years later.

Theatrically, the chief difficulties that WHEN WE DEAD AWAKEN offers are not, as Montague suggested, difficulties of staging; snow peaks and avalanches, which Montague thought it impossible to present, pose no insuperable problems to an imaginative producer, as the recent London performance of *Brand* proved. The real trouble with WHEN WE DEAD AWAKEN is that it is one of those plays, like *King Lear* and *Brand,* which, unless they are played big, had better not be played at all. Ibsen's realistic plays, such as *Ghosts,* can be presented as domestic melodramas with the subtleties and overtones ironed out, and can still be reasonably successful, just as a performance of *Hamlet* on a thriller level can be reasonably successful. One cannot do either of these things with WHEN WE DEAD AWAKEN. Although it exists on a realistic level, it exists much more powerfully on a symbolic level; Rubek and Irene are the shadows of mighty archetypal creatures moving near the sun.

A vital factor in any discussion or presentation of WHEN WE DEAD AWAKEN is Irene's age. This is not specified anywhere in the play, and although Ibsen once told Gunnar Heiberg that she should be twenty-eight, and then grudgingly allowed that she might be forty, I am sure Mr. Casper Wrede is right in suggesting that, for the play to seem plausible and achieve its full effect, she should be played as a woman of sixty-five and Rubek as a man of seventy. A mad woman of forty who complains that her life has been wasted arouses no-one's sympathy; a deranged woman of sixty-five who makes the same complaint is a much more tragic figure. The love affair that never was then becomes something dimly remembered from long ago. It is not a dozen years but half a century of wasted life that they are looking back on; and at the end, as Maja and Ulfhejm, the young and the strong, descend to the valley of what they call life, the two old people climb upwards to what they have come to believe is the only real life, the kind that is attained through the death of the body. If one thinks of Irene as an Edith Evans part, the play takes on an infinitely greater power and meaning.

WHEN WE DEAD AWAKEN is not only Ibsen's most experimental play; it is also his final account with himself. He had portrayed different facets of himself in most of his plays: the unsatisfactory husband preoccupied with his work (Tesman in *Hedda Gabler*, Allmers in *Little Eyolf*), the uncompromising idealist who brings unhappiness to those he loves most (Brand, Gregers Werle in *The Wild Duck*, Dr. Stockmann in *An Enemy of the People*), the egoistic artist (Ejnar in *Brand*, Hjalmar Ekdal in *The Wild Duck*, Lyngstrand in *The Lady from the Sea*), the ruthless old man who despises the world and neglects his wife (Solness in *The Master Builder*, John Gabriel Borkman). But nowhere do we find so complete and merciless a self-portrait as the character of Rubek in WHEN WE DEAD AWAKEN. The ageing artist, restless in his married life, restless in the homeland to which he has returned after a long sojourn abroad, restless in his art, shocked, like Brand, near the top of a mountain, into the realization that to reject love is to reject life; such is Ibsen's Portrait of the Dramatist as an Old Man, painted at the age of seventy-one.

Ibsen wrote WHEN WE DEAD AWAKEN in Christiania in 1899. Although, for the past eight years, he had been living in Norway, after twenty-seven years in Italy and Germany, he had never really settled down there. In a letter to Georg Brandes, dated June 3, 1897 (eight months after he had completed *John Gabriel Borkman*), he wrote: "Can you guess what I am dreaming of, and planning, and picturing to myself as delightful? It is to settle somewhere in the Sound, between Copenhagen and Elsinore, in a free, open place, where I shall be able to see all the deep-sea ships coming from afar and going afar. Here I can't do that. Here, every sound is locked (in both senses); every channel of understanding is stopped. Oh, my dear Brandes, one does not live for twenty-seven years out in the great, free, liberating world of culture for nothing. Here among the fjords is my native land. But—but—but—where shall I find my home? The sea is what draws me most. I live here alone and plan some new dramatic work. But I can't yet see clearly what shape it will take."

It was Ibsen's routine to begin a new play two summers after he had completed the previous one, but he was much distracted during 1898 by celebrations in honour of his seventieth birthday, not only in Norway, but also in Sweden and Denmark. At the banquet given for him in Christiania, he spoke of his wish "to dispel the misconception which in many ways has hampered me—I mean, the idea that unalloyed happiness must naturally have resulted from the unusual fortune which has been granted to me in winning reputation and fame in foreign lands. I have also found friendship and understanding there; which is much more important. But inward happiness, real happiness; that is not something which one just finds, or receives like a gift. It must be earned, at a price which often seems heavy. For the truth is that a man who has won for himself a home in many foreign lands feels in his heart of hearts nowhere truly at home, hardly even in his own fatherland."

He then surprised his hearers by announcing his intention to write a non-dramatic, autobiographical work: "a book which will knit my life and my work into a comprehensible whole. Yes, for I think I have by now reached a sufficiently ripe age to be granted a short breathing space—to take a year's holiday—for the writing of such a book would be a holiday in comparison with the vexatious and exhausting business of writing plays. I have never taken a real holiday since I left Norway thirty-four years ago; and I think I could do with one now. But, ladies and gentlemen, you must not therefore assume that I intend to lay down my dramatic pen. No; I intend to take it up again, and to hold on to it tightly until the end. I have, you see, a few crazy ideas left in my head which I have not yet found occasion to give expression to.

Not until I have rid myself of them will it be time for me to lay down my pen."

In Copenhagen that spring (1898), Ibsen, for the first time, saw *Brand* performed. The actress Oda Neilsen, who sat next to him during the performance (her husband was playing the title role) related that when it was over Ibsen said to her: "This moves me. This is—all my youth. I haven't thought about *Brand* for thirty years." We are told that he lay awake most of that night, thinking about the play he was going to write. As he lay there, he may have remembered, consciously or unconsciously, that, thirty years before, just after *Brand* had brought him the recognition from his countrymen that he had longed for, he had remarked to Georg Brandes (June 26, 1869) that Brand "could as well have been a sculptor or a politician as a priest." The chief character in his new play was to be a sculptor, of the same uncompromising ruthlessness as Brand; and, like Brand, he was to die in an avalanche near the top of a mountain, his pride crushed, with a Latin blessing cried out to him as though from a forgiving deity at the moment of death.

Later that month, he visited Stockholm and attended a dinner given for him at Skansen by two Swedish women's organizations. To entertain their guest they had arranged an exhibition of folk dancing, and among the dancers was one, a young girl, who especially attracted his attention. Her name was Rosa Fitinghoff; he talked to her several times before the evening ended, and asked her to see him off at the station the following day. On his return to Christiania he sent her his photograph, with an accompanying note:

"When I received your beautiful postcard, it was as though you had entered my house yourself with a spring greeting to warm my heart. There was music and dance in what you wrote; and it was through dance and music that we met. That is the happy part of the story. The sad part is that we did not meet until my last evening. Parties are often like life; people do not meet until they have to say goodbye. But go on writing to me."

During the past ten years Ibsen had entered into relationships of close affection with several young girls: Emilie Bardach, an eighteen-year-old Viennese girl; Helene Raff, a German painter; and Hildur Andersen, a Norwegian pianist. None of these relationships seems to have developed into an affair. Helene Raff, in a letter written in 1927, said: "Ibsen's relations with young girls had in them nothing whatever of infidelity in the usual sense of the term, but arose solely out of the needs of his imagination; as he himself said, he sought out youth because he needed it for his poetic production." His farewell message to Emilie Bardach, inscribed in her album on September 20, 1889, has a pathetic ring about it: *"Hohes, schmerzliches Glück—um das Unerreichbare zu ringen"—* "High, and painful fate—to struggle for the unattainable."

In 1895 Georg Brandes had sent Ibsen an essay he had written about the young Marianne von Willemer's infatuation for Goethe, when the latter was sixty-six, and its stimulating effect on the poetry of his old age. This essay had greatly interested Ibsen; in a letter dated February 11, 1895, he wrote to Brandes: "I cannot forbear to send you especial thanks for your *Goethe and Marianne von Willemer.* I didn't know anything about the episode you describe in it. I may have read about it years ago, in Lewis's book, but if so I had forgotten it, because at that time the affair held no particular interest for me. But now things are somewhat different. When I think of that quality that characterises Goethe's work during that period, I mean the sense of renewed youth, I ought to have guessed that he must have been graced with some such revelation, some such reassurance of beauty, as his meeting with Marianne von Willemer. Fate, Providence, Chance, can after all be genial and benevolent powers now and then."

In July 1898, three months after their meeting in Stockholm, Ibsen invited Rosa Fitinghoff to visit him in Christiania that summer. She did not come that year, but they continued to correspond; the following April we find him thanking her for a blue anemone she had sent him to mark the anniversary of their first meeting. He told her that he always glanced at where her letters lay before starting work. He had begun his new play that winter (an unusual time for him), or had, at any rate, written down his title page—*The Day of Resurrection* he called it at first—and his cast list, for these are dated February 22, 1899. But spring came, and summer, and still he, who normally wrote so rapidly, had not finished the first act. With the summer, however, Rosa came to Christiania, with her mother, the authoress Laura Fitinghoff; and her visit thawed his inspiration. On July 31 he finished the first act. On August 2 he began the second act, and finished it on August 23; and on August 25 he began the third act, which he finished on September 21. By this time, he had altered the title to WHEN THE (*sic*) DEAD AWAKEN.

It was, however, a further two months before the final fair copy was ready to go to the printer. The most notable piece of revision concerns the ending. In his original draft, Rubek and Irene reach their mountain peak, and the closing lines of the play read as follows:

> RUBEK, *to* IRENE. Up above the mists, I glimpse the moun-tain peak. It stands there, glittering in the sunrise. That is where our path lies. Through the mists of night, up into the light of morning.
>
> *The mist closes down more thickly over the scene.* RUBEK *and* IRENE *step down into the veil of mist, and gradually disappear from sight. The* NUN's *head appears in a rift in the mist, searching for them. High up above the sea of mist, the mountain peak shines in the morning sun.*

The Nun, one supposes, like the house in *Rosmersholm,* and the crutch in *Little Eyolf,* symbolizes the past that stands in the way of happiness. But Ibsen changed this ending. In the final version Rubek and Irene are killed by the descend-ing avalanche, the Nun's voice whispers a blessing on them, and the last sound as the curtain descends is Maja singing triumphantly as she descends into the valley. I think we must assume that, by this revision, Ibsen wanted to point the con-trast between the two different ideas of what is meant by life. Maja and Ulfhejm return to what they think is life, but what Rubek and Irene regard as death, while Rubek and Irene climb upwards to what the others regard as death but they regard as life. As long as people remain imprisoned in flesh, Ibsen seems to say, they are dead; it is only when the body dies that the dead awaken.

Ibsen completed his revision of the play on November 21,

1899, and sent it to the printer the following day. WHEN WE DEAD AWAKEN (as he finally entitled it, as though wishing to identify himself conclusively with the choice made by Rubek and Irene) was published on December 22 in an edition of 12,000 copies; a further 2000 were reprinted before publication. It received its first performance at the Hoftheater, Stuttgart, on January 26, 1900.[2] Within a month it had been played at many other theatres throughout Germany, as well as in Copenhagen, Helsinki, Christiania, and Stockholm. In 1902, a notable production was given at the Deutsches Theater in Berlin, with Albert Basserman and Irene Triesch. London saw the play in 1903, and New York in 1905, at the Knickerbocker Theatre, with Frederick Lewis as Rubek, Florence Kahn (later the wife of Max Beerbohm) as Irene, and Dorothy Donnelly as Maja. The acting is said to have been excellent, but, not surprisingly, the play failed to attract the interest of the general public.

In the spring of 1900 Ibsen had a stroke, and he spent the summer in a sanitorium at Sandefjord undergoing a cure for erysipelas. The following year, he spoke again of his intention to write a new play, but then he had a second stroke which left him unable to walk or write, and he remained virtually paralysed until his death on May 23, 1906.

M. M.

[2] As with all of his plays from *Hedda Gabler* onwards, however, a special edition of twelve copies in Norwegian, identical with the Copenhagen edition except for the title page, had been published in London by William Heinemann three days before the Copenhagen edition to secure copyright, since Denmark had not yet joined the Berne Convention. A public reading of the play in Norwegian had already been given at the Theatre Royal, Haymarket, on December 16, [at 10 A.M., a formidable hour at which to listen to such a play] to secure performing copyright.

CHARACTERS

PROFESSOR ARNOLD RUBEK, a sculptor
MAJA, his wife
THE INSPECTOR (at the Baths)
ULFHEJM, a country squire
A LADY TRAVELLER
A NUN
WAITERS, GUESTS and CHILDREN

The action takes place in Norway—the first act at a coastal watering place, the second and third acts in the grounds and vicinity of a mountain health resort.

ACT ONE

Outside the Spa Hotel at a watering place on the Norwegian coast. It is an open, park-like space, with fountains, shrubs, and clumps of large, old trees. On the left stands a little pavilion, covered with ivy and wild vine. In the background the fjord is visible, stretching right out to sea, with tongues of land and small islets in the distance. It is a still, hot summer morning.

PROFESSOR RUBEK and his wife, MAJA, are seated in basket chairs beside a laid table on the lawn outside the hotel. They have just lunched; now they are drinking champagne and seltzer, and each has a newspaper. The PROFESSOR is an elderly, distinguished-looking man wearing a black velvet jacket; apart from this he is in light summer clothes. MAJA RUBEK looks youthful and has a lively face and bright, provocative eyes; yet there is a hint of tiredness about her. She is dressed in elegant travelling clothes.

MAJA sits for a moment as though waiting for the PROFESSOR to say something. Then she lowers her newspaper and sighs.

RUBEK *looks up from his newspaper.* Well, Maja, what's the matter with you?

MAJA. Just listen to the silence.

RUBEK *smiles indulgently.* Can you hear it?

MAJA. Hear what?

RUBEK. The silence.

MAJA. I certainly can.

RUBEK. Perhaps you're right, my dear. One can sometimes hear silence.

MAJA. God knows one can. When it's as deafening as it is here——

RUBEK. Here at the spa, you mean?

MAJA. Everywhere in Norway. Oh, down in the city it was noisy. But even there, I thought all that noise and bustle had something—something dead about it.

RUBEK *looks hard at her.* Aren't you happy to be home again, Maja?

MAJA. Are *you?*

RUBEK. I?

MAJA. Yes. You've been abroad so much, much longer than I. Are you really happy to be home again?

RUBEK. No, to be perfectly honest. Not really happy.

MAJA. There, you see. I knew it.

RUBEK. Perhaps I have been abroad too long. This northern provincial life seems foreign to me.

MAJA, *eagerly, pulling her chair towards him.* Let's go away again! As quickly as possible.

RUBEK, *a trifle impatiently.* Well, we *are* going, Maja. You know that.

MAJA. Why not now, right away? We could be so comfortable down there, in our lovely new house——

RUBEK *smiles indulgently again.* Shouldn't you rather say "our lovely new home"?

MAJA, *curtly.* I prefer to say "house." Let's use that word.

RUBEK *gives her a long look.* You're a funny little creature, really.

MAJA. Am I so funny?

RUBEK. Yes, I think so.

MAJA. Why? Because I don't want to stay pottering around up here?

RUBEK. Who was it who was so insistent that we should come north this summer?

MAJA. It was I, I suppose.

RUBEK. Well, it certainly wasn't I.

MAJA. But, good God, how could I have known everything would have changed so dreadfully? And in such a short time! I mean, it's only just four years since I went away——

RUBEK. Since you got married, you mean.

MAJA. Married? What's that got to do with it?

RUBEK *continues.* Since you became Frau Professor, and the mistress of a beautiful home—— Oh, I beg your pardon, I should have said a handsome house. And a villa on the Taunitzer See—surrounded by all the best people. Yes, it's all very fine and handsome, Maja, there's no denying that. And very spacious. We don't have to sit in each other's laps all the time——

MAJA, *passing it off lightly.* No, no—we've got all the room we need——

RUBEK. Exactly. You've grown used to a more spacious and luxurious way of life. And a more gracious society than you'd been accustomed to at home.

MAJA. Oh, so you think it's I who've changed?

RUBEK. Yes, Maja. I do.

MAJA. Not the people here?

RUBEK. Oh yes, they've changed too, a little, no doubt. And not for the better. That I'm prepared to concede.

MAJA. I'm glad to hear it.

RUBEK, *changing the subject.* Do you know what I'm reminded of when I look at the people here and the way they live?

MAJA. No. What?

RUBEK. It reminds me of that night we spent in the train, when we were coming up from the Continent——

MAJA. You were asleep the whole time.

RUBEK. Not the whole time. I noticed how silent it was at all the little places we stopped at. I—heard the silence—like you, Maja—— And then I realised we had crossed the frontier. Now we were home. I knew it, because at every one of these little roadside halts, the train stopped, and stood quite still—though nothing ever happened.

MAJA. Why did it stop if there was no-one there?

RUBEK. Don't know. No-one got off, no-one got on—and yet the train stood there, absolutely silent, for minute after minute—as it might have been eternity. And at every station I heard two men walking down the platform—one of them had a lantern in his hand—and they muttered to each other, softly, tonelessly, meaninglessly in the night.

MAJA. Yes, you're right. There are always two men, who walk and talk together——

RUBEK. About nothing.

Changes his tone, and speaks more cheerfully.

Never mind, we only have to wait until tomorrow. Then the liner will put into harbour; and we shall go on board, and sail along the coast, northwards, as far as we can go— right up into the Arctic.

MAJA. Yes, but then you won't see anything of the country, and the people. And that's what you came for.

RUBEK, *curtly and irritably.* I've seen more than enough.

MAJA. Do you think a sea voyage'll be better for you?

RUBEK. Well, it's always a change.

MAJA. All right, if you think it'll be good for you——

RUBEK. Good for me? For me? There's nothing the matter with me.

MAJA *gets up and goes over to him.* Yes, there is, Rubek. And you know it.

RUBEK. But, my dear, what should be the matter with me?

MAJA, *behind him, leaning over the back of his chair.* You tell me. You've begun to wander round restlessly, as though you couldn't find peace, at home or anywhere else. And you've begun to avoid people lately.

RUBEK, *with a touch of sarcasm.* Really? *You've* noticed that?

MAJA. No-one who knows you could help noticing it. And I think it's such a pity you've lost your passion for work——

RUBEK. That, too?

MAJA. You used to work all the time. Day and night——

RUBEK. Used to.

MAJA. But ever since you finished your masterpiece——

RUBEK *nods reflectively.* "The Day of Resurrection."

MAJA. The masterpiece which has been exhibited all over the world, and has made you famous——

RUBEK. Perhaps that's where it began to go wrong, Maja.

MAJA. What do you mean?

RUBEK. When I completed my masterpiece——

Makes a passionate gesture with his hand.

For "The Day of Resurrection" is a masterpiece. Or was, when I first—— No, it still is! It must, must, *must* be a masterpiece!

MAJA *stares at him in surprise.* Yes, Rubek. The whole world knows that.

RUBEK. The world knows nothing. It understands nothing.

MAJA. At least they can sense *something*——

RUBEK. Something that isn't there, oh yes! Something I've never imagined. And that is what they all go mad about.

Growls to himself.

What's the use of working oneself to death to please them!

MAJA. Are you better occupied nowadays, churning out these portrait busts? Do you really think they're worthy of you?

RUBEK *smiles forbearingly.* They are not ordinary portrait busts, Maja.

MAJA. Oh, yes they are. These last two or three years—ever since you got that big group finished and out of the house——

RUBEK. Nevertheless, they are not ordinary portraits. Believe me.

MAJA. What are they, then?

RUBEK. There is something hidden within those faces. A secret meaning which people cannot see.

MAJA. Oh, really?

RUBEK. Only I can see it. And I find it intensely amusing. Superficially, there are these "striking likenesses" as they call them, at which people gape, entranced. But deep within, I have sculpted the righteous and estimable faces of horses, the opinionated muzzles of donkeys, the lop ears and shallow brows of dogs, the overgorged chaps of swine, and the dull and brutalized fronts of oxen.

MAJA, *indifferently.* All nice, domestic animals, poor dears.

RUBEK. Just nice, domestic animals, Maja. All the animals which man has corrupted in his own image. And which have corrupted him in return.

Empties his champagne glass and smiles.

And these disingenuous works of art are what our honest burghers commission from me—and pay for, in good faith and solid cash. Oh, they are almost literally worth their weight in gold.

MAJA *fills his glass.* Shame on you, Rubek. Drink, and be happy.

RUBEK *wipes his brow several times, and leans back in his chair.* I am happy, Maja. Really happy. In a way.

Is silent for a moment.

I mean, there is a certain happiness in feeling absolutely free and independent—in having everything one could possibly wish for. Everything material, I mean. Don't you agree, Maja?

MAJA. Oh yes, I suppose so. It's not to be despised.

Looks at him.

But do you remember what you promised me that day when we agreed on this arrangement——?

RUBEK *nods.* Agreed that we two should marry. It was a little difficult for you, wasn't it, Maja?

MAJA *continues deliberately.* And I was to go abroad with you, and stay there, and enjoy myself, always. Can you remember what you promised me then?

RUBEK *shakes his head.* I'll be damned if I can. What did I promise you?

MAJA. You said you would take me with you to the top of a high mountain, and show me all the glory of the world.

RUBEK *starts.* Did I promise that to you, too?

MAJA *looks at him.* Me too? Who else?

RUBEK, *casually.* No, no, I only meant, did I promise to show you——?

MAJA. All the glory of the world. Yes, that's what you said. And all that glory was to be mine, and yours, you said.

RUBEK. It was a phrase I used to be fond of.

MAJA. Only a phrase?

RUBEK. Yes. From my schooldays. I used to say it to the other children when I wanted to get them to come and play with me in the forest or up in the mountains.

MAJA. Perhaps that was all you wanted me for? To play games with?

RUBEK, *passing it off as a joke.* Well, it's been quite an enjoyable game, hasn't it, Maja?

MAJA, *coldly.* I didn't go away with you just to play games.

RUBEK. No, no, I daresay not.

MAJA. And you never took me with you up any mountain, to show me——

RUBEK, *irritated.* All the glory of the world? No, I didn't. The fact is, little Maja, you were not exactly made to climb mountains.

MAJA *tries to control herself.* You seemed to think I was, once.

RUBEK. Four or five years ago, yes.

Stretches in his chair.

Four or five years. That's a long, long time, Maja.

MAJA *looks at him bitterly.* Has it seemed so long to you, Rubek?

RUBEK. It begins to seem a little long now.

Yawns.

Just now and then.

MAJA *goes back to her chair.* Well, I won't bore you any longer.

She sits in her chair, picks up her newspaper, and turns the pages. Silence on both sides.

RUBEK *leans across the table on his elbows and stares banteringly at her.* Is the Frau Professor offended?

MAJA, *coldly, without looking up.* Not in the least.

Visitors to the spa, mostly ladies, wander singly and in groups through the park from the right, and go out left. Waiters carry refreshments from the hotel out past the pavilion. The INSPECTOR, *wearing gloves and carrying a stick, comes from his round of the park, meets the visitors, greets them respectfully, and exchanges a few words with some of them.*

INSPECTOR *comes forward to* PROFESSOR RUBEK's *table and takes his hat off respectfully.* May I have the honour to wish you a good morning, madam? Good morning, Professor.

RUBEK. Good morning, good morning, Inspector.

INSPECTOR, *addressing himself to* MAJA. May I enquire whether you have spent a good night?

MAJA. Thank you, yes, excellent—as far as I am concerned. I always sleep like a log.

INSPECTOR. I am delighted to hear it. One's first night in a strange bed can sometimes be a trying experience. And you, Professor?

RUBEK. Oh, I always sleep badly. Especially recently.

INSPECTOR *looks sympathetic.* Ah, I am sorry to hear that. But a few weeks here with us, and things will be different.

RUBEK *looks up at him.* Tell me, Inspector—have you a patient who is in the habit of bathing at night?

INSPECTOR. At night? No, I've never heard of such a thing.

RUBEK. You haven't?

INSPECTOR. No, I don't know of anyone here who's so ill as to require *that.*

RUBEK. Well, is there someone who takes a nightly walk in the park?

INSPECTOR *smiles and shakes his head.* No, Professor—that would be against the regulations.

MAJA, *impatiently.* For heaven's sake, Rubek, I told you this morning. You've been dreaming.

RUBEK, *dryly*. Really? Have I? Thank you.

Turns to the INSPECTOR.

It so happens I couldn't sleep last night, so I got up. I wanted to see what kind of a night it was——

INSPECTOR. Yes, Professor? And——?

RUBEK. So I looked out of the window. And I saw a figure dressed in white over there among the trees.

MAJA *smiles at the* INSPECTOR. And the Professor says this figure was wearing a bathing dress.

RUBEK. Or something of the sort, I said. I couldn't see closely enough. I could only tell it was something white.

INSPECTOR. Most remarkable. Was it a gentleman or a lady?

RUBEK. A lady, I'm almost sure. But behind walked another figure. And this second figure was quite dark—like a shadow——

INSPECTOR. A dark figure? Was it black?

RUBEK. Yes, it appeared so to me.

INSPECTOR, *beginning to understand*. And it walked behind the white figure? Close behind her?

RUBEK. Yes, a little behind.

INSPECTOR. Ah! Then I may be able to explain this mystery for you, Professor.

RUBEK. Well, tell me, who was it?

MAJA, *simultaneously*. You mean he wasn't dreaming after all?

INSPECTOR *whispers, and points upstage right*. Ssh! Look over there! Lower your voices for a moment, please!

A slender LADY, *dressed in fine, cream cashmere, enters past the corner of the hotel, followed by a* NUN *dressed in black, with a silver cross hanging from a chain on her breast. She walks through the park towards the pavilion downstage left. Her face is pale and drawn, as though numbed; her eyelids droop, and her eyes seem not to see. Her dress reaches to her feet, falling in long even folds close to her body. Over her head, neck, breast, shoulders and arms, she wears a large, white, crepe shawl. Her arms are folded across her breast. She carries her body stiffly, and her steps are measured and precise. The* NUN'S *demeanour is similarly precise, and suggests that of a servant. She watches the* LADY *ceaselessly with sharp brown eyes. Waiters with napkins on their arms come to the door of the hotel and stare curiously at the two strangers, who take no notice and, without looking round, enter the pavilion.*

RUBEK *has risen slowly and involuntarily from his chair, and is staring at the closed pavilion door.* Who was that lady?

INSPECTOR. A visitor who has rented that little pavilion.

RUBEK. Is she foreign?

INSPECTOR. I think she must be. They arrived here from abroad, anyway. About a week ago. They've never been here before.

RUBEK. She is the one I saw in the park last night.

INSPECTOR. It must have been. The thought occurred to me at once.

RUBEK. What is this lady's name, Inspector?

INSPECTOR. She registered as Madame de Satow and companion. That's all we know.

RUBEK, *reflectively.* Satow? Satow?

MAJA. Do you know anyone of that name, Rubek? Hm?

RUBEK *shakes his head.* No, no-one. Satow? That sounds Russian; or Slavonic, anyway.

To the INSPECTOR.

What language does she speak?

INSPECTOR. When the two ladies talk together, they use a language I don't understand, but at other times she speaks good honest Norwegian.

RUBEK. Norwegian? Are you sure you're not mistaken?

INSPECTOR. No, how could I be? I've talked to her several times. Only a few words, she's very reticent. But——

RUBEK. But she spoke Norwegian?

INSPECTOR. Good, pure Norwegian. Possibly with a slight northern intonation.

RUBEK, *to himself.* That too!

MAJA, *a little hurt and ill at ease.* Perhaps the lady has been your model at some time, Rubek. Think back, now.

RUBEK *looks sharply at her.* Model?

MAJA, *teasingly.* When you were young. Think of all those models you used to have. In the old days, I mean.

RUBEK. No, little Maja; to tell the truth, I have only ever had one model. Only one—for everything I have created.

INSPECTOR, *who has turned and stands looking away to the left.* I am afraid I must ask you to excuse me now. I see someone coming whom I would rather not speak to. Especially when a lady is present.

RUBEK *glances in the same direction.* Who's the hunter?

INSPECTOR. That is Squire Ulfhejm, from——

RUBEK. Oh, Squire Ulfhejm.

INSPECTOR. The bear-baiter, they call him.

RUBEK. I know him.

INSPECTOR. Yes, who doesn't?

RUBEK. Only slightly. Has he come here for treatment at last?

INSPECTOR. No, surprisingly enough, not yet. He just passes through once a year, on his way up to his hunting grounds. Please excuse me.

Turns to go into the hotel.

ULFHEJM, *offstage.* Wait a minute! Wait a minute, damn your eyes! Why do you always scuttle away when I come?

INSPECTOR *stops.* I was not scuttling, Squire Ulfhejm.

SQUIRE ULFHEJM *enters from the left, followed by a servant leading a pack of hounds. The* SQUIRE *is in shooting costume, with high boots and a felt hat with a feather in it. He is a lean, tall, sinewy man, with matted hair and beard, and a loud voice. His age is difficult to judge from his appearance, but he is no longer young.*

ULFHEJM, *pouncing on the* INSPECTOR. What kind of a way's that to receive visitors, eh? Running away with your tail between your legs as though the Devil was on your heels?

INSPECTOR, *calmly, ignoring the question.* Have you—ah—come with the steamer, sir?

ULFHEJM *growls.* Ain't had the pleasure of seeing any damn steamer.

With his hands on his hips.

Don't you know I always sail in my own cutter?

To the SERVANT.

Take good care of your fellow-creatures, Lars. Keep 'em ravenous, though. Fresh meat-bones—but not too much meat on 'em, mind! And be sure it's reeking raw, with plenty of blood in it. And get something in your own belly, too.

Aims a kick at him.

Well, get to hell out of here.

The SERVANT *goes out with the hounds past the corner of the hotel.*

INSPECTOR. Won't you go into the restaurant, sir?

ULFHEJM. What, among all those dead flies and half-dead people? No thank you, Inspector.

INSPECTOR. Well, well, just as you please.

ULFHEJM. Just get the housekeeper to fix me up as usual. No stinting with the food, mind; and bring out your best aquavit. You can tell her that I or Lars'll come and put the fear of God into her if she doesn't——

INSPECTOR *interrupts.* We know that from your previous visits.

Turns.

Can I tell the waiter to bring you anything, Professor? Or something for Mrs. Rubek, perhaps?

RUBEK. No, thank you, nothing for me.

MAJA. Nor for me.

The INSPECTOR *goes into the hotel.*

ULFHEJM *glares at them for a moment, then raises his hat.* Death and damnation! This is fine company for a yokel like me to stray into!

RUBEK *looks up.* I beg your pardon?

ULFHEJM, *more quietly and politely.* Isn't it master-carver Rubek himself?

RUBEK *nods.* We met once or twice socially, the last autumn I spent in this country.

ULFHEJM. Yes, but that was years ago; and you weren't as famous then as I hear you've become now, so that in those days even a dirty bear-baiter dared to come within range of you.

RUBEK *smiles.* Well, I don't bite, even now.

MAJA *looks with interest at* ULFHEJM. Do you really hunt bears?

ULFHEJM *seats himself at the next table, nearer the hotel.* Bears for choice, ma'am. But if they're not to be had, I'll take any wild thing that crosses my path. Eagles, wolves, women, elks, reindeer—as long as it's fresh and juicy and has good red blood in its veins.

Drinks from his hip flask.

MAJA, *looking at him intently.* But bears for choice?

ULFHEJM. For choice, yes. If they give any trouble, you can use your knife.

With a slight smile.

We both like tough material to work on, ma'am, your husband and I. He struggles with his blocks of—marble, I suppose it'd be—and I with the bear. And both of us conquer our material in the end; make ourselves masters over it. We don't give up till we've brought it to heel, however strongly it resists us.

RUBEK, *thoughtfully.* There's truth in that.

ULFHEJM. Yes; even stone's got something to fight for. It's dead, and'll do everything it can to save itself from being chiselled into life. Just like a bear when you creep up and prod it in its lair.

MAJA. Are you going up to shoot in the forests?

ULFHEJM. Yes, high up in the mountains. I daresay you've never been up to the top of a mountain, Mrs. Rubek?

MAJA. No, never.

ULFHEJM. Death and damnation, then, make sure you go up this summer! Come along with me. I'll take you both, gladly.

MAJA. Thank you. But my husband is thinking of going on a sea voyage this summer.

RUBEK. Only along the coast, among the islands.

ULFHEJM. Why the devil do you want to waste your time in those tepid gutters? I never heard of such an idea—frittering the summer away in that ditchwater! Dishwater, I call it!

MAJA. Do you hear that, Rubek?

ULFHEJM. No, come with me up to the mountains. It's clean up there; no people. You can't imagine what that means to me. But a little lady like you, Mrs.——

He stops himself. The NUN *comes out of the pavilion and goes into the hotel.* ULFHEJM *follows her with his eyes.*

Look at her, eh? That black crow. Who's going to be buried today?

RUBEK. No-one that I know of——

ULFHEJM. Well, someone must be at death's door. People who don't know how to keep themselves healthy ought to have the decency to get themselves buried, and not waste time about it.

MAJA. Have you ever been ill, Squire Ulfhejm?

ULFHEJM. Never. If I had, I wouldn't be sitting here. Some of my best friends have, though.

MAJA. And what did you do for them?

ULFHEJM. Shot them, of course.

RUBEK *stares at him.* Shot them?

MAJA *pushes her chair back.* Shot them dead?

ULFHEJM *nods.* I never miss, ma'am.

MAJA. But what could induce you to kill human beings?

ULFHEJM. Who's talking about human beings?

MAJA. You said your best friends.

ULFHEJM. I was referring to my dogs.

MAJA. Are they your closest friends?

ULFHEJM. None closer. Fine sense of honour—never let you down—hundred per cent loyal—grand sportsmen. As soon as one of 'em turns sick or starts to mope—bang! Off he goes. Into the next world.

The NUN *comes out of the hotel with a tray, on which milk and bread are set, and places it on the table outside the pavilion, which she then re-enters.*

ULFHEJM *laughs scornfully.* Look at that! Call that food for human consumption? Watered milk, and soft, mushy bread! Now you ought to see my fellows eat! Would you like to see 'em?

MAJA *smiles at the* PROFESSOR *and gets up.* Yes, I'd love to.

ULFHEJM *gets up too.* Spoken like a woman of spirit, ma'am. Come with me, then. Great red meat-bones—they swallow 'em whole—cough 'em up, and then gulp 'em down again. Does your heart good to watch 'em. Come along, and I'll show 'em to you. And we'll talk some more about this trip up into the mountains——

He goes out round the corner of the hotel. MAJA *follows him. A moment later, the* STRANGE LADY *comes out of the pavilion and seats herself at her table. She raises the glass of milk and is about to drink when she sees* RUBEK. *She stops, and looks at him with empty, expressionless eyes.* RUBEK *remains seated at his table, staring earnestly and intently at her. At length he rises, goes a few paces towards her, stops, and says softly:*

RUBEK. Irene!

IRENE, *tonelessly, setting down her glass.* You've guessed, have you, Arnold?

RUBEK. And you recognize me too, I see.

IRENE. That's different.

RUBEK. Why is it different?

IRENE. You're still alive.

RUBEK. Alive?

IRENE, *after a short pause.* Who was the other person? The one you had with you at the table?

RUBEK. That? That was—my wife.

IRENE *nods slowly.* Indeed? Good, Arnold. No concern of mine, then.

RUBEK, *uncertainly.* No, of course not.

IRENE. Someone you found after I died.

RUBEK. After you——? How do you mean, Irene?

IRENE. And the child? Our child is well? It has survived me, and become famous and honoured.

RUBEK *smiles, as though at some distant memory.* Our child? Yes, that's what we called it.

Trying to seem jovial.

Yes, Irene, now our child has become famous all over the world. You've read about it, I suppose?

IRENE *nods.* And has made its father famous. That was your dream.

RUBEK, *quietly, emotionally.* I owe everything to you, Irene, everything. Thank you.

IRENE *sits silent for a moment.* If I had done as I should have, Arnold——

RUBEK. Yes?

IRENE. I should have killed that child.

RUBEK. Killed it, did you say?

IRENE *whispers.* Killed it—before I left you. Smashed it, smashed it to pieces.

RUBEK. You could never have done that, Irene. You wouldn't have had the heart.

IRENE. No. I hadn't that kind of heart then.

RUBEK. But—afterwards?

IRENE. Since then I have killed it a thousand times. In the daylight and in the dark. Killed it in hatred, and revenge, and agony.

RUBEK *goes close to her table, and asks softly.* Irene, tell me now, after all these years. Why did you leave me? Vanish without a trace—nowhere to be found?

IRENE. Oh, Arnold. Why should I tell you that now—when I am dead?

RUBEK. Was there someone else you had fallen in love with?

IRENE. There was someone who had no use for my love. Or my life. Any longer.

RUBEK. Let's not talk any more about the past. Where have you been, Irene? All my efforts to find you came to nothing.

IRENE. I passed into the darkness. While our child stood transfigured in the light.

RUBEK. Have you travelled?

IRENE. Yes. Travelled through many countries.

RUBEK, *gently*. And what have you been doing, Irene?

IRENE. Well, now. Let me think. Yes, now I have it. I have stood like a statue, naked on a revolving platform, in music halls. I made a lot of money. That was something I'd never done when I was with you, because you hadn't any. And I've been with men, whom I could drive crazy. That was something I'd never been able to do to you, Arnold. You had such self-control.

RUBEK. You married, too, didn't you?

IRENE. Yes, I married one of them.

RUBEK. Who is your husband?

IRENE. He was a South American diplomat.

With a cold smile.

I drove him crazy. He went mad; incurably, hopelessly mad. It was amusing while it lasted.

RUBEK. Where is he now?

IRENE. In a graveyard, somewhere. With a fine big monument over him. And a lead bullet rattling in his skull.

RUBEK. Did he kill himself?

IRENE. Yes. He was kind enough to save me the trouble.

RUBEK. Aren't you sorry he's dead, Irene?

IRENE. Sorry who's dead?

RUBEK. Herr von Satow.

IRENE. He wasn't called Satow.

RUBEK. No?

IRENE. My second husband's name is Satow. He's Russian——

RUBEK. And where is he?

IRENE. Far away in the Ural Mountains. Among his gold mines.

RUBEK. He lives there?

IRENE *shrugs her shoulders.* Lives? Lives? I think I've killed him, too.

RUBEK. Killed?

IRENE. Killed him with a fine, sharp dagger I always take to bed with me—

RUBEK. I don't believe you, Irene!

IRENE *smiles gently.* It's true, Arnold, I promise you.

RUBEK, *sympathetically.* Have you never had any children?

IRENE. Yes, I have had many children.

RUBEK. And where are they now?

IRENE. I killed them.

RUBEK, *severely.* Now you are lying to me again.

IRENE. I killed them, I tell you! Without a moment's pity. As soon as they entered the world. No, long, long before that. One after the other.

RUBEK. There is another meaning in everything you say.

IRENE. I can't help it. Every word I say to you is whispered in my ear.

RUBEK. I think I am the only person who can guess that meaning.

IRENE. You should be the only one.

RUBEK *rests his hands on the table and looks deep into her eyes.* Some string inside you has broken.

IRENE, *gently.* Doesn't that always happen when someone dies?

RUBEK. Oh, Irene, forget these wild ideas! You are alive! Alive, alive!

IRENE *rises slowly from her chair, trembling.* I was dead for many years. They came and tied me up, tied my arms together behind my back. Then they lowered me into a tomb, with iron bars across the door, and padded walls so that no one up above could hear the shrieks of the dead. But now, slowly, I am beginning to rise from the dead.
She sits again.

RUBEK, *after a moment.* Do you blame me for this? Do you hold me guilty?

IRENE. Yes.

RUBEK. Guilty of—of your death, as you call it?

IRENE. Guilty of leaving me no future but death.

Changes her tone and says casually.

Why don't you sit down, Arnold?

RUBEK *moves a chair and sits down at the table.* Look, Irene. Now we two are sitting together as we used to in the old days.

IRENE. A little apart; as in the old days.

RUBEK, *moving nearer.* That's how it had to be, then.

IRENE. Had to?

RUBEK. There had to be a distance between us.

IRENE. Was it so necessary, Arnold?

RUBEK. Do you remember what you said when I asked you if you would leave home and come with me out into the world?

IRENE. I raised three fingers in the air and promised that I would go with you to the end of the world; and to the end of life. And that I would serve you in all things——

RUBEK. As a model for my work.

IRENE. Free and naked——

RUBEK. And you did serve me, Irene—joyfully, gladly, unstintingly——

IRENE. Yes; with all the trembling blood of my youth.

RUBEK. Too true you did.

IRENE. I knelt down at your feet, and served you, Arnold.

Shakes her fist at him.

But you—you—you——!

RUBEK. I never wronged you. Never, Irene.

IRENE. Yes, you did! You wronged my inmost being!

RUBEK. I?

IRENE. Yes, you. I stripped myself naked for you to gaze at me.

More quietly.

And you never once touched me.

RUBEK. Irene, didn't you understand that your beauty often drove me almost out of my mind?

IRENE. And yet, if you had touched me, I think I would have killed you on the spot. I had a sharp needle always with me; I hid it in my hair.

Wipes her forehead pensively.

Yes, but—but, no, no! How could you?

RUBEK. I was an artist, Irene.

IRENE, *darkly*. An artist. Yes.

RUBEK. Before all else, I was an artist. And I was sick—sick with a longing to create the one great work of my life.

Loses himself in memory.

It was to be called: "The Day of Resurrection." I conceived it in the likeness of a young woman, awakening from the sleep of death——

IRENE. Our child, yes.

RUBEK. She, this awakening girl, was to be all that is noble, all that is pure; perfection in woman. Then I found you. In you I saw all the things I wanted to express. And you agreed so gladly, so willingly. You left your family and your home, and came with me.

IRENE. When you took me away, I felt just as though I had become a child again.

RUBEK. That was why I was able to use you. You, and no-one else. To me, you were something sacred and untouchable, fit only to be adored. I was still young then, Irene. And I was convinced that if I touched you, if I desired you sensually, my vision would be profaned so that I would never be able to achieve what I was striving after. And I still think there is some truth in that.

IRENE. The child of the mind first; the child of the body second.

RUBEK. Condemn me if you will. But—I was so completely dominated by my task. And so exultantly happy in it.

IRENE. And you accomplished your task, Arnold.

RUBEK. Thanks to you, bless you, yes, I accomplished my task. I wanted to create woman as she will appear when

she wakes, pure and undefiled, on the day of resurrection.
Not marvelling at what is new, the unknown, the unim-
agined, but filled with a holy joy at finding herself un-
changed—she, a mortal woman!—in the higher, freer, happier
kingdom, after the long and dreamless sleep of death.

Quietly.

That is how I created her—I created her in your image,
Irene.

IRENE *places her hands flat on the table and leans back in
her chair.* And then you were finished with me——

RUBEK. Irene!

IRENE. You had no further use for me——

RUBEK. How can you say that?

IRENE. You began to look round for other ideals to inspire
you——

RUBEK. I found none after you.

IRENE. No other models, Arnold?

RUBEK. You were not a model to me. You were my inspiration.

IRENE, *after a moment.* What have you created since then?
In marble, I mean. Since the day I left you.

RUBEK. I have wasted the years carving trivialities.

IRENE. And the woman you're living with now——?

RUBEK, *sharply.* Don't speak of her now.

IRENE. Where do you intend to go with her?

RUBEK, *inert, tired.* On a long, tedious trip up north along the
coast.

IRENE *looks at him, smiles almost imperceptibly, and whispers.*
Go high up into the mountains; as high as you can go.
Higher, higher—always higher, Arnold.

RUBEK. Are you going up there?

IRENE. Dare you meet me again?

RUBEK. If only we could! Ah, if only we could!

IRENE. Why shouldn't we? If we want to. Come, come, Arnold! Oh, please come up to me——!

MAJA, *flushed and happy, comes past the corner of the*

hotel, and hurries over to the table where she and RUBEK *were sitting before.*

MAJA. You can say what you like, Rubek, but——

Stops as she sees IRENE.

Oh, excuse me! You've made a new acquaintance, I see.

RUBEK, *curtly.* I have renewed an old acquaintance.

Stands up.

What were you saying?

MAJA. I was saying, you may do as you like, but I am not going with you on that awful steamer.

RUBEK. Why not?

MAJA. I want to go up into the mountains, and the forests. I'd so love to.

Coaxingly.

Oh, you must let me, Rubek. I'll be so good if you do.

RUBEK. Who's given you these ideas?

MAJA. He—that horrible man who kills bears. Oh, you can't imagine what extraordinary things he's been telling me about the mountains! And the life up there! He's been making up the most horrible and frightening stories—I'm sure they're only stories—but somehow he makes it all sound wonderfully attractive. Oh, may I go up there with him? Just to see if all he says is true? May I, Rubek?

RUBEK. Go by all means, as far as I'm concerned. Yes, go up into the mountains, go as far as you please, stay as long as you please. I may possibly be going up there myself.

MAJA, *quickly.* No, no, you needn't trouble to come. Not for my sake.

RUBEK. But I want to go up into the mountains. I've made up my mind to it now.

MAJA. Oh, thank you, thank you! May I run and tell him at once?

RUBEK. Tell him anything you like.

MAJA. Oh, thank you, thank you!

Tries to take his hand, but he withdraws it.

How sweet and kind you are today, Rubek!

She runs into the hotel. At the same instant, the door of the pavilion is slowly and silently pushed ajar. The NUN *stands inside the doorway, watching them. They do not see her.*

RUBEK, *turning to* IRENE. Shall we meet up there, then?

IRENE *rises slowly.* Yes, we shall meet up there. I've been looking for you for such a long time.

RUBEK. When did you begin to look for me, Irene?

IRENE, *with an ironical smile.* From the moment I realised I had given you something I couldn't do without, Arnold. Something one should never part with.

RUBEK *bows his head.* Yes, that is true. You gave me four years of your youth.

IRENE. More; I gave you much more than that. I was too prodigal.

RUBEK. Yes, you were prodigal, Irene. All your naked beauty you gave me——

IRENE. To gaze at.

RUBEK. And immortalise.

IRENE. For your own glory. And for the child.

RUBEK. For you, too, Irene.

IRENE. You've forgotten the most precious gift I gave you.

RUBEK. The most precious——? What gift was that?

IRENE. I gave you my soul—young and alive. And left myself empty; soulless. Don't you see? That's why I died, Arnold. *The* NUN *opens the door wide, and stands aside for her. She goes into the pavilion.*

RUBEK *stands staring after her; then he whispers.* Irene!

ACT TWO

At a mountain health resort. The landscape, a vast treeless plateau, stretches away towards a long mountain lake. Beyond the lake towers a range of mountain peaks, with bluish snow in their crevices. Downstage left, a stream, divided into rivulets, ripples down a steep wall of rock and flows out smoothly across the plateau towards the right. The stream is lined with brushwood, plants and boulders. Downstage right, is a small hillock with a stone bench on its top. It is a summer evening, just before sundown.

In the distance, beyond the stream, a number of small children sing, dance and play. Some wear town clothes, some country clothes. Their merry laughter is heard faintly throughout the scene.

PROFESSOR RUBEK *is seated on the bench, with a plaid over his shoulders, looking down at the children playing. After a few moments,* MAJA *enters through some bushes left centre, and gazes with her hand shading her eyes. She is wearing a flat tourist bonnet, a short skirt gathered halfway up her legs, and tall, strong, laced boots. In her hand she carries a long vaulting-stick.*

MAJA *sees* RUBEK *at last, and calls.* Hallo!

She goes forward, vaults over the stream with the help of her stick, and climbs up the hill.

Out of breath. Oh, I've been looking for you everywhere, Rubek.

RUBEK *nods indifferently.* Have you come from the hotel?

MAJA. Yes, a moment ago. Ugh, that fly-trap!

RUBEK. You didn't come down to lunch, I noticed.

MAJA. No, we ate ours in the open. Under the sky.

RUBEK. We? Who are "we"?

MAJA. I and—and that awful bear-baiter.

RUBEK. Oh, him.

MAJA. Yes. And tomorrow we're going out again. At dawn.

RUBEK. After bears?

MAJA. Yes. Off to kill bruin.

RUBEK. Have you found any tracks?

MAJA, *superciliously.* One doesn't find bears as high up as this. Didn't you know?

RUBEK. Where, then?

MAJA. Far down. Down in the valleys, where the forests are thickest. Where people from the towns can't go.

RUBEK. And you two are going down there tomorrow?

MAJA, *throwing herself down in the heather.* Yes, that's what we've decided. Or we may even go this evening. If you've no objection?

RUBEK. I? No, far from it.

MAJA, *quickly.* Lars'll be coming with us, of course. With the pack.

RUBEK. I'm not interested in Mr. Lars and his pack.

Changing the subject.

Won't you come and sit here beside me?

MAJA, *drowsily.* No, thank you. I'm so comfortable in this soft heather.

RUBEK. I can see you're tired.

MAJA *yawns.* I think I'm beginning to be.

RUBEK. It always comes afterwards, when the excitement is over.

MAJA, *sleepily.* Yes. I think I'll close my eyes.

Short pause.

Suddenly, impatiently. Oh, Rubek, how can you bear to sit here and listen to those children yelling and watch them jumping around?

RUBEK. There's a kind of harmony in their movements; almost like music. At isolated moments, amid all that clumsiness. It amuses me to sit and wait for those moments.

MAJA. Always the artist, aren't you?

RUBEK. Yes, please God.

MAJA *turns on to her side, so that she has her back to him.* There's nothing artistic about him.

RUBEK. About whom?

MAJA, *sleepy again.* Him. You know.

RUBEK. The bear-baiter, you mean?

MAJA. Yes. Nothing artistic about him. Nothing at all.

RUBEK *smiles.* I don't doubt that for a moment.

MAJA. And he's so ugly!

Picks a tuft of heather, and throws it away.

So ugly, so ugly! Ugh!

RUBEK. Is that why you're so delighted to be going off with him into the forests?

MAJA, *curtly.* I don't know.

Turns towards him.

You're ugly, too, Rubek.

RUBEK. Have you only just discovered that?

MAJA. No, I've noticed it for a long time.

RUBEK *shrugs his shoulders.* One grows older. One grows older, Maja.

MAJA. I don't mean that. There's something so tired and resigned about your eyes—when you deign to look at me, which isn't often.

RUBEK. You've noticed that, have you?

MAJA *nods.* Little by little a kind of evil expression has crept into them. Almost as though you were plotting something against me.

RUBEK. Really?

Friendly, yet serious.

Come here and sit beside me, Maja, and let us have a little talk.

MAJA *raises herself half up.* May I sit on your knee, then? Like I used to?

RUBEK. No, you mustn't do that—people can see us from the hotel.

Moves slightly.

Come and sit here on the bench beside me.

MAJA. No, thanks, in that case I'd rather stay where I am. I can hear you quite well from here. Well, what was it you wanted to talk about?

RUBEK. What do you think was my real reason for suggesting that we should come up to this place?

MAJA. Well, you said among other things that it'd be so good for me. But——

RUBEK. But?

MAJA. But now I don't believe that was the real reason.

RUBEK. Well, what do you think was?

MAJA. I think it was because of that pale lady.

RUBEK. Madame von Satow?

MAJA. Yes, the one who follows us round all the time. Yesterday evening she turned up here too.

RUBEK. But why on earth——?

MAJA. Well, you knew her very well, didn't you? Long before you knew me.

RUBEK. I'd forgotten her, too, long before I knew you.

MAJA *sits up.* Do you forget so quickly, Rubek?

RUBEK, *curtly.* Exceedingly quickly.

Adds harshly.

When I want to.

MAJA. Even someone who's been your model?

RUBEK. When I no longer have any use for her.

MAJA. A woman who's stripped herself naked for you?

RUBEK. That means nothing. Nothing to us artists.

With a change of tone.

Besides, how, if I may venture to ask, could I possibly have guessed she was in this part of the country?

MAJA. You could have read her name in a visitors' list. In a newspaper.

RUBEK. Yes, but I didn't know that name she uses now. I'd never heard of any Herr von Satow.

MAJA, *pretending to be bored.* Oh, Lord, well I suppose you must have had some other reason for wanting to come here, then.

RUBEK. Yes, Maja. I had another reason. Quite a different reason. That's what we've got to talk about sooner or later.

MAJA, *stifling a giggle.* Lord, how solemn you look!

RUBEK. Unnecessarily so?

MAJA. What do you mean?

RUBEK. It's probably just as well, for us both.

MAJA. You're beginning to make me curious, Rubek.

RUBEK. Only curious? Not just a little bit worried?

MAJA. Not in the least.

RUBEK. Good. Then listen. You said that day down at the spa that you thought I'd become very nervous these past months——

MAJA. Yes, so you have.

RUBEK. Why do you suppose that is?

MAJA. How should I know? Perhaps you've grown tired of being continually together with me.

RUBEK. Continually?

MAJA. Yes. We've lived together down there for five whole years, just the two of us, and have hardly ever been away from each other for an hour. Just we two, all by ourselves.

RUBEK. Well?

MAJA. You don't like being with people, Rubek. You prefer to be by yourself, and think your own thoughts. And I can't talk properly to you about what interests you. About art and all that. God knows I don't care very much for it, either.

RUBEK. Poor Maja. So we spend most of our time sitting by the fire and talking about *your* interests.

MAJA. Lord, I've no interests to talk about.

RUBEK. Well, perhaps they are rather trivial. Still, time passes, Maja. Time passes.

MAJA. True enough. Time passes. It's running away from you, Rubek. I suppose it's that that makes you so uneasy.

RUBEK *nods vigorously*. And so restless.

Shifts on the bench.

No, I can't stand this miserable life much longer.

MAJA *gets up and stands for a moment looking at him*. If you want to be rid of me, just say so.

RUBEK. What on earth are you talking about? Be rid of you?

MAJA. Yes. If you want to be finished with me, say so straight out. And I'll go; at once.

RUBEK *smiles almost imperceptibly*. Is that meant to be a threat, Maja?

MAJA. What threat can there be in that for you?

RUBEK *gets up*. No, you're perfectly right.

After a moment.

You and I can't possibly go on living this kind of life together.

MAJA. Well, then obviously——

RUBEK. There is no "then obviously" about it. Because we two can't go on living together as we are, it doesn't necessarily follow that we have to get divorced.

MAJA *smiles acidly*. Just separate, you mean?

RUBEK. That isn't necessary, either.

MAJA. Well? Out with it. What you want to do with me, then?

RUBEK, *hesitantly*. What I feel so keenly—almost painfully— is the need of someone who is really close to me——

MAJA *interrupts*. Aren't I, Rubek?

RUBEK. Not in that way. I must live with someone who can make me complete—supply what's missing in me— someone who is one with me in everything I strive for.

MAJA, *slowly.* Yes; in big things like that, I can't be of any help to you.

Vehemently.

And God knows I haven't any desire to be, either!

RUBEK. I know that only too well. That wasn't what I had in mind when I married you.

MAJA. I can see you're thinking of someone else.

RUBEK. Indeed? I didn't know you were clairvoyant.

MAJA. Oh, I know you so well, Rubek. Too well.

RUBEK. Then perhaps you can also see of whom I am thinking?

MAJA. Indeed I can.

RUBEK. Well? Please tell me.

MAJA. You're thinking of that—that model you once used——

Suddenly changes her thread of thought.

Do you know, the people down at the hotel think she's mad?

RUBEK. Oh? What do the people down at the hotel think about you and our friend the bear-baiter?

MAJA. That has nothing to do with it.

Returns to her previous thread of thought.

It was that pale lady you were thinking of, wasn't it?

RUBEK. Exactly; of her. When I no longer had any use for her —and anyway, she left me—vanished, just like that——

MAJA. You took me as a kind of makeshift?

RUBEK. More or less, yes, to be quite frank, Maja dear. For a year or eighteen months, I had been alone, brooding in solitude. I had put the last touch—the absolutely final touch —to my work. "The Day of Resurrection" was exhibited all over the world. It brought me fame, and all the glory I could wish for. But I no longer loved my own work. The flowers and incense that were showered on me nauseated me, made me desperate; made me long to flee into the depths of the forest. Well, you are clairvoyant, can you guess what suddenly occurred to me?

MAJA. Yes, you decided to do portrait busts of ladies and gentlemen.

RUBEK *nods*. On commission. With animal faces behind the masks. They got *them* thrown in; free, gratis.

Smiles.

But that wasn't what I meant.

MAJA. Well, what did you mean?

RUBEK. I meant, it suddenly occurred to me that all this talk about the task of the artist and the vocation of the artist was empty, hollow, and meaningless.

MAJA. Well, what do you want instead?

RUBEK. Life, Maja.

MAJA. Life?

RUBEK. Yes. Isn't life in sunshine and beauty far more worthwhile than wasting one's years in a raw, damp cellar, wearing oneself to death wrestling with lumps of clay and blocks of stone?

MAJA, *with a little sigh*. Yes, *I've* always thought so.

RUBEK. Well, then I became rich enough to live in luxury and idly quivering sunlight. To build myself a villa on the Taunitzer See, and a mansion in the capital, and all the rest of it.

MAJA. And to cap it all, you could afford to buy me. And gave me leave to share your wealth with you.

RUBEK. Didn't I promise to take you with me up a high mountain and show you all the glory of the world?

MAJA. You may have brought me up quite a high mountain, Rubek. But you haven't showed me all the glory of the world.

RUBEK *laughs irritably*. How impossible you are, to please, Maja! Quite impossible!

Angrily.

But can you guess what it really is that has driven me to despair?

MAJA. Yes; the fact that you've tied yourself to me for life.

RUBEK. I wouldn't have put it quite so heartlessly.

MAJA. That doesn't make the thought less heartless.

RUBEK. You don't understand what really goes on in an artist's mind.

MAJA. Good heavens, I haven't the faintest idea what goes on inside my own mind.

RUBEK. I live so fast, Maja. We live like that, we artists. I have lived through a whole lifetime in the few years we two have known each other. And I've come to realize that it's not within my power to find happiness in idleness and soft living. Life is not shaped like that for me and my kind. I must go on working, creating incessantly, until I die.

With an effort.

That is why I can't go on with you any longer, Maja. Just you and I.

MAJA, *calmly.* Does that mean, in plain words, that you've grown tired of me?

RUBEK, *vehemently.* Yes, that is what it means! I've grown bored, intolerably bored and tired of living with you; it's drained all my vitality. Now you know!

Controls himself.

Those are hard and ugly words. I know that well. And you are not to blame, I admit that willingly. It's only in me that this change, this revolution has occurred.

Half to himself.

This awakening to the life that is really mine.

MAJA. Why in God's name can't we part, then?

RUBEK. Would you be willing?

MAJA *shrugs her shoulders.* Ye-es, if there's no alternative——

RUBEK. But there is an alternative. There is a way——

MAJA. Now you're thinking of that pale lady again.

RUBEK. Yes. To be honest, my thoughts always return to her. Ever since I met her again.

Moves closer to her.

I want to tell you a secret, Maja.

MAJA. Well?

RUBEK *taps himself on the chest.* In here, Maja—in here I keep a small casket, with a lock that cannot be picked. In that casket, all my visions lie. But when she left me, and vanished from my life, the lock of that casket snapped shut. She had the key, and she took it with her. You, my poor Maja, you had no key. So everything in it lies unused. And the years pass—and all that wealth lies there—and I cannot touch it!

MAJA. Then get her to unlock it for you.

RUBEK, *puzzled*. Maja——?

MAJA. She's here. No doubt it's because of this little casket that she has been following us.

RUBEK. I never mentioned a word of this to her. Never.

MAJA, *innocently*. But, my dear Rubek, is it worth making all this fuss and bother about such a simple matter?

RUBEK. You call this a simple matter?

MAJA. Certainly I do. You go to whoever you need the most. I shall always be able to find somewhere.

RUBEK. Where?

MAJA. Well, I could move out to the villa if necessary. But it won't be. Our town house is very large; with a little give and take, there should be room enough in it for three.

RUBEK. Do you think that could work? In the long run?

MAJA. Lord, if it doesn't work, it doesn't. We won't get any further by discussing it.

RUBEK. But what shall we do if it doesn't work, Maja?

MAJA, *cheerfully*. Then you and I will simply go different ways. Part. I shall find something new, somewhere. A place where I can be free. Free, free! You needn't worry about me, Professor Rubek.

Suddenly points away to the right.

Look! There she is!

RUBEK, *turning*. Where?

MAJA. Over there. Pacing along like a marble statue. She's coming this way.

RUBEK *stands up and stares, his hand shading his eyes*. Isn't she the incarnate image of "The Resurrection"?

To himself.

Why did I ever let her go? Drive her into the darkness? Change her into a——? Fool that I was, fool!

MAJA. What does all that mean?

RUBEK. Nothing. Nothing that you would understand.

IRENE *comes across the plateau from the right. The playing children have already seen her and run to meet her. Now she is surrounded by the whole crowd of them; some of them seem gay and trusting, some shy and nervous. She speaks quietly to them, and indicates that they shall go down to the hotel; she herself wants to rest for a while by the stream. The children run off down the hill to the left.* IRENE *goes over to the rock face and lets the rivulets run coolingly over her hands.*

MAJA, *softly*. Go down and talk to her, Rubek. Alone.

RUBEK. Where will you go?

MAJA. From now on I shall go my own ways.

She goes down the hillside and swings herself across the stream with her vaulting stick. She pauses beside IRENE.

Professor Rubek is up there waiting for you, madam.

IRENE. What does he want?

MAJA. He wants you to help him open a casket which has jammed shut.

IRENE. Can I help him with that?

MAJA. He says you're the only person who can.

IRENE. Then I'd better try.

MAJA. Indeed, madam, I think you better had.

She goes down the path towards the hotel. A few moments later, PROFESSOR RUBEK *descends to* IRENE, *but stops with the stream between them.*

IRENE. She said you've been waiting for me.

RUBEK. I have been waiting for you. For years. Without knowing it.

IRENE. I couldn't come to you, Arnold. I was lying down there, asleep. A long, deep sleep, full of dreams.

RUBEK. Ah, but now you have awakened, Irene.

IRENE *shakes her head*. The sleep is heavy in my eyes still.

RUBEK. The day will dawn and the sun will shine for both of us. You will see.

IRENE. Never believe that!

RUBEK. I do believe it! I know it! Now that I've found you again——

IRENE. Risen.

RUBEK. Transfigured!

IRENE. Only risen, Arnold. Not transfigured.

He crosses to her on the stepping stones beneath the water-fall.

RUBEK. Where have you been all day, Irene?

IRENE *points.* Far away, in the dead country yonder——

RUBEK, *trying to distract her.* You haven't your—your friend with you today, I see.

IRENE *smiles.* My friend keeps a close watch on me all the time.

RUBEK. How can she?

IRENE *glances around.* Oh, she can, she can! Wherever I go. She never lets me out of her sight.

Whispers.

Until, one fine, sunny morning, I shall kill her.

RUBEK. Do you want to kill her?

IRENE. Oh yes. If only I could.

RUBEK. Why?

IRENE. Because she's a witch.

Furtively.

Do you know, Arnold—she's turned herself into my shadow.

RUBEK, *trying to calm her.* Well, well, we all have to have a shadow.

IRENE. I am my own shadow.

Cries.

Can't you understand that?

RUBEK, *heavily.* Yes, yes, Irene. I understand.

He sits down on a stone by the stream. She stands behind him, leaning against the rock face.

IRENE, *after a few moments.* Why do you sit there with your eyes turned away from me?

RUBEK. I dare not—I dare not look at you.

IRENE. Why don't you dare to look at me any longer?

RUBEK. You have a shadow that torments you. And I a conscience.

IRENE, *with a happy cry, as though of liberation.* At last!

RUBEK *leaps up.* Irene! What is it?

IRENE. Be calm, be calm!

Takes a deep breath, and says, as though relieved of a burden.

All right. Now they let go of me. For a moment, anyway. Now we can sit down and talk. As we used to.

RUBEK. If only we could talk as we used to.

IRENE. Sit there where you were sitting before. Then I'll sit beside you.

He sits down again. She sits on another stone near him. A short silence.

Now I have come back to you from a far country, Arnold.

RUBEK. Yes; from an endless journey.

IRENE. Come home to my lord and master——

RUBEK. To ourselves; to our own selves, Irene.

IRENE. Have you waited for me every day?

RUBEK. How could I dare to wait for you?

IRENE, *with a sidelong glance.* No, I don't suppose you did. You never understood a thing.

RUBEK. Was it really not for someone else that you disappeared so suddenly?

IRENE. Couldn't it have been for you, Arnold?

RUBEK. But I don't understand——

IRENE. When I had served you with my soul and my body—and the sculpture stood there, finished—our child, as you called it—I lay at your feet the dearest sacrifice I could offer. I blotted myself out for ever.

RUBEK *bows his head.* And left my life a desert.

IRENE. Exactly. I wasn't going to allow you to create again,

ever. Once you had created this child of ours; our only
child.

RUBEK. Was it jealousy that made you do this?

IRENE, *coldly.* No. Hatred, I think.

RUBEK. Hatred? Hatred of me?

IRENE, *vehemently again.* Yes, of you! Of the artist who
lightly and casually took a warm living body, a young human life, and tore the soul from it, because you needed it
to create a work of art.

RUBEK. You say that? You, who shared my work so ardently,
with such a high, holy passion? That work for which we
met each morning as for an act of devotion?

IRENE, *coldly again.* There is one thing I must tell you,
Arnold.

RUBEK. Yes?

IRENE. I never loved your work, before I met you. Nor afterwards.

RUBEK. But—the artist, Irene?

IRENE. I hate the artist.

RUBEK. The artist in me, too?

IRENE. Most of all in you. When I stripped myself naked and
stood there before you, I hated you, Arnold.

RUBEK, *violently.* That's not true, Irene! You didn't!

IRENE. I hated you, because you could stand there so unmoved——

RUBEK *laughs.* Unmoved!

IRENE. Or so intolerably in control of yourself, then! And because you were an artist, only an artist, not a man!
Changes her tone, and speaks warmly, intensely.
But that statue of wet and living clay, her I loved—as she
rose out of that raw and formless mass, a human child, with
a soul. She was *our* creation, *our* child. Mine, and yours.

RUBEK. It was. In spirit and in truth.

IRENE. It's for our child that I have made this long pilgrimage.

RUBEK. For that marble image?

IRENE. Call it what you will. I call it our child.

RUBEK, *uneasily.* And now you want to see it? Finished? In marble, which you always said was so cold?

Eagerly.

Perhaps you do not know that it now stands far away in a great museum?

IRENE. I heard a story to that effect.

RUBEK. You always hated museums. You called them tombs.

IRENE. I want to make a pilgrimage to the place where my soul and the child of my soul lie buried.

RUBEK. You must never see that statue again! Do you hear, Irene? I beg you, never, never see it again!

IRENE. You think that I would die a second time?

RUBEK. I don't know what I think. How could I ever have known you would become so obsessed with this statue? You, who left me before it was complete!

IRENE. It *was* complete. That was why I was able to leave you. Leave you alone.

RUBEK *sits with his elbows on his knees, rocking his head from side to side, his hands over his eyes.* In the end, it— changed. Became—different, Irene.

IRENE, *quietly and swiftly, draws a thin, sharp knife from her bosom. She whispers.* Arnold, have you harmed our child?

RUBEK, *evasively.* Harmed? I'm not sure what *you* would call it.

IRENE. What have you done?

RUBEK. I'll tell you, if you promise to sit and listen calmly. And you mustn't look at me while I tell you.

IRENE *hides the knife and moves across to a stone behind him.* I shall sit here, behind you. Now tell me.

RUBEK *takes his hands from his eyes.* When I found you, I knew at once how I should use you. You were to be my masterpiece. I was young then. With no experience of life. I envisaged Resurrection as something perfect and beautiful—a pure young girl, unstained by life, awakening to light and glory without having to free herself from anything ugly or unclean.

IRENE. And that is how I stand there now?

RUBEK, *unwillingly*. Not—quite like that, Irene.

IRENE. Not quite——? Don't I stand there as I always stood before you?

RUBEK, *not replying*. In the years after you left me, Irene, I gained experience and knowledge. I began to envisage "The Day of Resurrection" as something bigger, something —something more complex. That small, round pedestal on which your statue stood erect and lonely—that was no longer big enough to hold all that I now wanted to express.

IRENE, *her hand moves towards the knife, but stops*. Well? Go on.

RUBEK. I portrayed what I saw with my own eyes in the world around me. I had to. I had no choice, Irene. I enlarged the pedestal, I made it broad and spacious. On it I set a small lump of our curved and fissured earth. And out of the fissures swarmed people, with the faces of beasts beneath their human masks. Women and men, as I knew them, from life.

IRENE. But in the middle of the throng the young woman stands, with the light of happiness transfiguring her face? I do, don't I, Arnold?

RUBEK, *evasively*. Not quite in the middle. Unfortunately I had to move the statue back a little—for the sake of the composition, you understand. Otherwise it would have dominated it too much.

IRENE. But the light of wonder and joy still shines on my face?

RUBEK. Yes, Irene, it does. In a way, that is. A little subdued, perhaps. To accord with the changed vision I had of life.

IRENE *rises silently*. And this new image expresses life as you see it now, Arnold?

RUBEK. Yes, I suppose so.

IRENE. And in this image you have portrayed me as a background figure, in a crowd?

She takes out the knife.

RUBEK. No, no. Not a background figure. No, at the worst I'd call it a middle-ground figure—or thereabouts.

IRENE *whispers*. Now you have pronounced judgment on yourself.

Is about to strike him with the knife.

RUBEK *turns and glances up at her.* Judgment?

IRENE *conceals the knife swiftly.* My whole soul—you and I—
we, we, we and our child, were in that lonely figure.

RUBEK *eagerly, tears off his hat and wipes the sweat from his
forehead.* Yes, but listen how I have portrayed myself in
this group. In the foreground, beside a spring, as it might
be here, there sits a man weighed down by guilt; he cannot free himself from the earth's crust. I call him remorse—
remorse for a forfeited life. He sits there dipping his fingers
in the rippling water, to wash them clean; and he is gnawed
and tormented by the knowledge that he will never,
never succeed. He will never, in all eternity, free himself,
and be granted resurrection. He must stay for ever in his
Hell.

IRENE, *coldly.* Poet!

RUBEK. Why poet?

IRENE. Because you're soft and self-indulgent, and so ready to
forgive all your own sins, everything you've ever done or
thought. You killed my soul, and then you model yourself
as a figure of penance and remorse.

Smiles.

And in your eyes, that settles your account.

RUBEK. I am an artist, Irene. I am not ashamed of the frailty
inherent in my nature. I was *born* to be an artist, you understand. And I shall never be anything else.

IRENE, *softly.* You are a poet, Arnold.

Strokes his hair gently.

You dear, big, ageing child, can't you see it?

RUBEK. Why do you keep on calling me a poet?

IRENE. Because there is something condoning in that word,
my friend. It is a word that condones all sins, and spreads a
cloak over every weakness.

Changes her tone suddenly.

But I was flesh and blood, once. I, too, had a life to live,
and a destiny to fulfil. But I turned my back on it all, threw

it away, to serve you. It was suicide; a mortal sin against myself. And that is a sin I can never expiate.

She sits down near him by the stream, keeping her eyes on him—though he does not see this. As though absent-mindedly, she picks some flowers from the bushes around them.

IRENE. I should have borne children into the world. Many children. Real children; not the sort that are hidden away in tombs. That should have been my calling. I should never have served you—poet!

RUBEK, *lost in memories.* But those were wonderful times we had, Irene. Miraculous, wonderful times—now that I look back——

IRENE. Can you remember a little word you said to me when you had finished? Finished with me and with our child? Do you remember that little word, Arnold?

RUBEK. Did I say something you still remember now?

IRENE. Yes, you did. Can't you remember it any longer?

RUBEK *shakes his head.* No, I can't say I do. Not at the moment, anyway.

IRENE. You took both my hands and pressed them warmly. I stood there, breathless, waiting. Then you said: "I am deeply grateful to you, Irene. This," you said, "This has been an inspiring episode in my life."

RUBEK. Episode? That's not a word I'm in the habit of using.

IRENE. "Episode" was the word you used.

RUBEK, *with attempted lightness.* Well, perhaps I may have—but so it was, really, an episode.

IRENE. At that word, I left you.

RUBEK. You take everything to heart so, Irene.

IRENE *wipes her forehead.* Yes. Perhaps you are right. Let us forget these things of the heart.

Picks the petals from a mountain rose, and scatters them in the stream.

Look, Arnold. There are our birds swimming.

RUBEK. What kind of birds are they?

IRENE. Can't you see? They're flamingoes. Red like roses.

RUBEK. Flamingoes don't swim. They only wade.

IRENE. All right, they're not flamingoes. They're gulls.

RUBEK. Oh, yes, red-billed gulls, I expect.

He plucks broad, green leaves and throws them on the water.

Now I am sending my ships after them.

IRENE. But there mustn't be any huntsmen on board.

RUBEK. No. There are no huntsmen on board.

Smiles at her.

Do you remember that summer when we sat like this outside the little farmhouse on the Taunitzer See?

IRENE *nods.* On Saturday evenings, yes. When we'd finished our work for the week.

RUBEK. We went out there by train. And stayed over till Sunday.

IRENE. An episode, Arnold.

RUBEK, *as though he has not heard.* You made birds swim in the stream then, too. Water lilies——

IRENE. White swans.

RUBEK. Yes, swans. And I remember I fastened a big hairy leaf to one of the swans. A dock leaf, wasn't it?

IRENE. And it became Lohengrin's boat, with the swan drawing it.

RUBEK. How you loved that game, Irene.

IRENE. We played it so many times.

RUBEK. Every Saturday, I think. The whole summer through.

IRENE. You said I was the swan who was drawing your boat.

RUBEK. Did I say that? Yes, I may well have.

Absorbed in the game.

Look, do you see how the gulls are swimming down the river, Irene?

IRENE *smiles.* And all your ships have run aground.

RUBEK *throws more leaves into the stream.* I have plenty of ships in reserve.

Follows the leaves with his eyes, throws more. After a moment:

Irene, I bought that little farmhouse on the Taunitzer See.

IRENE. Have you bought it? You often used to say you would if you could ever afford it.

RUBEK. Well, eventually I was able to. So I bought it.

IRENE, *glancing at him.* Do you live out there now, in our old house?

RUBEK. No, I had it pulled down long ago. And built myself a fine big villa in its place. With a park round it. That's where we——

Corrects himself.

Where I usually spend the summer.

IRENE. So you and—and that other woman live out there now?

RUBEK. Yes. When my wife and I aren't travelling; as we are this year.

IRENE. Beautiful, beautiful was life on the Taunitzer See.

RUBEK. And yet, Irene——

IRENE. And yet we let all that beauty slip from our grasp.

RUBEK, *softly, urgently.* Is it too late to find it again?

IRENE *does not answer him, but sits silent for a moment, then points across the plateau.* Look, Arnold. The sun is setting behind the mountains. See how redly it shines on all the heather.

RUBEK *follows her gaze.* It is a long time since I watched the sun set in the mountains.

IRENE. Or the sun rise?

RUBEK. I don't think I have ever seen a sunrise.

IRENE *smiles.* I once saw a miraculously beautiful sunrise.

RUBEK. Did you? Where was that?

IRENE. High, high up on a dizzy mountain top. You enticed me up there and promised you would show me all the glory of the world, if——

Stops sharply.

RUBEK. If——? Well?

IRENE. I did as you told me. Followed you to the mountain top. And there I fell on my knees and—worshipped you. And served you.

Is silent for a moment, then quietly:

Then I saw the sunrise.

RUBEK, *hesitantly.* Wouldn't you—like to come and live with us in the villa down there?

IRENE. With you and that other woman?

RUBEK. With me. As in the days when we created together. You can unfasten all the locks that have snapped shut inside me. Will you, Irene?

IRENE *shakes her head.* I haven't the key any longer, Arnold.

RUBEK. You have the key! You are the only one who has it.

Beseechingly.

Help me to start living again!

IRENE. Empty dreams. Idle, dead dreams. Our life together cannot be resurrected.

RUBEK, *curtly.* Then let us go on with our game.

IRENE. Our game, yes. Let us go on with our game.

They sit throwing leaves and petals into the stream, and watching them float and sail. Up the hill in the background to the left come SQUIRE ULFHEJM *and* MAJA, *in hunting costume. After them comes the* SERVANT *with the pack of hounds, which he leads out to the right.*

RUBEK, *catching sight of them.* Ah, there goes little Maja with her bear-baiter.

IRENE. Your lady, yes.

RUBEK. Or his.

MAJA *looks round as she walks, and sees the two figures by the stream. Shouts:* Goodnight, Professor! Dream about me! I'm going off on an adventure.

RUBEK *shouts back.* In quest of what?

MAJA *approaches.* Life. Real life. No substitutes.

RUBEK, *mockingly.* You, too, Maja dear?

MAJA. Yes. I've made up a song about it. It goes like this.

Sings happily.

> I am free! I am free! I am free!
> No longer imprisoned! I'm free!
> I can fly like a bird, and I'm free!

Yes, I believe I have awoken at last.

RUBEK. It sounds like it.

MAJA *takes a deep breath.* Oh, how heavenly it feels to be awake!

RUBEK. Goodnight, Maja, and good luck to your——

ULFHEJM *shouts warningly.* Don't say it! We don't want any of your goddam blessings! Can't you see we're going hunting?

RUBEK. What will you bring me home from the hunt, Maja?

MAJA. I'll bring back a fine hawk for you to model. I'll wing one for you.

RUBEK *smiles bitterly.* Yes, winging birds is rather in your line, isn't it?

MAJA *tosses her head.* Just let me take care of my own life from now on.

Laughs mischievously.

Goodbye! Have a nice quiet summer night on the mountain!

RUBEK, *jovially.* Thank you! And damn bad luck to you both —and to your hunting!

ULFHEJM *guffaws.* Now that's the kind of blessing I like to hear!

MAJA *smiles.* Thank you, thank you, Professor.

They go out through the brushwood to the right.

RUBEK, *after a pause.* Summer night on the mountain! Yes, that would have been life.

IRENE. Would you like to spend a summer night on the mountain? With me?

RUBEK *spreads his arms wide.* Yes! Yes! Come!

IRENE. My love, my lord and master!

RUBEK. Oh, Irene!

IRENE, *smiling, as she gropes for the knife.* It will only be an episode.

Whispers quickly.

Ssh! Don't look round, Arnold!

RUBEK, *as quietly.* What is it?

IRENE. There's a face staring at me.

RUBEK *turns involuntarily.* Where?

Starts.

Ah!

The NUN's *head is half visible among the bushes on the path down to the right. Her eyes are fixed on* IRENE.

IRENE *gets up and says softly.* We must part, now. No, don't move. Do as I say! You mustn't come with me.

Leans over him and whispers.

We'll meet tonight. On the mountain.

RUBEK. Will you come, Irene?

IRENE. Yes, I shall come. Wait for me here.

RUBEK *repeats, as in a dream.* Summer night on the mountain! With you!

His eyes meet hers.

Oh, Irene, that could have been our life. And we have wasted it——

IRENE. We only find what we have lost when——

Stops abruptly.

RUBEK. When——?

IRENE. When we dead awaken.

RUBEK *shakes his head sadly.* What do we find then?

IRENE. We find that we have never lived.

She walks across and climbs down the hill. The NUN *makes way for her, and follows her.* PROFESSOR RUBEK *remains seated motionless on the bench.*

MAJA *is heard singing happily higher up the mountain.*

> I am free! I am free! I am free!
> No longer imprisoned! I'm free!
> I can fly like a bird, and I'm free!

ACT THREE

A wild, broken mountain top, with a sheer precipice be-hind. To the right tower snowy peaks, losing themselves high up in drifting mist. To the left, on a scree, stands an old, tumbledown hut. It is early morning. Dawn is break-ing; the sun has not yet risen.

MAJA RUBEK, *out of breath and excited, comes down across the scree.* SQUIRE ULFHEJM *follows her, half angry, half laughing, holding her fast by the sleeve.*

MAJA, *trying to tear herself loose.* Let me go! Let me go, I tell you!

ULFHEJM. Steady, now, or you'll be biting me next! You're as snappish as a vixen.

MAJA *hits him over the hand.* Let me go, I say! Try to behave yourself!

ULFHEJM. I'm damned if I will.

MAJA. Then I won't go a step further with you. Do you hear? Not a step!

ULFHEJM *guffaws.* How do you think you'll escape from me up here?

MAJA *points down into the ravine.* I'll run down there, if need be.

ULFHEJM. And smash yourself into dog's-meat? A fine, sa-voury blood-pudding you'd make!

Lets go of her.

All right, go ahead. Run down the mountainside if you want to. It's as sheer as a wall, there's only one narrow path down, and that's as near as dammit impassable.

MAJA *dusts her skirt with her hand and glares angrily at him.* You're a fine one to go hunting with!

ULFHEJM. It's all in the sport.

MAJA. Oh, you call this sport, do you?

ULFHEJM. Yes, my fine lady, the kind of sport I like best.

MAJA *tosses her head.* Well, I must say!

After a moment.

Why did you let the hounds loose up there?

ULFHEJM *winks and smiles.* To give them the chance to hunt a little on their own, too.

MAJA. That's quite untrue. It wasn't for their sake you let them loose.

ULFHEJM, *still smiling.* Well, why did I, then? Tell me.

MAJA. Because you wanted to be rid of Lars. You told him to run after them and catch them; and meanwhile——

ULFHEJM. And meanwhile——?

MAJA. Never mind.

ULFHEJM. Lars won't find them. You don't need to worry about that. He won't come back before his time.

MAJA, *angrily.* No, I'm sure he won't.

ULFHEJM *tries to take her arm.* Lars knows my—my hunting habits, you see.

MAJA *evades his grasp and measures him with her eyes.* Do you know what you're like, Squire Ulfhejm? You're exactly like a faun.

ULFHEJM. A faun? Isn't that some kind of monster? A wood demon or something?

MAJA. Yes. Just like you. With a beard like a goat and legs like a goat—yes, and horns, too.

ULFHEJM. By Jove, horns too?

MAJA. A pair of beastly horns, just like you.

ULFHEJM. What, can you see my poor little pair?

MAJA. Yes, quite plainly.

ULFHEJM *takes the dog leash from his pocket.* Hm. I'd better tie you up, then.

MAJA. Have you gone mad? Tie me up?

ULFHEJM. If I'm a monster, I might as well play the part properly. So that's the way of it? You can see my horns, can you?

MAJA, *soothingly.* Now, now, please try to behave yourself, Squire Ulfhejm. But where's this hunting lodge of yours you were talking so much about? You said it was around here somewhere.

ULFHEJM *points with a flourish at the hut.* There it is, right in front of your eyes.

MAJA *stares at him.* That old pigsty?

ULFHEJM *chuckles.* It's housed more than one princess in its time.

MAJA. Was it there that that horrid man you told me about went in to the princess disguised as a bear?

ULFHEJM. Yes, my fair huntress, this was the very place. *With an inviting motion of his hand.*

If it should please you to step inside——

MAJA. Ugh! Set foot in that place? Ugh!

ULFHEJM. Oh, two people can while away a summer night very comfortably in there. Or a whole summer, for that matter.

MAJA. Thank you, I've no taste for that kind of thing. *Impatiently.*

Well, I'm tired of you and your hunting expedition. I'm going down to the hotel, before people wake up.

ULFHEJM. How do you suppose you're going to do that?

MAJA. That's your business. There must be a way down somewhere.

ULFHEJM *points upstage.* Bless you, yes, there's a way down. Down there.

MAJA. You see? You can be a gentleman when you want to——

ULFHEJM. Just you try it.

MAJA, *doubtfully.* Don't you think I dare?

ULFHEJM. You wouldn't have a chance. Unless I help you——

MAJA, *uneasily.* Well, come and help me, then. What else are you here for?

ULFHEJM. How would you rather I carried you, on my back——?

MAJA. Don't be ridiculous.

ULFHEJM. Or in my arms?

MAJA. For heaven's sake don't start that nonsense again!

ULFHEJM. I did that to a young girl once. Picked her up out of the gutter, and carried her away in my arms. Carried her on my hands; I'd have carried her right through life like that, so that she shouldn't hurt her pretty foot against a stone. Her shoes were worn to shreds when I found her——

MAJA. And yet you picked her up and carried her on your hands?

ULFHEJM. Lifted her up out of the mire, and carried her as high and as gently as I knew how.
Laughs roughly.
Do you know what thanks she gave me?

MAJA. No, what?

ULFHEJM *looks at her, smiles, and nods.* She gave me horns. The ones you can see so clearly. Isn't that a funny story?

MAJA. Oh yes, quite funny. But I know one which is even funnier.

ULFHEJM. What's that?

MAJA. Once upon a time there was a silly girl. She had a father and mother, but they were very poor. One day a great and powerful man appeared in their poor little house and picked the girl up in his arms, just like you, and carried her far, far away.

ULFHEJM. Wanted to live like he did, eh?

MAJA. Yes. She was stupid, you see.

ULFHEJM. And he was tall and handsome, no doubt.

MAJA. No, he wasn't so terribly handsome. But he made her believe he was going to take her up to the top of the highest mountain, where the sun would always shine.

ULFHEJM. He was a mountaineer, was he?

MAJA. Yes. In his way.

ULFHEJM. So he took the wench up with him?

MAJA *tosses her head.* Took her up with him? Oh yes! No— he led her into a cold, damp cage, which the sun and the fresh air never reached—or so it seemed to her—though the walls were gilded, and lined with great stone ghosts.

ULFHEJM. Serve her right, damn it!

MAJA. Yes, serve her right. It's a funny story, though, isn't it?

ULFHEJM *looks at her for a moment.* Look now, listen to me——

MAJA. Well, what is it now?

ULFHEJM. Why don't we two stitch our tattered lives together?

MAJA. Is the Squire turning poor man's tailor?

ULFHEJM. Yes. Couldn't we try to draw the rags together here and there so as to patch some kind of a life out of them?

MAJA. And when those poor rags have quite worn out, what then?

ULFHEJM. Then we shall stand there, free and unashamed. Ourselves, as we really are.

MAJA *laughs.* You with your goat's legs?

ULFHEJM. And you with your—well, let that pass.

MAJA. Come on, let's go.

ULFHEJM. Where to?

MAJA. Down to the hotel, of course.

ULFHEJM. And then?

MAJA. Then I shall bid you a polite farewell, and say: "Thank you, sir, for the pleasure of your company."

ULFHEJM. I can offer you a castle——

MAJA, *pointing to the hut.* Like that?

ULFHEJM. It hasn't fallen down yet.

MAJA. And all the glory of the world?

ULFHEJM. A castle, I said——

MAJA. Thank you. I've had enough of castles.

ULFHEJM. With splendid hunting grounds for miles around——

MAJA. Is it full of great works of art, this castle of yours?

ULFHEJM. I can't offer you any of those.

MAJA. I'm glad to hear it.

ULFHEJM. Will you come with me, then?

MAJA. There is a tame bird of prey which keeps guard over me.

ULFHEJM. We'll wing him, Maja.

MAJA. Come and carry me down this path, then.

ULFHEJM *throws an arm round her waist.* Yes, it's time we went. The mist is on us.

MAJA. Is it very dangerous, the way down?

ULFHEJM. Not as dangerous as a mountain mist.

She tears herself loose, goes to the edge and looks down, but starts quickly back.

ULFHEJM *goes over to her and laughs.* Does it make you giddy?

MAJA. Yes, it does. But look down there! Those two climbing up——

ULFHEJM *leans over the edge.* It's only your bird of prey. And his strange lady.

MAJA. Can't we get down without their seeing us?

ULFHEJM. Impossible. The path's too narrow. And there's no other way down.

MAJA. Oh, well. Let's face them here, then.

ULFHEJM. Spoken like a true bear-baiter!

PROFESSOR RUBEK *and* IRENE *come into sight above the edge of the ravine. He has his plaid over his shoulders, she a fur coat thrown loosely over her white dress and a swansdown hood over her head.*

RUBEK. Hallo, Maja! So we meet again?

MAJA. At your service. Come right up.

RUBEK *climbs up and reaches down his hand to* IRENE, *who joins him.*

RUBEK, *coldly, to* MAJA. So you've been on the mountain all night too? Like us.

MAJA. Yes, I've been hunting. With your permission.

ULFHEJM *points over the edge.* Have you come up that path?

RUBEK. As you see.

ULFHEJM. The strange lady, too?

RUBEK. Yes, of course.

With a glance at MAJA.

The strange lady and I will not be going separate ways any more.

ULFHEJM. Don't you know that this path you've just climbed is a deathtrap?

RUBEK. We tried it, anyway. It didn't look too difficult at first.

ULFHEJM. Nothing looks difficult at first; but then you come to a tight corner where you can't go on to turn back, and you're stuck there fast, Professor. Fast as a rock.

RUBEK *smiles.* Are these meant to be words of wisdom, Squire?

ULFHEJM. Words of wisdom be damned!

Points up towards the mountain top.

Can't you see the storm's about to break? Don't you hear the wind rising?

RUBEK *listens.* It sounds like the prelude to the Day of Resurrection!

ULFHEJM. It's the wind blowing from the mountain, man! Look how the clouds are heaving and sinking! They'll be all round us soon like a winding-sheet.

IRENE. A winding-sheet! I know that feeling!

MAJA *pulls at his arm.* Let's go down, quickly.

ULFHEJM, *to* RUBEK. I can't take more than one. Get into that hut and stay there till the storm's past. Then I'll send men up to fetch you down.

IRENE. To fetch us! No, no!

ULFHEJM, *roughly*. Take you down by force, if need be. This is a matter of life and death. Now you know!

To MAJA.

Come on; now don't be afraid, trust me.

MAJA, *clinging to him*. Oh, get me down, get me safely down!

ULFHEJM, *as he begins to climb down, shouts to the others*. You wait in the hut. Till they come with ropes to fetch you.

ULFHEJM, *with* MAJA *in his arms, descends hastily, yet cautiously, down the mountainside.*

IRENE *stares frightened at* RUBEK. Did you hear that, Arnold? They are coming up here to fetch me. Men—coming here——!

RUBEK. Be calm, Irene.

IRENE. And she—the one in black—she'll come too! She must have missed me long ago by now. She'll take hold of my arms, Arnold! And put me in the strait jacket! She's got it with her, in her trunk. I've seen it!

RUBEK. No-one will be allowed to touch you.

IRENE *smiles*. Oh no. I've a way to stop them.

RUBEK. What do you mean?

IRENE *takes out the knife*. This.

RUBEK *tries to take it*. A knife?

IRENE. Always, always. Day and night. In bed, too.

RUBEK. Give me the knife, Irene.

IRENE. I meant it for you, Arnold.

RUBEK. For me?

IRENE. As we were sitting there last night, down by the Taunitzer See——

RUBEK. The Taunitzer——?

IRENE. Outside the farmhouse. Playing at swans and water lilies——

RUBEK. Go on.

IRENE. I heard you say, clear as ice, cold as the grave, that I was only an episode in your life——

RUBEK. You said that, Irene, not I.

IRENE *continues.* I took out my knife. I was going to stick it in your back.

RUBEK. Why didn't you?

IRENE. I suddenly realised you were already dead. You'd been dead for years.

RUBEK. Dead?

IRENE. Dead. Like me. We sat there by the Taunitzer See, two clammy corpses, playing our little game together.

RUBEK. I don't call that death. But you don't understand me.

IRENE. Then where is that burning passion for me which you fought against when I stood naked before you as the woman rising from the dead?

RUBEK. Our love is not dead, Irene.

IRENE. That love which belongs to our life on earth—that beautiful, miraculous life so full of riddles—that love is dead in us both.

RUBEK. I tell you, that love throbs and burns as passionately in me now as it ever did!

IRENE. And I? Have you forgotten who I am now?

RUBEK. Whoever you are, whatever you are, to me you are only the woman I see in my dreams of you.

IRENE. I have stood on a stage, naked, and showed my body to hundreds of men since you——

RUBEK. I was blind, I drove you to it. I set that dead figure of clay above life, and happiness, and love.

IRENE. Too late. Too late.

RUBEK. Nothing that has happened since has cheapened you one whit in my eyes.

IRENE, *raising her head.* Nor in mine!

RUBEK. Well, then! We are free! There is still time for us to live, Irene!

IRENE *looks at him sadly.* The desire to live died in me, Arnold. Now I am risen from the dead, and look for you, and find you. And I find that you are dead, and life is dead—as I have been.

RUBEK. No, you are wrong, wrong. Both in us and around us life rages as fiercely and joyously as ever.

IRENE *smiles and shakes her head.* The woman whom you created, rising from the dead, sees life cold and lying on its bier.

RUBEK *throws his arms tightly round her.* Then let us two dead people live life to the full for one short hour before we go down again into our graves!

IRENE. Arnold!

RUBEK. But not here in this half-darkness. Not here, with this hideous dank shroud flapping around us.

IRENE. No, no. Up into the light, where glory shines. Up to the promised mountain top.

RUBEK. Up there we shall celebrate our wedding feast, Irene, my beloved.

IRENE, *proudly.* The sun may look on us, Arnold.

RUBEK. All the powers of light may look on us. And all the powers of darkness, too.

Grips her hand.

Will you come with me now, my bride of grace?

IRENE, *as though transfigured.* Freely and willingly, my lord and master.

RUBEK, *leading her.* First we must pass through the mists, Irene. And then——

IRENE. Yes, through the mists. And then up, up to the top of our tower, where it shines in the sunrise.

The mist closes tightly over the scene. RUBEK *and* IRENE, *hand in hand, climb upwards over the snowfield to the right, and soon disappear into the low clouds. Sharp gusts of wind hunt and whine through the air.*

The NUN *comes over the scree to the left. She stops, and looks round silently, searchingly.*

MAJA *is heard singing happily from far down in the ravine.*

> I am free! I am free! I am free!
> No longer imprisoned! I'm free
> I can fly like a bird, and I'm free!

Suddenly a roar like thunder is heard from high up on the snowfield, which rushes down, whirling, at a fearful pace.

RUBEK *and* IRENE *are glimpsed momentarily as they are whirled round in the snow and buried beneath it.*

THE NUN *utters a shriek, stretches out her arms towards them as they fall, and cries.* Irene!

She stands silent for a moment, then makes the sign of the cross in the air before her.

Pax vobiscum!

MAJA'S *song continues from further down the mountain-side.*

NOTE ON THE TRANSLATION

I have translated Ibsen's text faithfully, but have allowed myself a certain amount of liberty as regards cutting. I do not
think Ibsen can be played without cuts today, any more than
Shakespeare, and judicious cutting seems to me to be almost
as essential as accurate translation.

Ibsen, though marvellously taut in his construction, was
not always taut in his phrasing and, especially in the opening and expository scenes of a play, underlined his points to a
degree which today would sound tiresomely repetitive. I have
trimmed these repetitions and have thinned out the language elsewhere.

Above all, I have not hesitated to strip the dialogue of
many of its stage directions. Ibsen's descriptions of the appearance of his characters, and of the rooms and landscapes
through which they move, are indispensable, and his directions for moves remain surprisingly valid. But—largely, one
supposes, for the benefit of his readers, for he was consid-
erably dependent on book sales for his income—he prefaced
many of his lines of dialogue with an adjective or adverb,
usually of a highly melodramatic nature. These single-word
directions are continually demanding that the characters shall
start backwards, shrink horrified, whisper hoarsely, rise
threateningly from their chairs, etc. (Agnes, in *Brand,* is
called on to deliver one of her most moving lines "shrinking
behind a tree".) No modern producer can be expected to

follow these directions, and they are extremely distracting to any reader and, more particularly, to any actor or actress. I have retained only those which seem to me essential and helpful.

I have not modernised Ibsen's dialogue, but have tried to translate it into a language common to the period in which his plays are set, and to the present. I have, however, retained certain turns of phrase which look Victorian on the printed page but have proved effective in the theatre when spoken by an actor in nineteenth-century costume in a nineteenth-century room. Above all, I have tried to convey that mixture of sharpness and evasiveness which is the peculiar characteristic of Ibsen's dialogue. His leading characters are usually inhibited by a deep sense of guilt, and for much of the time they speak evasively, like the characters of Conrad. Suddenly there is an exchange of knife-thrusts; then they return to their evasions. Ibsen is never obscure, but frequently the real meaning of a line is implied rather than stated; there is a meaning behind the meaning.

I gladly acknowledge my debt to Mr. Casper Wrede for much minute criticism, and more valuable suggestions than I can list.

M. M.